# AN INTRODUCTION TO SHAKESPEARE

# An Introduction to Shakespeare

The Dramatist in His Context

Peter Hyland

First published in Great Britain 1996 by
**MACMILLAN PRESS LTD**
Houndmills, Basingstoke, Hampshire RG21 6XS and London
Companies and representatives throughout the world

A catalogue record for this book is available from the British
Library.

ISBN 0–333–59880–6

---

First published in the United States of America 1996 by
**ST. MARTIN'S PRESS, INC.,**
Scholarly and Reference Division,
175 Fifth Avenue, New York, N.Y. 10010

ISBN 0–312–16274–X (cloth)
ISBN 0–312–16276–6 (paperback)

Library of Congress Cataloging-in-Publication Data
Hyland, Peter.
An introduction to Shakespeare : the dramatist in his context /
Peter Hyland.
p.   cm.
Includes bibliographical references (p.    ) and index.
ISBN 0–312–16274–X (cloth) — ISBN 0–312–16276–6 (pbk.)
1. Shakespeare, William, 1564–1616—Stage history—To 1625.
2. Shakespeare, William, 1564–1616—Contemporary England.
3. Theater—England—History—16th century.  4. Theater—England–
–History—17th century.  5. England—Civilization—16th century.
6. England—Civilization—17th century.  I. Title.
PR3095.H95  1996
822.3'3—dc20                                          96–19741
                                                         CIP

---

This book is printed on paper suitable for recycling and made from fully  managed and sustained forest sources.

10   9   8   7   6   5   4   3   2
06   05   04   03   02   01   01   99   98

Printed in Hong Kong

# Contents

*For Theresa*

# Prefatory Note

Dr Johnson once wrote, 'Notes are often necessary, but they are necessary evils.' Anyone who writes about Shakespeare has inherited a vast amount of knowledge, and it is impossible to assign all of it to its original source. I have tried to keep to a minimum my own footnotes by acknowledging only direct quotation or citation, but all the sources I have used are to be found in the 'Suggested Reading' list.

I have quoted throughout from the New Arden editions of Shakespeare's plays, published by Routledge. Documentary matter taken from E.K. Chambers, *The Elizabethan Stage* (Oxford: Clarendon Press, 1923) is noted in the text, using the abbreviation *ES* and volume and page numbers. In the interests of consistency I have modernized spelling when appropriate.

P.H.

# Introduction: Approaching Shakespeare and His Stage

In 1623, seven years after Shakespeare's death, two members of his acting company, John Heminges and Henry Condell, published 36 of his plays in a volume now known as the First Folio. The collection was prefaced by a number of documents, including an elegy to Shakespeare by the poet and dramatist Ben Jonson. Jonson had been at different times a colleague and a rival of Shakespeare's; he had written plays in which Shakespeare himself had acted, and he had also written plays for acting companies that were in competition with Shakespeare's own.[1] In his elegy, Jonson wrote of Shakespeare, 'He was not of an age, but for all time!' (43) Now in one sense it is clearly true that Shakespeare is 'for all time', since his plays, after 400 years, are still the most popular in the English language and are still performed throughout the world. But Jonson's words imply more than this, for, whether or not he intended to do so, he effectively characterized Shakespeare, the 'Sweet Swan of Avon', as the Bard, the universal figure of the poet existing in a transcendent world of Truth and Beauty: 'But stay, I see thee in the Hemisphere / Advanc'd, and made a Constellation there!' (75–6). This Shakespeare, the 'Star of Poets', has had his ups and downs, but it is safe to say that the history of Shakespearean appreciation and criticism, especially since romantic readings of him in the early nineteenth century, has been dominated by the figure of the timeless Bard, watching, omniscient and god-like, over the great moral and philosophical questions that petty men and women struggle with: 'Others abide our question. Thou art free. / We ask and ask – Thou smilest and art still, / Out-topping knowledge.'[2] This is how the Victorian poet Matthew Arnold presented him: mysterious, distant, all-knowing.

So compelling was this idea of Shakespeare in the early part of the twentieth century that he was incorporated into the English education system as its cornerstone, as a kind of summation of all that was valuable in the culture. According to the Newbolt Report on the teaching of English in England of 1921, which led

1

to the loading of Shakespeare into the school curriculum, 'Shakespeare is an inevitable and necessary part of school activity because he is . . . our greatest English writer.'[3] The assumption here, of course, is that in teaching Shakespeare one is teaching 'truth' – otherwise, why teach him? Thus Shakespeare ceased to be a man, a playwright who wrote for a specific audience at a specific time, and became his work, a kind of holy writ or dogma, a body of unquestionable writings, like the Bible.

The tendency to render Shakespeare's works into a kind of pure essence, to turn the author into an object of worship, has been called Bardolatry. Of course, not all lovers of Shakespeare have been so extreme, but the desire to bring readings of his plays into conformity with a preconceived notion of the 'Shakespearean' has often limited or blinkered interpretation. This tradition of Shakespeare appreciation, by defining him as a poet rather than a dramatist, and by concentrating on the poetic language of the plays, had a major part in transforming the play-texts into literary texts. It also tended to treat literature as a realm apart from ordinary life, uncontaminated by the local, the topical, the political – that is, the historical. The context in which Shakespeare wrote his plays was seen as mere background material, essentially irrelevant to their universal meaning.

Since the mid-1970s a great deal has changed. New schools of criticism (poststructuralism, Marxism, feminism, new historicism and cultural materialism are only a few) have fragmented the monolithic idea of Shakespeare. The ideological positions visible in the plays have been attacked, and the political context and the material conditions of their production have been more thoroughly scrutinized. The stability of the texts has been brought into question, so that we cannot now say that there is such a thing as a definitive text of, say, *King Lear*. There has been greater emphasis on the plays as texts for performance. Above all, there has been rigorous analysis of how the image of 'Shakespeare' has been constructed and reconstructed by particular ideological interests.

Let us go back to Ben Jonson's presentation of Shakespeare as a poet 'for all time'. In reality Jonson did not fully approve of Shakespeare's work, because he himself believed in a classical theory of poetry that did not leave much room for a kind of writing that apparently lacked control. He certainly did not see Shakespeare as the ultimate artist, for he told a colleague, William

Drummond, that 'Shakespeare wanted art', and he wrote in his own commonplace book, *Discoveries*, that Shakespeare 'had an excellent fancy; brave notions, and gentle expressions: wherein he flowed with that facility, that sometime it was necessary he should be stopped'.[4] But in his elegy he had a particular purpose. First, of course, he had to fulfil the requirements of decorum by saying positive things about the author of the volume to which his poem was a preface, and so he constructed a glowing image of the poet, but it is as much an image of the poet in abstract as it is of the particular poet Shakespeare. Throughout his own career Jonson was concerned to give dignity to the profession of the poet, and to promote himself within that profession. The figure of the poet he constructed in the elegy, characterized less by fancy and facility than by 'art', which to Jonson meant sweating over his lines, is closer to Jonson himself than it is to Shakespeare.

Shakespeare the Bard was there from the beginning, and from the beginning he was a construct, a figure created to fit Ben Jonson's needs and the commercial needs of the publishers of the 1623 Folio. There was a real Shakespeare (although, as we shall see, there are those who deny it), but for us he can only be reconstructed from slim or opaque evidence: a few biographical details, some understanding of the conditions in which his plays were written, the evidence of the plays themselves. The plays continue to fascinate us; they have generated a vast secondary literature and will no doubt continue to do so. The man who stands behind them, however, remains enigmatic: in a sense, we can never know the real Shakespeare, only 'Shakespeare'.

Although, in presenting Shakespeare as the supreme poetic genius, history has handed him down to us as a man standing outside history, his work needs to be understood in the context of the conditions in which it was produced. Shakespeare was a professional dramatist writing for a particular market-place, the public theatre; he did not create art for art's sake, but wrote to make a living, and he was very successful at this. Although nowadays we think of his plays as 'high art', he actually wrote for a popular medium, and he wrote under the many constraints that this entailed. Apart from having to be aware of the risks of offending the authorities, he had to keep in mind the demands of a fickle audience with a thirst for novelty, the possibilities and limitations of the theatrical space for which he was writing, and the needs of the individual members of the acting company for which he worked. Like most professional writers, he must have been plagued by deadlines and by the pressure to produce yet another success.

In fact, we can learn more of interest about Shakespeare from the conditions under which he had to work than we can from what is known about his life, most of which comes from official records and documents. His contemporaries had surprisingly little to say about him, a fact that has given fuel to the so-called anti-Stratfordians, people who for various reasons believe that some-one other than Shakespeare wrote the plays: Sir Francis Bacon and Christopher Marlowe have been favoured candidates in the past, but the current favourite is Edward de Vere, seventeenth Earl of Oxford. There are, of course, events in Shakespeare's life that we can be fairly sure about, but much of what is 'known' about Shakespeare is really only myth. Samuel Schoenbaum, in his book *Shakespeare's Lives*, spends a little over 30 pages on what can be known about the dramatist from documentary evidence, and rather more than 500 pages on the subsequent embroideries of that evidence.

Even apparent certainties about Shakespeare raise questions. We all know what he looked like, or at least we think we do: the high forehead rising to a bald dome, the waving side-locks of hair, the neatly trimmed beard are as familiar to us from pub signs as they are from books. In fact, there are only two 'reliable' sources for his image. One of these is the sculpted effigy that stands above his grave in Holy Trinity Church, Stratford-upon-Avon. Made by a Dutch immigrant stonemason called Gheerhart Janssen, it presents a picture of a successful middle-class business-man (which in a sense Shakespeare was), prosperous-looking and self-satisfied. The other is the portrait engraved by the Flemish artist Martin Droeshout that appears on the title-page of the First Folio edition of Shakespeare's plays. By our standards both images might seem inept and unflattering; the Droeshout portrait particularly, with its grossly exaggerated forehead, has made the drama-tist appear ridiculous to many, though the bulging dome may simply be intended to signify the magnitude of his intellectual accomplishment. Both images, however, might make us wish to ask what kind of man this really was.

Once we begin to question our idea of Shakespeare, we find ambiguities everywhere. What was his name? In official documents connected with his life it appears in many variants – he is Shackspere, Shaxper, Shagspere, Shaxberd. It was not unusual, in a time before spelling became fixed by dictionaries, for a man to spell his name inconsistently, but the variants increase the sense of a man hard to pin down. Even the date of his birth is a problem. He was baptised on 26 April 1564, and it is generally accepted that he was born three days earlier, but the only evidence for this is the fact that children were usually baptised two or three days after birth. The idea that he was born on 23 April has special appeal, however. First, this is St George's Day, so it might seem particularly appropriate that the man who has been made into England's national poet should have been born on the day named for its patron saint. Second, Shakespeare died on 23 April 1616, giving his life a neat circularity. Ambiguities of this sort are in themselves minor, and they certainly do not prove that Shakespeare did not exist, but they should alert us to the fact that much of what we think we know about him is really a part of a myth that has generated the figure of the English national poet.

When all is said, however, we are left with the plays. Even if we accept that much of the concept 'Shakespeare' is myth, and even if we accept that the plays can no longer be seen as repositories of universal truth and, in some cases, embody attitudes that we find repugnant, this does not mean that they are thereby drained of value for us. Shakespeare's plays are immensely complex structures which push language to its extremes to embody the felt experience of history. They put conflict into words, and the pressures and stresses they represent and the emotions they generate, whether or not we call them universal, are recognizable to us. Reading and coming to some understanding of a Shakespeare play is hard work. Language changes, and his meanings are sometimes difficult for us to discover. Furthermore, they reflect a time long gone, and it is not easy for us to recover a sense of that time. But after 400 years Shakespeare's plays remain living things; that is why they still hold the stage so well. We can find in them moments of human suffering and human joy, confrontations with mystery and with truth, universal or not, and that is why they are worth the effort.

The sub-title of this book, 'The Dramatist in His Context', expresses its central theme. My aim is to present as clearly and comprehensively as possible, given the constraints of space, an account of the complex, often ambiguous conditions under which Shakespeare produced his plays. I am consequently asking the reader to understand the word 'context' here in its broadest possible sense. It refers to the historical moment at which the plays were written, including the shifting political pressures that had their source in the needs of monarch and government, but reflected also the growing needs of other more or less powerful groups. It refers to the communal, ideological and commercial pressures exerted by a society going through profound and unprecedented changes. It refers to the ideas and beliefs of the time, not just those that were inherited from the medieval past, but also the new ones generated by this turmoil. It refers to the theatre in which the dramatist worked, and the playwrights and actors who made up his profession; the audiences for which he wrote; and the literary and dramatic traditions that provided him with much of his material and techniques. All these elements and more, intimately inter-connected and inter-dependent, formed Shakespeare's context.

# 1
# Life and Times

## LIFE

According to the Parish Register of the town of Stratford-upon-Avon in the county of Warwickshire, 'Gulielmus filius Johannes Shakspere' was baptised on 26 April 1564. He was probably but not certainly born on 23 April. His mother, Mary Arden, was the daughter of a wealthy landowner, and his father, John Shakespeare, was a glovemaker who held a number of prominent positions in local politics. In the year of William's birth more than 200 Stratford people out of a population of fewer than 1500 died of bubonic plague. The harshness of life at the time can be gauged from the fact that of John and Mary's eight children only five survived into adulthood.

John Shakespeare's father had been a farmer, but John himself was apprenticed to become a glover and leather-dresser. This was a good trade, and he seems to have done well enough in it to attract the attention of the affluent Arden family. As well as bringing him a good settlement, his marriage to Mary Arden was a move upward in the social scale, for the Ardens were minor gentry. By 1556 John was prosperous enough to be able to buy and convert the two houses that were to become William Shakespeare's birthplace. He was also active in local politics; in 1558 he became town constable, and then held various important offices, but around 1576 it appears that he got badly into debt, and his affairs went into a decline.

It is impossible to tell how this decline affected William because very little is known about his life in Stratford. As for his formal education, there is no documentary evidence, but the evidence to be found in his plays indicates that he had a good one, and there is no reason to doubt that he attended the King's New School in Stratford. This was an excellent grammar school, which provided its scholars with much more than the basics of reading, writing and arithmetic. They would have been trained in rhetoric, logic and history, and would have read widely in Latin literature and contemporary European humanist writing and less widely in Greek (in his elegy on Shakespeare Jonson refers to Shakespeare's 'small Latin, and less Greek', but he was inviting comparison with his own erudition, of which he often boasted, and we should not take this comment too literally). The Arden family were staunch Catholics, and Shakespeare himself may have had Catholic leanings, but his religious education would have been orthodox Protestant. From 1559 everyone was required to attend church, and there were mandatory readings from the Bible, the Prayer Book and the *Homilies*. Whether or not Shakespeare accepted these teachings uncritically, hearing them week after week he could hardly have avoided taking them in as a rich part of his mental furniture, and there are echoes of more than 40 books of the Bible in his works.

Amongst the few events from Shakespeare's Stratford years that are documented is his marriage, in November 1582, to Anne Hathaway. Shakespeare was 18 at the time, and Anne, seven or eight years older, was pregnant (their first daughter Susanna was christened in May of the following year). Two years later twins were born (Hamnet and Judith, christened 2 February 1585). There has been a lot of the obvious kind of speculation about the circumstances of this marriage but in truth we know nothing about it. We do not know, either, whether Shakespeare had any trade to support his family, although there has been speculation about this too, and in legend he has been apprenticed as a butcher, a lawyer, a physician, a schoolmaster. The foreign settings of many of his plays have suggested to some that he must have been a soldier or sailor, and the desire to romanticize his image has led others to turn him into a drinker and a poacher. Some or none of these legends may be true; the fact is that for the years from 1585 to 1592, the so-called 'lost years', there is no documentary evidence whatever to suggest what he might have been doing. All that is known is that at some point during those years he left Stratford for London and began working in the theatre.

He would certainly have had the opportunity to develop an interest in theatre while he was living in Stratford. He could have seen one of the last performances of the miracle plays in nearby Coventry. He must have seen performances by some of the London acting companies, who toured the provinces when there was plague or excessive heat in the city. A number of them visited

Stratford between 1569 and 1586, and it is reasonable to suppose that Shakespeare in some way became connected with one of them, since it is unlikely that he would have been able to go to London and seek his fortune in the profession without some such contact. It is possible that he became attached to the Earl of Leicester's Men, at that time one of the most prestigious of the acting companies. Leicester's Men were led by James Burbage, builder of the first public playhouse in London; he was the father of Richard Burbage, who became a long-time associate of Shakespeare's in the company that started out as the Lord Chamberlain's Men. This is only a matter of speculation, for the next time we hear of Shakespeare is in 1592, when he was already a working playwright.

There had been bands of travelling actors in England for many years, but the first permanent public playhouse, the Theatre, did not open in London until 1576. At around the same time the Children of the Queen's Chapel, one of a number of companies of child actors that had for many years entertained the nobility with amateur performances, acquired a permanent hall in the Blackfriars precinct, which was operated as a private theatre. Other theatres quickly followed, and with them developed an exciting and risky profession. Amongst the earliest writers for these theatres was a group known as the University Wits, one of whom was Robert Greene. A brilliant university-educated man who squandered his talents and himself in dissolute living, Greene tried his hand at all kinds of writing: plays, poems, pamphlets and prose romances. He was not particularly successful, and was deeply embittered by this. In 1592 when he was close to death, though barely in his 30s, he wrote a pamphlet entitled *Greene's Groatsworth of Wit*, as a warning against a life like his. In it appears this attack on one of his rivals:

> there is an upstart crow, beautified with our feathers, that with his *Tiger's heart wrapt in a player's hide*, supposes he is well able to bombast out a blank verse as the best of you; and being an absolute *Johannes Factotum*, is in his own conceit the only Shakescene in a country.[1]

It has been suggested that the 'Shake-scene' derided here is Christopher Marlowe, a writer who 'bombasted out' many a blank verse and who, by 1592, had certainly made a name for himself as a playwright. It has also been suggested that Greene was not referring to a playwright at all, but to the clown Will Kempe, or to the well-known actor Edward Alleyn, whose ranting style of acting probably could be said to 'shake the scene'.[2] But the orthodox view of this passage seems sound: that it contains clear allusions to Shakespeare, and that it therefore constitutes the earliest known evidence of his presence in London.

The hostility in Greene's tone could be attributed to a sense of his own intellectual and social superiority to this 'upstart', or simply to resentment of Shakespeare's success. His motives are not important, however; what concerns us here is what we can learn of Shakespeare's career. What Greene tells us is that Shakespeare must have been in London for some years, because by 1592 he was already successful enough to generate such resentment. The term '*Johannes Factotum*' means 'Jack-of-all-trades'; Shakespeare had probably begun his career as an actor ('player') before taking up writing, and he may have gained entry into play-writing by providing additions to extant plays by established dramatists like Greene (this is one possible meaning of 'beautified with our feathers', though this phrase could also be an accusation of plagiarism, implying that Shakespeare made his plays out of materials stolen from others). The comment about the tiger's heart is a reference to a line in *3 Henry VI*: 'O tiger's heart wrapped in a woman's hide!' (1.4.137), so it is reasonable to assume that Shakespeare had written all three parts of that history play by this time. Apart from this, we can only conjecture, because the chronology of his early plays is obscure, but it is possible that he had also written *Richard III*, *The Comedy of Errors* and *The Taming of the Shrew*, and the revenge tragedy *Titus Andronicus*. If so, then the popularity that so incensed Greene is not surprising, for we see him experimenting with all three of the main dramatic forms (history, comedy, tragedy) current at the time.

Greene was one of the better-known of the dramatists working at the time when Shakespeare began to write for the stage. He was a member of the group of academic writers already mentioned, the University Wits; others of them, notably George Peele, Thomas Lodge and Thomas Nashe, also wrote plays, for both children's and adult companies, though only Peele had much success. A more important figure was John Lyly, who wrote for the children's companies, and whose comedies had an important influence on Shakespeare's early work. Thomas Kyd's play *The Spanish Tragedy* had an extraordinary and long-lived popularity, but he appears to have written nothing else of importance. The most significant dramatist was Marlowe, a notorious figure who nevertheless, with plays that included *Tamburlaine the Great*, *The Jew of Malta* and *Doctor Faustus*, had made an astounding start to a writing career that was cut sadly short by his violent death at the hands of one Ingram Frizer, a spy and informer.

Few playwrights were also actors, but Shakespeare may well have continued to act for as long as he worked in the theatre. The only plays that he certainly acted in are two by his fellow dramatist and rival Ben Jonson, the comedy *Every Man in His Humour* (1601) and the tragedy *Sejanus* (1603). We know that he also acted in his own plays, because at the beginning of the First Folio there is a list of 'the principal actors in all these plays', and Shakespeare's name appears at the head of it. Nothing is known about the roles he took, though legend has it that he played the ghost of Hamlet's father and the old servant Adam in *As You Like It*, which are both minor roles. If he had been a notable actor there would surely be some contemporary evidence about his acting skills, as there is, for example, about those of Richard Burbage and Will Kempe, respectively the leading actor and the comedian in the Lord Chamberlain's Men. Faced with the lack of any evidence to the contrary we can only conclude that he was not an outstanding actor.

By 1593 Shakespeare had a patron, to whom he dedicated his narrative poem *Venus and Adonis*, and in the following year another long poem, *The Rape of Lucrece*. The cause of this burst of non-dramatic writing is not clear, but in 1592 there was a severe outbreak of the bubonic plague which led to a two-year ban on performances in playhouses, and it is possible that this temporary relaxation of the need to turn out plays led him to direct his energies elsewhere. His patron, Henry Wriothesley, Third Earl of Southampton, was a brilliant, handsome young man who encouraged other poets and writers besides Shakespeare. Many scholars believe that Southampton was the 'Fair Youth' addressed in the poet's sonnets, and it is indeed likely that Shakespeare began to write his sonnets around this time, though they were not published until 1609 and there are many doubts as to their sequence and dating. For the moment we can limit ourselves to asking why Shakespeare needed a patron. At that time, it was virtually impossible for poets, or indeed any writers apart from those working in the theatre, to make a living out of writing. Some nobles wrote poetry as a kind of hobby, but writers without an independent income depended on wealthy and influential patrons to give them financial support or lucrative positions (Edmund Spenser is a good example of this; his epic poem *The Faerie Queene* was, amongst other things, a massive attempt to win the favour of Queen Elizabeth). It may be that Shakespeare, still new to the professional theatre, was hedging his bets, seeking powerful patronage in case he failed as a dramatist. He need not have worried.

We do not know which acting company Shakespeare worked for when he first arrived in London. It may have been Leicester's Men, or he may have joined the company belonging to Ferdinando, Lord Strange, who became the Earl of Derby in 1593. Lord Strange's Men included a number of actors who later became members of the Lord Chamberlain's Men, including Will Kempe and John Heminges. However, according to the title pages of some of Shakespeare's plays, they were acted by various companies: Pembroke's Men and the Earl of Sussex's Men, as well as the Earl of Derby's. It is possible that, at the beginning of his career, Shakespeare had to offer his plays to whomever would take them. When the theatres re-opened in 1594 after the plague epidemic, he joined the Lord Chamberlain's Men, then newly-constituted, as actor–playwright; we know this because he is listed along with Kempe and Burbage as being paid for court performances for the Christmas season.

Shakespeare remained with this company until he retired in 1612. It was the most successful of the acting companies of the day. During Elizabeth's reign its closest rival was the Lord Admiral's Men, led by the famous tragedian Edward Alleyn, but their relative popularity can be judged from the fact that, in 1603 when James I acceded to the throne, the Lord Chamberlain's Men were honoured by being allowed to change their name to the King's Men, while their rivals had to be content with the patronage of his son Prince Henry. When Shakespeare joined them the Lord Chamberlain's Men were performing at the Theatre, which was built on land leased from one Giles Alleyn. When the lease expired the company became involved in an argument with Alleyn over its renewal, and so on 28 December 1597 they dismantled the building and carried its timber across to the other side of the Thames, where they began the construction of what was to become the Globe. Shakespeare himself was a shareholder in both the building and the company; this, rather than his plays, was the source of his later great prosperity.

During his early years with the Lord Chamberlain's Men Shakespeare continued to write history plays, and also the series of romantic comedies that culminates with *As You Like It* and *Twelfth Night*. During these years his only attempt at tragedy after *Titus Andronicus* was *Romeo and Juliet*, though some of his histories, most notably *Richard II*, have a tragic structure. Around the year 1600 his writing took on a new direction with a series of puzzling plays, *Troilus and Cressida*, *All's Well That End's Well* and *Measure for Measure*, that may be called comedies but are much harsher in tone than anything he had written before. He also embarked on his major tragedies, *Hamlet*, *Othello*, *King Lear* and *Macbeth*. Some critics have accounted for the darkening of tone in his works by assuming that there must have been some personal tragedy in his life, but there is no evidence for this. It seems more likely that he simply needed to move in a new artistic direction, or that he was responding to the growing mood of pessimism and uncertainty in the country that developed during Elizabeth's declining years and was not dispelled for long by the accession of James. Around 1608 he changed direction again, ending his career with the group of plays of forgiveness and reconciliation known as romances. One reason for this change must have been that in 1608 the King's Men took over a second theatre, the Blackfriars; this was a private indoor theatre that catered for a more sophisticated audience than those that attended public theatres, and the romances would have been intended to provide suitable fare for them.

*The Tempest*, the last of these romances, has often been seen as Shakespeare's farewell to the stage, since its central figure, Prospero, is a creator of illusions who finally breaks his magic wand and throws away his books. He does indeed give a speech that seems to dismiss the magic of the theatre:

Our revels now are ended. These our actors,
As I foretold you, were all spirits, and
Are melted into air, into thin air:
[. . .]
                the great globe itself,
Yea, all which it inherit, shall dissolve,
And, like this unsubstantial pageant faded,
Leave not a rack behind.

                              (4.1.148–50, 153–6)

However, if we have to equate Prospero with Shakespeare all manner of problems are raised in the play; for the present, suffice it to say that it is always risky to assume that any voice is speaking directly for the dramatist. Nevertheless, it appears that Shakespeare did intend *The Tempest* to be his final play, because he retired to Stratford after it. He came out of retirement at least twice, to collaborate with John Fletcher on *The Two Noble Kinsmen*, and to write *Henry VIII*. This latter play was first performed on 29 June 1613 at the Globe; during the performance the theatre caught fire and burned to the ground.

In 1597 Shakespeare had bought a house in Stratford called New Place, and it was there that he spent his last, sadly few years, from his retirement in 1612 to his death on 23 April 1616 at the age of 52. Nothing is known about the circumstances of his death. He lies buried in Holy Trinity Church in Stratford; on his gravestone are these words, popularly supposed to have been written by Shakespeare himself:

Good friend, for Jesus' sake forbear
To dig the dust enclosed here.
Blessed be the man that spares these stones
And cursed be he that moves my bones.

As we shall see, there have been those who wanted very much to move Shakespeare's bones.

In his own time Shakespeare seems to have been amongst the most popular of the many writers working for the stage, and he was certainly the most successful. The publication in 1623 of the First Folio collected edition of his works indicates that, ten years after he had ceased to write, his plays were still of commercial value to the King's Men. There have been numerous attempts to calculate his income from the theatre; the most probable figure seems to be around £200 a year.[3] This can be compared with the earnings of Ben Jonson, who claimed in 1619 that 'Of all his plays he never gained two hundred pounds.'[4] If these figures are accurate it means that Shakespeare earned from the stage in a year as much as Jonson earned over some 20 years. Shakespeare's income did not simply come from his plays, however, for much of it would have come from the shares he held in the company and the theatres. He invested his profits wisely: New Place was the second finest house in Stratford, and in subsequent years he bought more land and property. In 1596 his father had applied to the College of Heralds for a family coat of arms, which was granted to him, so that when Shakespeare retired he was a very respectable member of the gentry. Any account of Shakespeare has to take into consideration this prudential, even materialistic aspect of his character.

This is most of what can be said with much certainty about Shakespeare's life, and even so I have had to use words like 'suppose' and 'speculate'. The scarcity of details has inevitably prompted the generation of myths and legends to fill in the gaps. I have already mentioned the attempts to show what he might have been doing during the 'lost years', but there are many other legends, such as the rumour that the Caroline dramatist Sir William Davenant was his illegitimate son (a rumour encouraged by Davenant himself), or the story that he died of a fever contracted as the result of a drinking session with Ben Jonson and the poet Michael Drayton. However attractive such stories might be as indicators of Shakespeare's human frailties, we have to treat them with caution due to the lack of evidence.

Evidence. The most persistent questions about Shakespeare are those asked by the bone-movers, the anti-Stratfordians, who have tried to prove that he was not the author of his own plays. The problem with the documentary evidence concerning Shakespeare is that very little of it connects the man from Stratford to the London playwright. For that matter, there is little to connect the London man-of-the-theatre to the plays that appeared under his name. There is a body of evidence that some but not all of the plays were published under the name William Shakespeare. A smaller body of evidence shows that a man called William Shakespeare was a sharer in the Lord Chamberlain's/King's Men. There is not much evidence at all that the Shakespeare of Stratford was the same man as the Shakespeare of London, although there is the Stratford man's will, in which he made bequests to Heminges, Burbage and Condell, all actors with the King's Men. It is, of course, both puzzling and frustrating that there is not more evidence about such a major figure, that so few of his contemporaries had anything to say about him, but this does not prove that Shakespeare did not write the plays. Nevertheless, there are those who suggest that no such person even existed, that 'Shakespeare' was a pseudonym for some other writer or writers; others have accepted his existence but have claimed that he allowed his name to be used by the true author who wished to remain anonymous.

There seem to be two main reasons for these anti-Stratfordian myths. The first is based on a misunderstanding of the nature of both Shakespeare's education and the learning to be found in his plays. This misunderstanding assumes that only a university training could account for the intellectual content of the plays, but in fact, as we have seen, the grammar school in Stratford would have provided a rigorous education, and many of the ideas in the plays would have been common in the fashionable circles to which Shakespeare had a degree of access. Furthermore, the example of Ben Jonson, the son of a bricklayer, who did not attend a university and still managed to turn himself into the leading classical scholar in England, shows what an autodidact can achieve. The favourite candidate of those who prefer an alternative, more erudite author was for a long time Sir Francis Bacon. Bacon is certainly an important figure in the history of English thought, a pioneer of the scientific method of enquiry. His interests as a writer were scientific and rational, and in many ways he stands out as the most representative man of his age. But he was by no means a poet, and even a cursory reading of his works shows how improbable it is that he could have written Shakespeare's plays.

The other main reason for doubting that Shakespeare wrote his own plays seems to be more a matter of social snobbery, an unwillingness to believe that the works that have become the cornerstone of English culture could have been written by the son of a glovemaker from a tiny country town. Doubters have sought amongst noble literati for the real author: the Earl of Essex, the Earl of Derby, Sir Walter Raleigh, even Queen Elizabeth herself, all have had their champions. The current favourite is the Earl of Oxford (even Freud thought that the Earl of Oxford might have written the plays), but none of them wrote anything that would convince most people that they were capable of writing Shakespeare's plays, and arguments in their favour have to depend on ingenuity rather than evidence.

These two kinds of snobbery, intellectual and social, help to explain the motives of some anti-Stratfordians. But there are others who, without any apparent grounds at all, have tried to assign Shakespeare's plays to other dramatists. Thomas Dekker, Thomas Heywood, John Webster and Thomas Middleton, either individually or in collaboration, have all been credited with the writing of

Shakespeare's plays, though no one has explained why they should have been unwilling to identify themselves as their author. The most favoured candidate here is Christopher Marlowe. Marlowe was a dramatist of great abilities who in his brief lifetime wrote some half-dozen plays, the best-known of which is the tragedy *Doctor Faustus*. Marlowe was born in the same year as Shakespeare, and there seems to have been some degree of rivalry between them. Unfortunately he died in 1593, before most of Shakespeare's plays were written. The only way to support the claim that Marlowe wrote Shakespeare's plays is to argue that his death was a hoax, and that he was somehow spirited away from the murder scene and enabled to continue writing under the pseudonym 'Shakespeare'. This might seem ridiculous, but some have been willing to believe it.[5]

All of the anti-Stratfordian theories depend on belief in some such massive conspiracy. If the Earl of Oxford wrote the plays, why did he need to hide the fact? How can we explain the plays that appeared after his death in 1604? Why, since such a conspiracy, continued for so many years, must have been known to many people, did not a single one of them ever mention it? The supporters of the Oxfordian case do provide answers to these questions, but they are characterized more by ingenuity than by sense. It is true that the evidence about Shakespeare's life is sparse (though no more so than the evidence about the lives of other dramatists of the time, with the exception of Jonson), but even so, it takes a great leap of imagination to accept any of the alternative theories.

I have given up what might seem to be an excessive amount of space to these attempts to obliterate Shakespeare. I should certainly wish to assert, against them, that in a period of something more than 20 years, encompassing the last decade of the sixteenth century and the first decade of the seventeenth, a man named William Shakespeare created a body of dramatic and literary work that has subsequently become the foundation stone of the canon of English literature and has turned its author into the national poet. I see no reason to deny his existence, or to deny the quality of his work. However, recent critical theory has raised questions about *how* this work has been given value. Structuralist readings have denied that an author has a limiting 'authority' over his text, since language is independent of its author's intentions. If we accept this view, then it does not matter who wrote the plays. Poststructuralist or deconstructive readings, focusing on the 'free play' of language, try to show that all writing resists any reduction to an authoritative 'meaning'. Performance criticism diverts attention away from the 'poetic text' to a larger whole that includes costume and make-up, movement and gesture, properties, music, and all the other aspects of performance, including actors' and directors' views of how a play should be presented.

All of these approaches to Shakespeare's plays minimize the importance of Shakespeare's as the originating 'mind', or deny the possibility of access to it. Other recent theoretical movements have accepted a 'mind', but have not necessarily liked what the mind seems to represent. Feminist readings, especially, have tended to see Shakespeare as endorsing a phallocentric view of society that insists on the subjugation of women. New historicist or cultural materialist readings have looked at the plays as sites for a conflict of ideologies, and Shakespeare has been seen both as a spokesman for established power and as a radical critic of it. So perhaps 'Shakespeare's life' does not matter very much.

I think, however, that without rejecting all that comes out of these approaches it is possible to appreciate the plays in a complex context that includes a measure of understanding of what it was like to live in Shakespeare's time, as well as what it is like to live in our own. The author of the plays, and I do want to call him Shakespeare, was a playwright and poet of genius, and he was also a man who early on gained bitter experience of the brutal realities of life when he married the pregnant Anne; who faced the grim prospect of spending his life in his father's business in order to provide for a growing family; and who instead went to London, taking with him the scepticism and the cunning protean energies as well as the fresh perspective of an outsider. His marginal status, as a man from the provinces, must have assisted him in establishing himself in a profession that was defined by its own marginal status and that nevertheless had more to say to and about its time than any other. He was an outsider looking in on the centre of power, which through imaginative identification he was able to know and represent to itself. Anti-Stratfordians ask how a non-aristocrat was able to understand the aristocratic life so well, but the fact is that he understood it without wholeheartedly endorsing it. There is always in the margins of his plays a voice that mocks or questions, that is able to criticize in an oblique way the follies and abuses of the powerful. Shakespeare was a leading practitioner of an occupation that could minutely reflect changes, not just in fashion, but also in thought and feeling.

Many today deny that there is any such thing as universal value or essential humanity, but the fact remains that Shakespeare's plays speak to us down the centuries as complex structures that do comment on our own situation, that continue to mock and question as well as to comfort and console – even if what they say is no longer quite what Shakespeare thought they said.

## SHAKESPEARE'S CONTEXT

It has become customary to divide the historical context within which Shakespeare wrote into two broad areas: the 'times', meaning the historical and political events that took place and the social conditions that existed during his lifetime; and the 'background of ideas', that more abstract area of beliefs that were then current, the social, political and religious concepts often referred to as the 'Elizabethan world picture'. This is, however, an artificial distinction, for the 'times' is really a cultural context in which the events that we think of as the history of the period, and the structures of thought that dominated or competed within it, were really aspects of the same thing. Cultural events cannot be detached from their originating history, and for Shakespeare the 'times' and the 'background of ideas' were equally informed by crisis and controversy. Within that context the theatre in which he worked was more than simply a form of entertainment, more than an art form; it was a dynamic place that reflected and influenced political and religious pressures and social and cultural assumptions.

Anyone with more than a cursory knowledge of Shakespeare's plays will have recognized that both their figurative language and its philosophical underpinnings appear to reflect a deep concern, amounting almost to obsession, with order and disorder. In this Shakespeare was not different from other dramatists of his time or, for that matter, from poets and prose writers. The concern with order is so prevalent in Elizabethan documents that one modern scholar, E.M.W. Tillyard, understood it to be the shaping spirit of Elizabethan thought. Tillyard's book, *The Elizabethan World Picture*, first published in 1943, had an immense influence on Shakespeare studies for the four decades that followed its publication. In it he argued that Elizabethans had a world view governed by a conception of universal order that was 'so taken for granted, so much a part of the collective mind of the people, that it is hardly mentioned except in explicitly didactic passages'.[6] This conception was, according to Tillyard, implicit everywhere in the writing of the time. The 'collective mind' he proposed was a deeply conservative one so terrorized by the threat of disorder that dissent was, in effect, a psychological impossibility.

The fact is, however, that both Elizabeth I and James I ruled over a state that was not merely threatened by disorder, but heading towards the political, social, ideological and spiritual division that culminated in the Civil War of 1642. Shakespeare's world was dominated by the needs of the reigning monarch in ways that today are difficult for us to comprehend. The monarch was at the centre of political power, the key agent in a system that depended on the control and balance of the competing needs of ambitious individuals and factions. Beyond this, the *figure* of the monarch was at the centre of a symbolic system that gave religious and cultural authority to the political system, and that provided narratives and metaphors for poets and playwrights. Shakespeare's working career spanned the last 15 years of the reign of Elizabeth I and the first ten years of that of James I, a period when the whole system was under pressure. Both monarchs were concerned to maintain political control in a situation where many things threatened their own safety as well as the stability of the state.

The 25 or so years of Shakespeare's theatrical career coincided with the most productive years of the explosion of English theatre that happened between the 1570s and 1642. They also marked the climax of literary and artistic activity that was a part of the Renaissance in England. 'Renaissance' or 'rebirth' is the name that has been given to the extraordinary years that marked the transition in Western Europe from the medieval to the modern world. It is impossible to define with any degree of precision the boundaries of the period. It is usual to place it in the span of years from the fourteenth to the early seventeenth century, but its roots in Italy went further back than that, while in England it did not make much impact until the end of the fifteenth century. The word 'Renaissance' implies a fixed moment of renewal, however, and that is misleading because the phenomena to which it relates were diverse, and embraced continuities as well as discontinuities, clinging to past certainties as well as advancing into an unknown future, loss as well as gain. Some recent critics avoid the ambiguity inherent in the term by referring instead to the 'early modern' period.

There are, nevertheless, broad progressions that we can identify. A major one was the rediscovery of Classical culture. One change that marked the waning of the Middle Ages was a growth of scepticism about the traditional authority of the Church. Established religion was subjected to pressures that led to the Protestant Reformation, which substituted a belief in the absolute authority of the Bible for the acceptance of the absolute authority of the Church. But the search for an alternative source of ethical authority led some scholars to Classical writings and to the 'renaissance' of Greek and Roman culture; much effort went into the project of reinterpreting Christian thought so as to harmonize it with this revived pagan culture. This intellectual counterpart of the Reformation was termed 'humanism'. It replaced blind acceptance of authority and dogma with a new spirit of sceptical and empirical enquiry.

These new ideas were introduced into England around the turn of the sixteenth century by a group of men who gathered round the Dutch scholar Desiderius Erasmus and the English scholar–statesman Sir Thomas More. They included John Colet, who founded St Paul's School in 1509, and William Grocyn, who introduced Greek into the university curriculum. Their efforts fostered a more widespread desire for education; the first printing press had been set up as recently as 1476, and it was obviously crucial as a means of disseminating the multiplying fruits of intellectual exploration. The results of this excitement of ideas are too extensive to be considered here, but for the moment suffice it to say that the possibilities opened up for empiricism and scepticism were no small part of the nexus of problems, both ideological and practical, faced by Elizabeth and James.

## POLITICS AND HISTORY

Some problems had their origins in the distant past, and we need to know something of their history. The Tudor dynasty was founded in 1485 by Elizabeth's grandfather, who ascended the throne as Henry VII after he defeated the army of Richard III at the Battle of Bosworth Field. Henry's defeat of Richard put an end to that long period of civil strife, known as the Wars of the Roses, that had marked the struggle between the Houses of Lancaster and York for possession of the English crown (the red rose was the symbol of the House of Lancaster, the white rose of the House of York). This was a dynastic struggle between the descendants of John of Gaunt, Duke of Lancaster, and Edmund Langley, Duke of York, the third and fourth sons of Edward III. In 1399 Gaunt's son Henry Bolingbroke had taken the crown from his cousin and rightful king, Richard II, to become Henry IV, thus distorting the line of inheritance. Henry's reign was troubled by dissention and revolt, but his son Henry V, a very able king, restored domestic peace. However, Henry V died while his own son was still an infant, and Henry VI grew up to be a weak king, controlled by protectors and ambitious rivals, and finally overthrown by the Yorkist descendants of Edmund Langley and displaced by Edward IV.

The struggles between Lancaster and York, bitter as they were, were essentially a gigantic family struggle for the crown amongst contenders who all claimed a blood tie to the throne, and many of them died in the struggle. They did, of course, involve the country at large, though in comparison with civil wars as we observe them today these were rather minor ones. However, as Elizabethan writers never tired of pointing out, a disease of the head infects the entire body. Henry Tudor's removal of Richard was a welcome act of surgery, and his coronation as Henry VII and subsequent marriage to Elizabeth of York, daughter of Edward IV (Henry was himself a remote descendant of the Lancastrian line) continued the healing process by uniting the warring factions. The Wars of the Roses retained a powerful significance throughout the Tudor period, which is why Shakespeare made use of them in his history plays. They offered a warning, frequently used by Tudor propagandists, of the dangers of rebellion, though they could just as easily be used to warn of the dangers of tyranny. In spite of the obviously positive outcome of his defeat of Richard III, Henry's right to the English throne was weak, and his reign was plagued by opposition, though he managed to control it. He and his successors expended much energy in trying to prove the legitimacy of the Tudor dynasty.

The need to consolidate the Tudor hold on power and to project the family name into the future became an obsessive concern for Henry's son, who in 1509 succeeded him as Henry VIII. Henry

VIII was well aware of the fragility of human life, for his older brother Arthur, who should have succeeded Henry VII, had died in 1502. Shortly after Henry's coronation he married Arthur's widow, Catherine of Aragon. This was largely because of pressure from his father, who wanted to maintain the ties with Spain, as well as the dowry that came with Catherine. Their marriage had caused deep discomfort within the Church because of the Biblical prohibition of the marriage of a man to his brother's widow, and a papal dispensation had been necessary. Catherine was a good wife to Henry, and the marriage lasted for more than 20 years, but it was darkened by Henry's increasing resentment at her failure to produce a male heir. She did give birth in 1516 to a daughter, Mary, but a series of miscarriages made it clear to Henry that she was unlikely to produce the son he so desperately wanted both as a means of continuing his name and in order to secure the stability of the kingdom. His efforts to remedy this added religious division to dynastic instability.

In 1527 Henry initiated an attempt to divorce Catherine on the grounds that the marriage and the papal dispensation that allowed it had not been valid. Negotiations with Rome proceeded uneasily, but in 1532 Henry learned that his mistress Anne Boleyn was pregnant. He married her secretly in January of the following year, and in May Thomas Cranmer, Archbishop of Canterbury, dissolved the marriage to Catherine, making Mary illegitimate and giving a doubtful legitimacy to Anne's child, which, ironically, was also a girl, the future Elizabeth I. Little more than three years after this second marriage Henry accused Anne of adultery; this was probably a trumped-up charge, but she was executed for it. The day after the execution Henry married Jane Seymour, who did produce a son, Edward, the heir that Henry wanted, though she died as a result of giving birth. As is well known, Henry had three more wives, but he fathered no more children. All three of those he did produce had their turn at ruling England.

Henry's efforts at producing an heir had other results. Rome refused to accept the annulment of his marriage to Catherine, so denying the validity of his marriage to Anne. The man who in 1527 began the negotiations with Pope Clement VII for annulment on Henry's behalf was his Lord Chancellor, Thomas, Cardinal Wolsey. Wolsey had already set about reforming the Church in England when he was sent by Henry on what should have been a relatively straightforward mission. It was complicated, however, by the fact that the Pope was under the control of the Holy Roman Emperor, Charles V of Spain, who was Catherine's nephew. What was, for Henry, primarily a domestic problem was, for Wolsey, a political one about control of the Papacy, for the Pope's spiritual sway over European states was really a political hold. Wolsey found himself working towards incompatible goals; he was unable to accept the compromises that would have been necessary to gain Papal agreement, and in the struggle that followed England was forced to watch the Pope being placed more firmly under the control of the Empire.

The failure to get his way was also a humiliation for Henry, who removed Wolsey from the Chancellorship in 1529. The following years saw, inevitably, increasingly strained relations with Rome, until the news of Anne's pregnancy drove Henry to the action we have already seen. His act of defiance pushed those relations to breaking point: not only was his new marriage declared invalid, but Cranmer, who had legitimized it, was excommunicated, and Henry was warned that he would suffer the same penalty. His excommunication was carried out in September 1533, to which he responded by proclaiming himself 'Protector and only Supreme Head of the Church and Clergy of England'. This was the initiating act of the Henrician Reformation, which divided Church and nation and set in motion the long internal struggle in England between Catholic and Protestant factions.

Henry's son by Jane Seymour was a sickly child who acceded to the throne at the age of ten as Edward VI (1547–53), though for most of this time the country was governed by the Lord Protector, the Duke of Northumberland. This put power into Cranmer's hands, giving him the opportunity to develop Protestant reforms by instituting his 42 articles of religion (1551) and introducing an English prayer book, measures which led to the foundation of the Anglican Church in Elizabeth's reign, although these developments were anything but smooth. On the death of Edward, Northumberland attempted to extend Protestant power (and his own) by effecting the marriage of his son to Lady Jane Grey, granddaughter of Henry VII, and proclaiming her queen. He did not succeed in this, and all three of them were executed.

It is ironic that Henry's attempts to secure the future of his dynasty by producing a male heir should have created the conditions that jeopardized the security of both his daughters. Mary, who succeeded Edward and reigned for five years, was  considered illegitimate by Protestants because in their eyes the marriage of Henry to her mother, his brother's widow, had never been valid. Elizabeth's legitimacy had been proclaimed both in her father's will and by Act of Parliament, but the Catholic Church had never recognized the divorce and considered her to be illegitimate, so from the start her reign was plagued by questions about her right to govern. In the shadow of these conflicting claims Mary and Elizabeth embodied the division between Catholics and Protestants. Mary, as soon as she became queen, set about reversing the religious reformation initiated by her father. Within months of her accession she had reinstated Catholicism in England and encouraged the persecution of prominent Protestants that led to the martyrdom of many and the exile of many more, ensuring a lasting English hatred of Rome. She married Philip II of Spain, partly to consolidate Catholic power, partly in the hope of producing an heir to prevent her sister from ascending the throne and restoring Protestantism. In this latter she was disappointed, but she did create in Philip a claimant to the English throne and in Spain a potential enemy to England for most of Elizabeth's reign, even after the defeat of the Armada in 1588.

Although Elizabeth was guilty of the persecution of Catholics, during her own very long reign she did much to heal the division and to promote tolerance by effecting a compromise in the Church. Still, she was left with the religious and political repercussions of the division, and for the duration of her reign there were many plots to overthrow her. Some were devised by foreign Catholic enemies, particularly by Spain and France. There were also strong internal Catholic interests, which promoted the right to the throne of Elizabeth's cousin Mary Stuart, Queen of Scots.

Mary was the daughter of Henry VIII's sister Margaret, who had married James IV of Scotland. The Catholic faction, still refusing to accept Elizabeth's legitimacy, now claimed that Mary was first in line to the throne. In 1558 Mary married the heir to the French crown, giving another powerful Catholic force an interest in the English throne. Mary's sexual adventurousness was her downfall, however: her jealous second husband Lord Darnley murdered her lover David Rizzio, and was in turn murdered by another lover, the Earl of Bothwell, probably with Mary's connivance. Her subsequent marriage to Bothwell was too much for the Scots, and in 1567 she was forced to abdicate in favour of her infant son James. In the following year, after a failed attempt to regain power, she fled to England. This created a dilemma for Elizabeth; Mary was a source of danger, but she was also her cousin, and an exiled monarch. In spite of the advice of her advisers to be rid of the problem, Elizabeth retained Mary in custody, as prisoner and guest, and this remained her state for 19 years. During that time she figured in numerous conspiracies against Elizabeth, but it was only in 1586, when there was documentary evidence of Mary's involvement in yet another conspiracy, the Babington plot, and only at the strong urging of Parliament, that Elizabeth was finally prevailed upon to order Mary's execution, which was carried out in the following year. This did not put an end to the Catholic problem, but it did remove one of its central emblems.

Elizabeth's dealings with religious issues seem to have been driven by political expediency and by her sense of the prospect of national greatness and unity. She might have followed her sister's return to Rome, which would certainly have made relations with Spain and France easier, as well as neutralizing Mary Stuart, but it would also have reversed the move to an independent nationhood that her father had initiated, and it would have ignored the inclinations of an increasing number of Englishmen. She began her reign, therefore, with the Elizabethan Settlement. This was passed, not without strenuous opposition, by her first Parliament in 1559. It made Elizabeth 'Supreme Governor' of Church and state, establishing a Church of England that incorporated Cranmer's reforms and was independent of Papal authority, though retaining traditional forms of worship. It also required that everyone attend church.

Elizabeth's compromises obviously did not appease most Catholics. They were also seen as insufficient by radical Protestants, often misleadingly called 'Puritans'. Many of the most ardent reformers, who under Mary had been driven into exile in Europe, returned with even more extreme ideas. Their hostility to the ritual and excess of Catholicism and to priestly power was not satisfied by moderate adaptations, and many were as reluctant to obey a monarch as head of the Church as they had been to obey the Pope.

Elizabeth's hold on power had to contend with another major difficulty: as a woman ruling a patriarchal system she was an anomaly. Renaissance England inherited and generally accepted a hierarchy in which women were legally and culturally subject to men. As we shall see, Elizabeth countered this problem in subtly theatrical ways, transforming herself into the central figure in a complex of myths. This only served to disguise the fundamental issue raised by her unmarried state, however, and for this her sister Mary stood as a warning. In marrying Philip of Spain Mary had risked putting the control of England into the hands of a foreign monarch, and after her death Philip did indeed lay claim to the English throne. If Elizabeth were to marry an equal, she too would have to wed a foreigner, and nationalist feeling was not open to a repeat of that experience. Any English husband she might choose, however, would necessarily be an inferior, and that would not do either.

Through the early years of her reign Elizabeth frequently teased her subjects with the possibility of one marriage or another, to a foreign prince (King Philip of Spain, the Archdukes Ferdinand and Charles, the Duke of Anjou were all suitors at various times), or to a favourite like Robert Dudley, Earl of Leicester, but she diplomatically remained single. This, however, created a further problem. It left open the question of who would succeed her after her death, a question to which she refused to offer any answer. The Wars of the Roses were a reminder to the English of the competing factions and potential civil strife that could arise when there was no indisputable candidate for the succession. This unknown future was a constant source of national concern and anxiety, increasing as Elizabeth grew older and beyond the age of possible motherhood, and resolved only on her deathbed, when she named James VI of Scotland as her successor.

Nevertheless, for 45 years she performed a brilliant and, for the most part, effective political balancing act. She was an erudite and astute woman, a consummate politician who knew how to manipulate her own image into a symbol of national unity, glory and power: she made herself into Gloriana, the Virgin Queen, embodiment of English magnificence. Although she fostered belief in royal absolutism, which taught that the monarch was God's deputy on earth, she was always willing to listen to trusted advisers and to take note of the opinions of the Privy Council. Until late in her reign she made a judicious choice of counsellors, like Sir Francis Walsingham and William Cecil, Lord Burleigh, without allowing any of them to engross too much power. She exerted control over the factional interests that were always ready to erupt in the Tudor court, and managed to maintain genuine internal order most of the time and its semblance at other times. She watched over the growth of English power beyond her borders:

the rise of power at sea was to a large extent rooted in piracy, but the defeat in 1588 of the Spanish Armada, which Philip had intended as the vehicle of a decisive Spanish invasion, gave England naval supremacy.

Perhaps Elizabeth's greatest achievement was the explosion of national pride that characterized the middle years of her reign. Her father's break from Rome had been a dangerous move, and its perils became fully apparent in the many Catholic conspiracies against her. Her success in foiling these, and in thwarting French and Spanish designs on England, was part of the reason for the increased sense of national identity, of England as a state able to resist foreign political interference. This perception of a national identity is closely tied in with the phenomenal growth of a national literature. Writers whose works we still read today – poets like Sidney, Spenser and Donne, dramatists like Marlowe, Shakespeare and Jonson, prose-writers like Bacon and Burton – represent a literary flowering that marked English as the language of a new national culture fit to exist alongside the older, more prestigious cultures of France and Italy.

Her achievements notwithstanding, Elizabeth ruled for too long; in her final years the shine had faded from her image. She allowed too much power to Sir Robert Cecil and too much favour to his rival the Earl of Essex, giving the latter ambitions that tempted him in 1601 to lead a rebellion against her, creating what was potentially the most serious threat to her rule at any time during her career. The post-Armada years had involved England in futile wars on the Continent. There was economic disturbance in the realm and her refusal to settle doubts about the national future imparted a tinge of bitterness to the declining years of her reign, as well as encouraging the development of factions. Her death came as something of a relief.

The accession of James I in 1603 should have resolved all these problems. As a descendant of Henry VII his claim to the throne was strong, and he was a candidate with an appeal for both Protestants and Catholics. Furthermore, after 50 years of rule by women he restored patriarchy, which for most people implied stability, and as a father of sons he offered the assurance of a smooth succession that had been impossible for Elizabeth. In spite of the hostility of the English to the Scots, he ascended the throne with the nation well-disposed towards him. He was an intelligent and cultured man, a poet who had also written political treatises.

As King James VI of Scotland he had been a strong and successful monarch; but his experience did not prepare him for the more complex interests and rivalries that Elizabeth had been so adept at balancing. As King of England he showed himself to be a vacillating defender of the Protestant cause, and alienated the Puritan faction that was increasingly dominating Parliament, where he was perceived as being insufficiently firm against Catholic interests.

Many of the difficulties James faced were inherited from Elizabeth, particularly the decline in royal revenue and the economic problems caused by disastrous famines in the last decade of her reign. But he proved a wasteful and ineffectual ruler, countering the increasing influence of Parliament by a stronger affirmation of the concept of royal absolutism or the divine right of kings, which merely served to obscure his weakness in dealing with political realities. The national optimism of the beginning of his reign quickly soured, and people forgot the disappointments of Elizabeth's regime and looked back on it as a golden age.

This political, religious and constitutional history is not simply 'background' to Shakespeare's writing. Rather, it is the framework within which he wrote, and its preoccupations, its disturbances and anxieties, are what he wrote about, however obliquely. The disturbances in the political sphere had wider ramifications, for they reflected and were reflected by the troubled and shifting social circumstances of Elizabethan and Jacobean England. The model of the state was organic: the state was like a body – was, indeed, the 'body politic'. In this model, the body was perceived as a hierarchy, healthy when all its parts were working in good order, the lower parts serving the head, the head in control of the lower parts. Throughout his career Shakespeare monitored the health of this body.

## SOCIAL MODELS

Tudor England was a hierarchical society based on differences in 'degree' or rank. Its structure had its origins in the feudal system of the Middle Ages, but due to various pressures the breakdown of the structure was well advanced. The feudal system of law and government was imposed on England by William the Conqueror after the successful Norman invasion of 1066. He rewarded his followers with lands taken from the defeated English nobles, which they could hold for as long as they provided the king with military support when he needed it, but he retained jurisdiction over them. In effect the king owned all the country, which he ruled through a hierarchy of lords and barons. Each lord administered the land around his own manor, and generated support by leasing out part of it to lesser nobles. The system continued down the scale to the villeins and serfs at the bottom, who worked the fields of the lord of the manor and received food, shelter and protection. Thus, the mass of people were peasants, essentially enslaved to the land they worked, and with little freedom to leave the estates on which they lived. Their lord had a theoretical duty to protect them, but this system of ties of obedience was held together by military and economic force – a man remained in his 'rightful' place because he had little choice in the matter. It is important to note that although the Church reinforced this organisation by teaching that it was a man's Christian duty to carry out the responsibilities of his place, it did not claim that a king was king by divine right. This was a Tudor invention.

Elizabethan writings are full of the language and imagery of this hierarchical system, but circumstances had changed. The feudal system had broken down in the later Middle Ages, and by Elizabeth's time the increase in social mobility was such that the old distinctions were wearing away too quickly for the entrenched orders to cling on to them. As the historian D.M. Palliser puts it, 'the very period – from say 1540 to 1640 – when society was especially fluid was the time of greatest stress upon order, degree, the Chain of Being, genealogy and the cult of ancestry'.[7] The reactionary emphasis on the concepts of a world view fast becoming obsolete was an attempt to halt change by pointing insistently to the dangers of disorder and the rightness of the 'Chain of Being', and it blurred or even denied the distinction between social unrest and social change.

There were clear causes of social unrest during Elizabeth's last years, and they persisted into James's reign. The economy of England was still based on agriculture. The defeat of the Spanish Armada in 1588 had boosted national pride and fostered a sense of unity that distracted attention from the effects of very poor harvests in 1586 and 1587. The euphoria soon evaporated in a decade of famines and protest against their economic effects. There was a run of meagre harvests between 1594 and 1597, and food prices rose while the wages of labourers fell. In 1595 there were food riots in London, and Elizabeth was forced to impose martial law on the city. In 1596 starving workers rioted in Oxfordshire. The consequences of bad harvests were exacerbated by the effects of the enclosure system, which had allowed wealthy landowners to convert arable land into pasture. Raising sheep was an efficient way to use land and a far less labour-intensive activity than growing crops, so many labourers were displaced from the land and without work.

As a result there was a steady migration of rural workers to the towns, especially to London. Increased opportunities for education produced a growing number of intelligent and ambitious men who moved to the capital in search of opportunities and employment that might advance them (we could count Shakespeare as one of them). But if many migrants were able to offer useful skills and were employable, many more became vagrants, the 'masterless men' who so terrified Tudor and Stuart authorities obsessed with place and order and yearning for stability, to whom they represented the ultimate threat to hierarchy. Masterless men included wage-labourers unable to find work, and unemployed soldiers returning from the European wars. Vagrancy was defined in terms of three main characteristics: poverty, fitness for work and unemployment. Because the established view was that those who remained unemployed did so through choice, they were treated as criminals and punished harshly for a condition that they could not remedy.[8] In the early years of Elizabeth's reign, unprotected actors were classed as vagabonds and ran the risk of being so treated.

Paradoxically, as the numbers of the poor increased, so did the numbers of the prosperous. England's naval power had opened up new opportunities for trade. Industries were developing, notably cloth manufacturing, and coal, iron, tin and copper were mined on an increasing scale. A growing merchant class was able to exert an upward pressure on the social dividing-lines. The upper level of the aristocracy had already been forced to open itself up to the 'new men', able advisers and supporters who had been raised and enriched by Henry VII and especially by Henry VIII. They had long defended their privilege and kept wealth and power within their own hands by inter-marrying; a glance at the genealogies of the great families shows how close and complex these ties had been. Between 1485 and 1569 more than half the peers and their male heirs married within the peerage. During Elizabeth's reign this figure changed significantly, however: between 1570 and 1599 the proportion dropped to one third.[9] The growing number of peers marrying outside their class indicates an increasing need to bring money into the aristocracy through the daughters of wealthy citizens; it also indicates the increasing influence of those wealthy citizens.

Although in its broad outlines the social hierarchy in Shakespeare's time still reflected the medieval feudal structure, there were these important differences. The move away from a rural, agriculture-based economy to an urban economy based on trade created the accompanying social movement that advanced the development of new strata. Beneath the monarch herself the Elizabethans recognized three classes, though within the classes there were levels of differentiation: the nobles and gentlemen; the citizens and burgesses and the rural yeomanry; and a lower class of artisans, servants, labourers and apprentices. Beneath these, having no official standing at all, was the impoverished underclass of the unemployed: rogues, beggars, vagabonds, masterless men. The authorities tried many measures to enforce these divisions, from the enactment of sumptuary laws that prescribed the kind and quality of clothing for different social groups, to regulation of movement from town to town. However, the shifts taking place in society made such control increasingly difficult.

The highest social rank, the nobility, were also those closest to the seat of power, since it was from amongst them that Elizabeth chose her Privy Council, the body through which she governed. They also represented the greatest threat to her security. She surrounded herself with brilliant courtiers; some were dangerously ambitious, driven by self-interest, and part of her own genius was to be able to deal with political intrigue. Court culture was sophisticated and even cosmopolitan. The language of education was still Latin, and Elizabeth herself often used it to write letters to foreign dignitaries, though she could also communicate in French, Italian, Dutch and Spanish. The highest level of the nobility beneath the queen herself was very small, consisting of the lay peers and their families. Only the monarch could create peerages, and a peerage died out if there was no hereditary succession. Elizabeth clearly saw it as in her best interests not to allow the numbers of these powerful men to increase, for when she came to the throne in 1588 there were 57 lay peers, and at her death in 1603 there were 55.

The peers were really the top level of the gentry, which included knights, usually given the title for some service done to the country. Originally, as the title implies, that service would have been military, but Elizabeth could also bestow knighthoods for political and personal service, and even in recognition of outstanding wealth. The rest of the gentry was made up of esquires and gentlemen, men who possessed land and wealth and were entitled to a coat of arms (the application of the Shakespeare family in 1596 for a coat of arms indicates how they evaluated themselves on the social scale). Their substance and abilities supposedly gave them the capacity to govern at a local level. It is impossible to know the exact number of members of the gentry, but Palliser estimates it at no more than 2 per cent of the population.[10]

The line dividing gentry from commoners was important but intangible, and it was a line often crossed. Gentlemen were usually landowners, but they did not farm their own land; landowners who did were known as yeomen. Commoners had their own hierarchy. The yeomen at the top were often as wealthy as many of the gentry. Townsmen of equivalent rank were known as burgesses: these were usually men of some local importance who held civic positions, or members of the rising merchant classes. Below the yeomen were husbandmen, farmers who did not own the land they worked but were tenants of it, and at the bottom of the recognised social heap were craftsmen such as tailors and carpenters, and day-labourers and farm-workers – men who owned no land, who worked for wages and who were generally poor. Access to skilled trades and crafts was controlled through the regulation of apprenticeships. Only the sons of families that had estates with income valued at more than 40 shillings were allowed to be apprenticed to a trade. They were taken on at about the age of 14, and remained as apprentices for seven years, during which time they lived in the household of their employer. Without the training given through apprenticeship it was almost impossible to enter a skilled trade, so those who fell beneath the minimum financial requirement were doomed to stay there; even at these lower levels of society, the lines between classes were policed.

Since all able-bodied men were expected to work, those who did not have a craft became labourers or farm-workers and remained poor. They were the lowest of the classes, but this does not mean that they had no one to look down on. As we have seen, there was the vagabond under-class who threatened the hierarchy by having no place in it. Our knowledge of Elizabethan life is derived from whatever documents remain, and since literate people tended to write about their own surroundings we know more about the upper and 'middle' classes than we do about the poor, but it is certain that the poor far outnumbered the wealthy.

The basic Elizabethan social unit was the household rather than the family because it included servants and employees. Its hierarchy reflected that of the state. The patriarch was like a king; his wife was subordinate to him, and his sons remained under his authority until they married and set up their own households. His daughters, on marriage, were passed from his authority to that of their husbands (the echo of this remains in modern wedding ceremonies when a father 'gives away' the bride as if she were a possession rather than a person). In theory a woman did not have control over her person or her property unless she was a widow. The Widow who marries Hortensio in *The Taming of the Shrew* obviously has authority over her person.

Marriage amongst the gentry was a means of providing heirs to secure the family name and property, and most Church teaching still stressed that procreation was the primary purpose of marriage. Marriages were often arranged, so as to unite families to consolidate wealth or power or social status. Enforcement was rarely necessary, since everyone understood the social, political and economic foundations of such arrangements. A man might marry a woman of his own social level, or from a class beneath him if her family was wealthy. Sexual desire as a basis for marriage was constantly attacked by commentators of the time; the interest in the relationship between romantic love and marriage shown in so many of Shakespeare's plays does not indicate that it was commonplace. Affection might well develop within a marriage, but it was not the same as our modern notion of romantic love. Children of wealthy commoners had more freedom in this, and Puritan belief did stress the importance of mutual esteem and companionship between marriage partners, but even for them duty took precedence over impulse. Amongst the lower classes, poverty ensured that practical needs excluded much possibility of romance.

Modern ideas about the importance of individual fulfilment make it difficult for us to understand such a willingness to subordinate desire to duty, but as Lawrence Stone has shown, in the sixteenth and seventeenth centuries people did not draw a clear distinction between marriage for material reasons and marriage for reasons of sentiment, nor did they believe that a sexual relationship should of necessity be accompanied by an emotional one.[11] This does not mean that they did not understand the passions that we call 'love', only that they did not give them the same value that we do today. Their ability to perceive marriage in terms of duty meant that the breakdown of marriage was comparatively rare – a good thing, since divorce was out of the question.

In the families of the gentry both boys and girls were educated, and were expected to be able to read and write; they received their basic education from tutors. At the age of 12 a boy might be sent to another household, usually of higher rank, where he would serve as a page. He was not actually a servant, however, because he would learn all the skills demanded of a young gentleman: riding, hunting, archery and military skills, as well as the rules of etiquette. Schools were for the sons of families of lower rank (though not, generally speaking, of the poor), and provided the kind of education that young men hoped would help them to secure social advancement. The schools were usually run by clergymen, who taught the boys to read and write in English, though some offered much more than this. The majority of commoners remained illiterate, however; most could not even sign their names.

There were only two universities in England at this time, Oxford and Cambridge, which had been founded to train clerics. The Inns of Court in London provided a higher education in the law. The universities and the inns catered mainly for the sons of gentlemen, though wealthy yeomen saw them as a means of advancing the fortunes of their own sons; their function was from this point of view as much social as educational. Many university graduates did go into the ministry and the law, as well as into other areas of public life. Some who could not find employment set up village schools. There were many ambitious men who, like Greene and other of the University Wits, were drawn to London and found themselves embittered inhabitants of the fringes of a life they coveted. Such men figure in many plays of the period as malcontents, satirist–observers of a social world they despise and yet envy, like Jaques in *As You Like It* or, on a different level, Hamlet.

## LONDON

This was the state of England as Shakespeare experienced it, and it informs the material of his plays, but in a particular way. History has identified him with his country as a kind of patron artist, England's national poet and playwright. This is somewhat misleading, however, because to Shakespeare England was London. It is undeniable that he loved the life outside London: his upbringing gave him a deep knowledge of country life, which is clearly reflected in his plays. The fact that when he ended his London career he retired to Stratford indicates how assiduously he maintained his ties with that small provincial town; and since he could easily have afforded to remain in London, it might also suggest that he preferred the simpler life beyond the metropolis. But the profession he had entered was a London phenomenon. There were times, as we know, when his acting company had to take to the road and perform in the provinces; its plays were nevertheless written for London audiences and reflected their tastes, their interests, their preoccupations. As the historian Peter Laslett has suggested, Tudor and Stuart England was 'a large rural hinterland attached to a vast metropolis through a network of insignificant local centres'.[12] For Shakespeare it was the concerns of the denizens of this 'vast metropolis' that were of consuming interest. To understand those elements of Shakespeare's experience we have to begin in London.

During the 25 or so years that Shakespeare spent in London, it was a place that united great splendour and great squalor. It had the royal court as its symbolic centre and its centre of power. It embraced fine churches and palatial mansions and estates, the homes of aristocrats and powerful churchmen. It contained the houses and businesses of the growing merchant middle class, and was a magnetic centre for ambitious and energetic men. But it also contained the ruins of religious houses (the 'bare ruined choirs' of Sonnet 73), a reminder of the devastation carried out through Henry VIII's reforming zeal; and it contained the cottages or hovels of the poor. Many of the increasing numbers drawn to London in search of a better life found that the streets they had hoped would be paved with gold were actually covered in dung.

Between 1560 and 1603 the population of London almost doubled, from approximately 120 000 to something over 200 000. This might not seem especially large to us today, but it was the largest city in Europe, and no other city in England had a population of more than 15 000 (the total population of England was about five million). London was the centre of England's political and economic life and, increasingly, of its cultural life. Its existence depended on the River Thames: the city proper, holding about half of London's population within its protective wall, stretched along the north bank for a distance of something more than a mile, but its suburbs spread out in all directions. The entrance to the city from the south was London Bridge, an impressive structure with shops lining its length. The river itself teemed with activity, criss-crossed by ferries that were an important means of transportation for the populace. The boats and barges that sailed up and down it were the key to both local and international trade, while downriver were the ships that gave Elizabethan England the control of the seas that led to the beginnings of empire.

The Thames was also a sewer, recipient of the refuse that collected in the city's open ditches. In this it reflected the obverse side of London's reality: houses and shops were built very close together and disease could spread very rapidly. This was an overcrowded, insanitary city, visited almost every summer by the bubonic plague, also known as the Black Death. It is impossible to give any sense of the average toll taken by the plague; during Shakespeare's London career the worst years were 1592–3 and 1603. In 1603 perhaps 23 per cent of the London population died of it. The word 'plague' took on something of the ugliness that 'cancer' has for us today, and sometimes hid the facts of other diseases: death from malnutrition, for example, was common and was often ascribed to the plague. Smallpox too was frequently epidemic; in 1562 the queen herself almost died of it.

The crowding that encouraged the spread of disease was also the source of much of the dangerous excitement of Shakespeare's London. The noble, or the fashionable 'gallant', or the respectable citizen who ventured out into the streets joined a vital throng of tradesmen and pedlars, street-boys and apprentices, prostitutes and unemployed soldiers. It was often difficult to find passage, and the unwary might fall victim to tricksters or cutpurses, or find themselves drawn into brawls. The playhouses attracted both nobles and apprentices, but so did a cock-fight or a bear-baiting – or an execution. This was, after all, a society in which punishment was a form of public spectacle. Executions, even of the most noble of 'criminals', such as Mary, Queen of Scots, were carried out in public, and their grisly results were left on public display: the bodies of thieves and murderers were left hanging on the gibbet, and the heads of traitors were exhibited at the tower on London Bridge as a warning against rebellion. At the lower end of the social scale, as we have seen, harsh corporal punishment was often inflicted on beggars and paupers for no other reason than that they were poor. Apart from being flogged, beggars and petty criminals might be put into the stocks or the pillory, so that the townsfolk could take pleasure in pelting them with stones or rotten fruit.

London was an unruly organism, and governing it was a matter of conflict and compromise. Because the city was the seat of the court, the crown obviously had a stake in its government. The monarch ruled the country by hereditary right, with the guidance of a group of hand-picked advisers known as the Privy Council. The monarch did not have to accept the advice of the Privy Council, but Elizabeth usually managed to give the impression at least of listening. Orders of the Privy Council were binding on the country and could be issued for particular areas, so the Privy Council was able to exert a degree of control over London.

The city also had its own government, however, a Corporation led by the Lord Mayor and two sheriffs, elected annually by powerful groups of merchants and tradesmen, and 26 aldermen elected for life. Since many London citizens were increasingly drawn to Puritanism, the city authorities were often hostile to what they saw as the frivolous or wasteful ways of the crown. The crown, on the other hand, was dependent on the city in many ways, particularly for loans, and whenever possible avoided blatantly opposing city wishes, though as we shall see the theatres became the centre of an on-going struggle between crown and city.

The paradoxical juxtaposition in London of magnificence and barbarity reflects the complex tensions that existed in all areas of English life – social, political, religious and cultural. In this account of England in the late sixteenth and early seventeenth centuries I have stressed the antithetical pressures generated by an official vision of an ordered society faced with a reality of potentially explosive strain and unrest. Elizabeth and James were both well aware of their own vulnerability and of the threat to national stability. Each was at the centre of a political machine that monitored the state through surveillance and the gathering of intelligence and that used much more subtle means to forestall and defuse dangers, including historical distortion, poetic myth, theatrical illusion and personal symbolism.

## BELIEFS AND MYTHS

I want to return to the questions raised earlier about the 'Elizabethan world picture' and the 'collective mind' that Tillyard believed was represented by it, because to understand Shakespeare's plays we do need to know something of it, and of how it related to the historical, political and social energies we have examined.

The doctrine fundamental to this world picture was derived from medieval teachings that had their roots in Greek philosophy. This doctrine apprehended the universe as a system of parallel and interlocking hierarchies. The word 'hierarchy' itself properly refers to the groupings of three divisions and nine orders of angels with different levels of power. The hierarchy that gives validity to all others has God at its head, and descends through levels of angels, men, animals, and the vegetable and mineral worlds. Within each level of this major hierarchy are others that replicate it: the lion is the head of the hierarchy of animals, the rose of flowers, the oak of trees, the sun of stars and planets, and gold of metals. The hierarchy of men has the king at its head. This vast system of hierarchies is sometimes known as 'the great chain of being'. It was believed that, because it was God's will, the natural and universal structure of things was right.

The human body itself is a hierarchy, a microcosm that reflects the macrocosmic order of the universe, as do all human systems. The system of social order has the monarch at its head and all local systems are similarly hierarchical. Within the family fathers rule over children, husbands over wives, older brothers over younger. Royal privilege, patriarchy, the rights of primogeniture, the ascendancy of the aristocracy over commoners: all these were considered 'right' because they are an image of cosmic order. The subordinate hierarchies within this system are connected one to another, which allows the system to generate a metaphorical or analogical language, because the members of one hierarchy can be spoken or written of in terms of the members of another. My statement above that the monarch is the 'head' of the social order is one such metaphor, and the language of royal symbolism, in which the sun, gold, the lion, the oak, etc. are used to character-ize the monarch, depends on metaphorical transference. Much of the imagery of Shakespeare's plays has this doctrine behind it.

The most significant public statement of the concept comes in a homily or sermon entitled 'An Exhortation Concerning Good Order and Obedience to Rulers and Magistrates', one of 12 homilies published at Cranmer's instigation in 1547. These homilies were intended to be read in all churches on appointed days of the year, and this was the case for the remainder of the Tudor period. As people were obliged to attend church the homilies were, in effect, heard by all Tudor subjects at the same time. This is how the homily on obedience begins:

> Almighty God hath created and appointed all things in heaven, earth and waters in most excellent and perfect order. In heaven, he hath appointed distinct orders and states of archangels and angels. In earth, he has assigned kings, princes, with other governors under them, all in good and necessary order. The water above is kept and raineth down in due time and season. The sun, moon, stars, rainbow, thunder, lightning, clouds and all birds of the air do keep their order. The earth, trees, seeds, plants, herbs, corn, grass and all manner of beasts keep them in their order. . . . Every degree of people, in their vocation, calling and office, hath appointed to them their duty and order. Some are in high degree, some in low, some kings and princes, some inferiors and subjects, priests and laymen, masters and servants, fathers and children, husbands and wives, rich and poor, and every one has need of other: so that in all things is to be lauded and praised the goodly order of God, without the which, no house, no city, no common wealth can continue and endure. For where there is no right order, there reigneth all abuse, carnal liberty, enormity, sin and babylonical confusion.[13]

We can only guess at how many times Shakespeare heard those words. They are echoed over and over in his plays.

Shakespeare's main presentation of these ideas of cosmic order comes in Ulysses' speech on 'degree' in the first act of *Troilus and Cressida*:

> The heavens themselves, the planets, and this centre
> Observe degree, priority, and place,

Insisture, course, proportion, season, form,
Office, and custom, in all line of order:
[. . .]
How could communities,
Degrees in schools, and brotherhoods in cities,
Peaceful commerce from dividable shores,
The primogenity and due of birth,
Prerogative of age, crowns, sceptres, laurels,
But by degree stand in authentic place?

(1.3.85–8, 103–8)

The concept that all things existed in a divinely-appointed order was, indeed, a commonplace amongst writers of Shakespeare's time; Tillyard quotes passages from Spenser, Elyot, Hooker and Raleigh. It has analogues in earlier writers too, such as Homer, Virgil, Ovid and Chaucer.

The concept of cosmic order and the rightness of the *status quo* that underlay the 'Elizabethan world picture' reinforced and was reinforced by other Tudor myths of absolutism, such as the idea of the divine right of kings, which claimed that a monarch was appointed by God and that even a weak or tyrannical monarch could not be deposed. This principle, a Tudor invention in essence, was taken over and forcefully propagated by James I. In a speech made before Parliament in 1609 James went so far as to claim that monarchs partake of the divine:

> Kings are justly called Gods, for that they exercise a manner or resemblance of Divine power upon earth: For if you will consider the Attributes to God, you shall see how they agree in the person of a King. God hath power to create, or destroy, make, or unmake at his pleasure, to give life or send death, to judge all, to be judged nor accomptable to none: To raise low things and to make high things low at his pleasure, and to God are both soul and body due. And the like power have Kings.[14]

This mystification of royal power was underpinned by the doctrine of 'the king's (or queen's) two bodies', which proposed that the monarch had a 'body natural' and a 'body politic'. The body natural contained the body politic; the body natural could die, but the body politic was immortal and passed on to a dying monarch's rightful successor, which in England would normally be his or her first-born son. It is clear that, in the case of Elizabeth, neither a first-born son herself nor having one of her own, this doctrine was problematic and in need of continual readjustment, and that it must have generated problems in the debates over who would succeed her. The term 'body politic' was apposite, however, because it identified the immortal essence of the monarch with the line of monarchs who had gone before as well as with the (metaphorical) social body of those he or she ruled.

Historical continuity of line was fundamental to arguments about royal legitimacy. Henry Tudor, when he displaced Richard III, had only a very tenuous claim to the throne. The Tudors needed to demonstrate their continuity with earlier dynasties, and so attempted to revive belief in the pseudo-history that connected England with Troy. This dated back at least to Geoffrey of Monmouth's *Historia regum Britanniae* (1136), which claimed that after the fall of Troy, Brutus, the grandson of the Trojan hero Aeneas, wandered through Europe with his army of followers, finally arriving on the island of Albion. After defeating the giants who inhabited the island he re-named it 'Britain' after himself, settling on the River Thames and founding the city he called Troia Nova or New Troy, which eventually became London. The line of kings that descended from him culminated in King Arthur, the most potent figure of British national legend and identity. Geoffrey's book was very popular and seems to have been taken by later medieval historians to be actual history. Both Henry VII and Henry VIII had encouraged historiographers to attempt to connect the Tudor lineage to Arthur and thus to the supposed ancient origins of British kingship, and although by the later Tudor period Geoffrey's stories had been discredited as history, they nevertheless retained something of their mythical power.

The problem with Tillyard's treatment of the great chain of being is not the philosophical concepts themselves, for they were generally known and many people did believe in them. But Tillyard's idea of a collective Elizabethan mind so immersed in the world picture as to accept it completely has been profoundly misleading. Applied to Shakespeare and his fellow dramatists, it makes impossible any dissent from a rigidly-established doctrine and forces us to see the dramatist as the spokesman for a conservative vision of the world, simple-mindedly defending aristocratic, hierarchical values, incapable of any sceptical questioning. Thus

Ulysses, presenting Tudor doctrine to the Greek leaders, is really Shakespeare reminding his audience of what they are all supposed to believe.

We might, however, wish to ask why the Tudor authorities thought it necessary to have such things frequently read out to a captive audience if the audience already took these concepts of order for granted? The answer that seems to force itself upon us we have already seen: the Tudor establishment feared that the people did *not* take them for granted, and the homily and many other similar texts are not so much statements of philosophical commonplaces as pieces of political propaganda. After all, in the homily's title the subject is not being exhorted to give obedience to God, but rather to obey *earthly* rulers and magistrates. The restatement of authoritarian commonplaces in the homilies seems to be a response to a real threat of disorder, to the feared ramifications of the unprecedented changes taking place. The authorities were looking not at a society unanimous in its belief in the absolute rightness of hierarchical order, but at one increasingly divided in its needs and interests. The doctrine of the homilies did not represent the furnishings of the collective mind so much as a set of beliefs that were fast becoming archaic but that retained power as an officially-fostered myth, to generate belief and thereby obedience.

The great chain of being, then, and the associated myths of hierarchy, mystical royal continuity and the absolute power of the monarch, were commonplaces, but not because everybody believed in them. They all figure in Shakespeare's plays, but that does not mean that he accepted them as unquestionable truth. He fully understood their significance as instruments of political indoctrination. Indeed, when in *Troilus and Cressida* Ulysses makes his speech about universal hierarchical order, he is quite clearly using the concept for political ends, to restore authority to Agamemnon, whose own inept leadership has been the cause of disorder in the Greek camp. Ulysses is a cynical manipulator, and Shakespeare would surely have expected his audience to recognize the distance between the noble rhetoric and the machiavellian uses to which it is being put.

Many aspects of Elizabethan doctrine were troubled. Long-held beliefs were being put to the test of a scepticism that had arisen out of scientific discovery, especially in astronomy and medicine, out of exploration and the discovery of the New World and 'new found lands', and out of changing ways of thinking about the individual, his role in society and his relationship with God. Some beliefs resisted, some were modified, some were supplanted, and if there was an Elizabethan world picture it was marked by diversity rather than uniformity. John Donne wrote in 'The First Anniversary' (1611):

And New Philosophy calls all in doubt,
The Element of fire is quite put out;
The Sun is lost, and th'earth, and no man's wit
Can well direct him, where to look for it.

(205–8)[15]

Donne's doubts were more extreme than those of many of his contemporaries, but the difference was in magnitude rather than in kind.

One of the fundamental supports of the doctrine of cosmic order and hierarchy was a concept of the universe that was derived from Aristotelian philosophy, formalized by Ptolemy of Alexandria in the second century AD, and augmented by borrowings from, among many others, Pythagoras and Plato. From the Middle Ages scholars worked to harmonize this doctrine with Christian teaching. The cosmic system as the Renaissance understood it had the earth fixed at its centre with a series of nine concentric spheres, corresponding to the nine angelic orders (Seraphim, Cherubim, Thrones, Dominions, Powers, Virtues, Principalities, Archangels, Angels), revolving around it. Beyond the ninth sphere was the Empyrean or heavens, the domain of God. Each of the spheres was the province of a heavenly body: the moon was closest to the earth, followed by Mercury, Venus, the sun, Mars, Jupiter, Saturn and the 'fixed' stars (that is all the named and nameless stars we can see at night). The ninth sphere was that of the *primum mobile* which imparted motion to the entire system, with one revolution around the earth every 24 hours. The division between the changing and the unchanging was represented by the moon, with its monthly phases; beneath the moon the 'sublunary', fallen world of human experience was conditioned by time and death, but in the spheres beyond was permanence. The vibration of each revolving sphere caused it to emit a musical note inaudible to earthly ears, the system as a whole producing the music of the spheres. The inter-connectedness of the system meant that the movement of the stars and planets influenced events on earth and in human lives; what we call astrology was not differentiated from astronomy.

The loss of sun and earth brought about, according to Donne, by the new philosophy was a loss of old certainties. The work of Nicolaus Copernicus had been published in 1543. Copernicus saw that problems with the Ptolemaic model could be settled when it was understood that the earth was not at the centre of the universe, but revolved around the sun. He was well aware of the far-reaching implications of his proposal, and was cautious in his statement of it, but later astronomers, Tycho Brahe, Johannes Kepler, and especially Galileo, elaborated his work. Resistance to these new ideas was strong, however, for in displacing the earth as the centre of the universe astronomers were displacing much more: they were displacing man himself. The belief that the earth was at the centre of the universe was of profound theological significance, because it affirmed the importance of man at the centre of God's creation, a status validated by the account in Genesis. If the earth were demoted to a subsidiary position revolving around the sun, what would this imply about man's place?

The concept of the chain of being had also given man a pivotal position: poised between the angelic and the bestial he was a microcosm, uniting spirit and body, and containing all that constituted terrestrial matter. All physical matter was made up of four elements which, like everything else, formed a hierarchy: earth (cold and dry), water (cold and moist), air (hot and moist) and fire (hot and dry). The lower, earth-bound elements were earth and water, while air and fire aspired upwards. The human temperament was conditioned by four 'humours' which corresponded to these elements: melancholic, phlegmatic, sanguine and choleric; individual personality depended upon the mixture of these elements. The pseudo-medicine that attempted to heal through the manipulation of the humours was closely related to alchemy, the pseudo-science that aimed, through manipulation of the hierarchy of metals, to transmute base metal into gold. A more rigorous application of what we would today recognize as scientific method was supplanting such beliefs in much the same way as astronomy was purging astrology.

Astrology, alchemy, humours – all these seem to most of us today to be mere superstition. It is important to understand that the move away from these modes of belief was not a simple move from a kind of primitive fiction to scientific truth, because many important discoveries grew from them and they represented an important stage in what we like to think of as progress. There was no clean break, and old ways of thought persisted in the face of what could be put down as novelty or fashion. Shakespeare's works frequently set new views alongside the old. In the second scene of *King Lear*, for example, Gloucester relates the disturbances in the kingdom and in his family to the 'late eclipses in the sun and moon' (1.2.107). His illegitimate son Edmund, much more up-to-date in his beliefs, mocks his father's superstition, asserting individual freedom against 'heavenly compulsion': 'I should have been that I am had the maidenliest star in the firmament twinkled on my bastardizing' (1.2.138–40). From a modern perspective Edmund is right in his insistence on human responsibility, but his intellectual freedom brings about much of the suffering in the play, and Shakespeare does not allow us to believe that 'truth' will inevitably lead us in a better direction, or even that it will help us to know where we are going. For him too the new philosophy called 'all in doubt'.

It is here, in the domain of moral action, that the changes that characterize Renaissance thought and belief have their greatest significance, for moral action embraces religious, political and personal experience. If the old certainties were no longer dependable, what then was the nature of humanity, and how should men and women deal with one another? The concept of man as inhabiting a plane between the angelic and the bestial defined him as a divided being with the potential to be drawn upwards by his reason or downwards by his baser passions. The Classical basis of much Renaissance thinking concurred with the biblical story of the Fall: there had been a Golden Age, like the biblical Eden, in which man had enjoyed perfection and from which he had fallen through a failure of right reason. His fall had caused also the fall of nature from timeless perfection to a state of decay (hence the prevalence of 'unweeded gardens' as an emblem of human and political disorder in Renaissance poetry). Human existence is a struggle to recover the Golden Age through reason, but men are troubled by their passions, which draw them downwards; as Sidney put it, 'our erected wit maketh us know what perfection is, and yet our infected will keepeth us from reaching unto it'.[16]

Early in the sixteenth century humanist teachers, following

Erasmus and More, took an optimistic view, arguing that man's central position in the universe gave him dignity, and that through his God-given faculty of reasoning he could control his instincts or passions and ascend towards the divine. Later in the century Sidney argued that man could perceive the golden world through poetry; the theological equivalent was that man could achieve salvation through Christ, the second Adam whose sacrifice paid for the disobedience of the first. There were, contemporary with Erasmus, more radically pessimistic beliefs that saw fallen man as unable to redeem himself through his own efforts. Martin Luther believed that the salvation of each individual is entirely dependent on God's grace. A man's faith is the gift of God, and a man with true faith is one of the elect; his good works are a sign of his election, but not a cause of it. John Calvin took Luther's arguments to their logical conclusion: because God foreknows all, the election of the individual is predestined and human will can do nothing to save the man who is preordained for damnation. Thus the question of freedom of will became a hotly contested theological issue. Luther's ideas had arisen out of his struggle against what he saw as the corruption and profligacy of the medieval Church, especially its concern with outward show rather than inner truth, but his more significant struggle was against the rigidity of Catholic dogma and its attachment to Aristotelian systems. He attempted to free the individual conscience from its subservience to traditional doctrine, and in doing so he reflected and facilitated the fragmentation of the monolithic concept of feudal order.

The chain of being had tied together theology, politics and history in a concept of order as the expression of the will of God and the ruler as the instrument of that will. In *The Prince* (c. 1513) Niccolò Machiavelli proposed a secular, pragmatic concept of political action that was essentially outside morality. He understood that 'the gulf between how one should live and how one does live is so wide that a man who neglects what is actually done for what should be done learns the way to self-destruction rather than self-preservation'.[17] For Machiavelli order was an expression of the will of the politician, a man able to make immediate and firm decisions. Like the Calvinists, Machiavelli saw men as being essentially evil, and believed them to be in need of powerful control. What he called 'virtue' in a ruler was the ability to be ruthless when necessary in exerting control; his observations of successful leaders showed him that they were men willing to use any means to a desired end, men who combined the qualities of the lion and the fox, strength and cunning.

Machiavelli's empirical realism or *realpolitik* was well understood by many Elizabethan writers, including Shakespeare, who in his history plays and elsewhere explored the means by which governors imposed control. However, Machiavelli was popularly misunderstood: his realism was seen as cynicism, and in England his name became synonymous with Italianate villainy and the sinister threats of Catholicism – ironically so, considering that the Roman Church also hated him. While editions of his works were officially banned in England, on the stage his ideas were debased into a caricature of horror-comic wickedness representing political dissimulation and trickery, as in Marlowe's *The Jew of Malta*, where 'Machiavel' speaks the Prologue:

> To some, perhaps, my name is odious,
> But such as love me guard me from their tongues,
> And let them know that I am Machiavel,
> And weigh not men, and therefore not mens words.
> Admired I am of those that hate me most. . . .
> I count religion but a childish toy
> And hold there is no sin but ignorance.
>
> (5–9, 14–15)[18]

In Elizabethan England Machiavelli's disturbing ideas caused him to lead a double life, as a serious political analyst and as the theatrical bogey-man termed the 'machiavel'.

All these disturbing ideas – the cracking of the rigidity of feudal order, the discovery that the individual might have a self beyond his limited function in a hierarchical system, the interrogation of long-held certainties by sceptical and empirical perspectives – threatened to disrupt the supposed order of things. Even geographical exploration and the discovery of new countries shook the old certainties. The New World disclosed paradisal lands inhabited by 'savages' who spoke no recognizable language and therefore no language: in *The Tempest* Miranda says to Caliban:

> I pitied thee,
> Took pains to make thee speak, taught thee each hour
> One thing or other: when thou didst not, savage,
> Know thine own meaning, but wouldst gabble like

A thing most brutish, I endow'd thy purposes
With words that made them known.

(1.2.355–60)

Because Caliban had no language that she comprehended, Miranda thinks he had no language at all and no thoughts until she gave him her language. Indians like Caliban posed a problem for traditional views of human nature, their 'natural' qualities forcing Europeans to rethink the meaning of civilized life.

Ideas that threatened the edifice of traditional doctrine threatened especially those in power. In England, as we have seen, the Elizabethan establishment countered change by constant reiteration of the orthodox view, and by retrogression into medievalism and myth, seeing their Golden Age in codes of chivalry and service. Authoritarian instructions on how the monarch and the system of which she or he was the head were to be valued were not sufficient in themselves; even the mystification of a God-given pattern for human society required something visible to sustain it. What was needed was a glorious vision of the monarch's personal and symbolic significance. Both Elizabeth and James were fully aware of the political power of theatrical display. Elizabeth is recorded as saying: 'We Princes are set as it were upon stages in the sight and view of the world.'[19] James echoed her words in *Basilikon Doron*, his treatise on kingship: 'A King is as one set on a stage, whose smallest actions and gestures, all the people gazingly do behold.'[20] Both monarchs offered spectacular visions to the view of the world, but while James resented having to appear before his people, Elizabeth invested huge energy in the creation of mythic versions of herself. She fully understood the implications of the idea that she was the object of the public gaze, and from the moment of her coronation she ensured that the public had something marvellous to gaze at. One witness of the ceremony commented:

> So that if a man should say well, he could not better term the city of London that time, than a stage wherein was showed the wonderful spectacle, of a noble hearted princess toward her most loving people, and the people's exceeding comfort in beholding so worthy a sovereign.[21]

Elizabeth already knew how to play a part that would send her audience away happy.

The essential function of Elizabeth's self-staging was to turn her weaknesses into strengths, to transform her reality into myth. Her 'weaknesses', of course, were that she was a woman (her language was often evasive about this: her reference to herself as 'We Princes' carefully elides her sex) and that she was unmarried. To transform them, she fostered the cult of Gloriana, the Virgin Queen. The figure of the Virgin Queen united multiple identities and resolved contradictions. She was Diana or Cynthia, goddess of chastity and constancy, yet associated with the moon. She was Venus-as-Virgo, figure of love and beauty. She was Astraea, the virgin goddess of justice who left the earth when the Iron Age destroyed all virtue in men, and whose return to earth, Virgil had foretold, would usher in the return of the Golden Age of peace and plenty. She displaced the figure of the Virgin Mary, just as she had replaced her own sister Mary, representing the Protestant triumph over Catholicism, the English triumph over Rome. The religious implications of this last facet of the figure were not accidental. Elizabeth-as-Astraea too had religious associations, since Astraea's return suggested a second coming or resurrection. The connection of the Virgin Queen with the moon, with its cyclic disappearance and growth to fullness, extended such associations, and Elizabeth also used the emblem of the phoenix, the mythical bird that arose from its own ashes.

All of this was powerful stuff, a complex structure that implied Elizabeth's continuity with figures of myth and history, her immortality and her embodiment of national identity and fortune. It was elaborated through public processions and entertainments, through literary texts, through paintings. Royal celebrations included tournaments at which Elizabeth's courtiers made triumphal entries as knights with a full entourage of squires and pages, evoking an idealized image of medieval romanticism. Sir Philip Sidney, who competed in tournaments under the name Sir Philisides, wrote his sonnet sequence *Astrophil and Stella* at least in part as an act of political courtship of the queen at a time when he was out of favour (it is worth noting where the romantic word 'courtship' originated). These tournaments were more than an aristocratic game, for through the Order of the Garter and the absorption of the popular cult of St George, England's patron saint, they drew together influential nobles as defenders of English Protestantism and its goddess–queen against the dragon of Rome.

Edmund Spenser began his vast project *The Faerie Queene*, also a pseudo-medieval romance, as an attempt to win royal patronage, and explained the allegorical meanings of his central figure Gloriana in a letter to Sir Walter Raleigh:

> In that Faery Queen I mean glory in my general intention, but in my particular I conceive the most excellent and glorious person of our sovereign the Queen, and her kingdom in Faery land. And yet in some places else, I do otherwise shadow her. For considering she beareth two persons, the one of a most royal Queen or Empress, the other of a most virtuous and beautiful Lady, this latter part in some places I do express in Belphoebe, fashioning her name according to your own excellent conceit of Cynthia, (Phoebe and Cynthia being both names of Diana.)[22]

Shakespeare too indulged in celebration of Elizabeth through her mythic attributes, though not on such a large scale. In *A Midsummer Night's Dream* Oberon tells a story of Cupid's failed attempt to arouse an 'imperial votaress' who surely represents Elizabeth:

>                          a certain aim he took
> At a fair vestal, throned by the west,
> And loos'd his love-shaft smartly from his bow
> As it should pierce a hundred thousand hearts.
> But I might see young Cupid's fiery shaft
> Quench'd in the chaste beams of the watery moon,
> And the imperial votress passed on
> In maiden meditation, fancy-free.
>
>                                   (2.1.157–63)

In the context of the treatment of chastity elsewhere in this play there may be a certain irony here, but it is difficult to see how the passage could be understood as anything but a compliment paid to England's fair and chaste maiden-queen.

Perhaps the myth of Gloriana is detailed most evidently in the iconography of royal portraits. From the 1580s Elizabeth appeared in a series of paintings in which she wore dress so elaborate and was surrounded by images and devices so arcane that they demanded to be read allegorically. The 'Armada' portrait, for example, painted around 1588, shows the Queen with her hand on a globe, indicating her power over land and sea; behind her we see images of English fire-ships being sent into the Spanish fleet, and the later shipwreck of the Spanish fleet off the coast of Scotland. The painting cannot be understood realistically; rather, it sets a triumphant representation of Elizabeth amidst images of the key moments of that triumph. The 'Ditchley' portrait of 1592 shows her standing on a map of her kingdom as if the two were fused together, ruler and realm inseparable. Behind her we see a cosmic image of sunshine replacing storm, as if by her control. One of the last paintings of her, the 'Rainbow' portrait of around 1600, reiterates this idea of cosmic power by depicting the queen holding in her right hand God's sign of his covenant with man, the rainbow. One significant element of most of the paintings of Elizabeth that survive is that her face hardly differs from one portrait to another; even in the 'Rainbow' portrait, painted when she was nearing 70, she appears youthful. This is because what we are offered in these paintings is not a 'real' image of the queen at all, but a representation of her unchanging value, what Roy Strong describes as a mask 'that totally ignored reality and instead gave visual expression to the final cadences of her cult in which the poets celebrated her seemingly eternal youth and beauty'.[23]

The cult of Gloriana the Virgin Queen worked well for many years as a means of presenting to the nation a constant image of its own power and worth as represented in the figure of its monarch. It generated much public devotion, and in its echoes of the medieval ideals of courtly love and service it also provided a means of keeping control of ambitious courtiers. As Elizabeth grew older, of course, the gap between the splendid ideal image and the actual parsimonious and aging spinster grew wider, and this myth, like the other Tudor myths we have considered, fitted only loosely. Nevertheless, for much of Elizabeth's reign it was a potent means of generating and controlling loyalty and nationalistic fervour. When James I came to the throne he understood the power of royal theatricality, as his words in *Basilikon Doron* show, but he was a much more private man, and through the encouragement of the court masque, a complex mixture of poetry, music, dance and spectacle, he gradually withdrew nationalistic myth and self-idealization from public view into the closed arena of aristocratic circles. In doing so he removed an important unifying element in national culture, creating further reason for popular disillusionment with his rule, and moving a little closer to the radical separation that let to the Civil War.

For a society with increasingly disparate interests the main-
tenance of national order needed something more than a glam-
orous myth, and something more sinister. In the 'Rainbow' portrait
the golden cloak worn by the queen is decorated with eyes and
ears, representing her as the receiver of intelligence, hearing and
seeing all. The court was a place of secrets and spying, and there
was a need to keep constant watch on potential Catholic plotters;
until his death in 1590 Sir Francis Walsingham, Elizabeth's Sec-
retary of State, was her eyes and ears in this matter, and ran a
very efficient machine. But court factions also spied on each other,
and few were safe from such intrusions (this is reflected in *Hamlet*: consider how many denizens of the Danish court spy on that
prince). In his poem 'Inviting a Friend to Supper', Ben Jonson
presents as one of the attractions of the feast the fact that there
will be no spies around; he will provide excellent wine, he says,
and,

> Of this we will sup free, but moderately,
> And we will have no Pooly, or Parrot by;
> Nor shall our cups make any guilty men:
> But, at our parting, we will be, as when
> We innocently met.
>
> (35–9)[24]

Robert Pooly was a government spy who, in 1586, betrayed the
Babington Plot and seven years later was present at the murder
of Christopher Marlowe. Parrot has not been identified, but the
name characterizes him as an informer.

Much official effort, then, went into fostering beliefs that would
validate royal claims to a divine as well as a historical right to
rule, and impose upon the subject the duty of order and obedience, as well as watching to ensure that people did obey. The
effort was needed precisely because there was not universal agreement about order and the rightness of things. It is an exploration
of the tensions and divisions implied by this, rather than a vision
of universal harmony, that underlies the plays of Shakespeare
and his fellow dramatists. The tensions are fundamental to the
material of Shakespeare's plays, and they are the dynamic source
of the value that the plays continue to hold for us today. That
value has changed in the course of time and we now find unac-
ceptable many of the attitudes that are reflected in the plays. But

those attitudes are never simple; they exist within a structure that accommodates and questions a diversity of views and opinions, and if we find ourselves arguing with one of Shakespeare's plays, that is a good thing. Shakespeare's own audience contained those who argued as well as those who agreed, though as I have tried to show, agreement was a lot safer than argument in a society that was, from a modern democratic point of view, repressively authoritarian.

# 2

# Theatrical Professions

For most of us today attendance at a professional performance of a play by Shakespeare is a special event. Tickets are expensive, so we dress up for it. We have been taught from childhood that what we are experiencing is the pinnacle of literary art, so we sit quietly and reverentially in the darkened, cathedral-like space of the theatre, listening to (and perhaps not fully understanding) words that have somehow become part of our cultural heritage, spoken by actors who may themselves be national figures. A visit to such a theatre is a very respectable thing, but in Shakespeare's London theatre-going was an experience of a very different sort. Performances at public playhouses were given in daylight, and even in private indoor theatres the space occupied by the audience was illuminated. Members of the audience could see each other as clearly as they could see the performers, and many of those who dressed up for the occasion went to be seen as much as to see. Some of those who frequented the theatre would be rowdy in their behaviour and loud in their criticisms if a play did not hold their attention or if it failed in other ways to please them. People ate and drank during the performance, and enjoyed the new fashion of smoking clay pipes. Some men went there to pick up women (who, presumably, were there to pick up men). In 1597, as part of the London authorities' ongoing efforts to have the theatres closed down, the Lord Mayor wrote a letter to the Privy Council complaining 'They are the ordinary places for vagrant persons, Masterless men, thieves, horse stealers, whoremongers, Cozeners, Conycatchers, contrivers of treason, and other idle and dangerous persons to meet together . . .' (*ES* 4: 322). Obviously, to many of Shakespeare's contemporaries, a visit to the theatre was *not* a respectable thing.

The London theatrical profession of Shakespeare's time had grown out of a complex, even contradictory, set of conditions. On the one hand acting was a marginalized activity: players and others associated with the theatres were often reviled by their

55

enemies as vagabonds, and indeed were in the early years of the profession legally defined as such. Players and plays were feared and hated by Puritan authorities, especially the authorities in the fast-growing City of London. Plays were feared because they were seen as a cause of riot and immorality, hated because theatre and playing were associated in the reforming Protestant mind with the Roman Church. Thus the players were prohibited from building their playhouses within the City of London, being limited to those marginal suburban locations in which inns, brothels and animal-baiting arenas already flourished. On the other hand, each of the acting companies was given at least the nominal protection of a powerful aristocratic patron, who employed them as servants, lent them his title, allowed them to wear his livery and often used them for his own political advancement. And, particularly during Queen Elizabeth's reign, the clearest sign of a company's success was an invitation to perform before her, either in the Banqueting Hall at Whitehall or in Great Wall at Hampton Court. If we are to come to some understanding of Shakespeare's plays, we have to know something about the conditions that created the paradoxical state and status of his theatre.

## THE RISE OF PLAYING

When Shakespeare began writing for the stage in the last years of the 1580s he joined a profession that was in one sense new – the first permanent public theatres had opened a little more than a decade before his arrival in London. However, the roots of popular theatre in England reached a long way back into the medieval past and beyond, into folk rituals and games of which the origins can barely be mapped. The disruptive potential of such activities has often aroused the hostility of authority, and certainly the relationship between theatrical activity and Christian authority in Europe seems always to have been uneasy. The collapse of the Roman Empire brought with it the end of the Roman theatre, the last decayed remnant of the great classical theatre whose origins were in rituals and ceremonies that predated by many centuries its own finest flowering in Athens in the fifth century BC. From the sixth century AD theatre was officially discouraged by the Catholic Church, though it is difficult to believe that this put a stop to all of those vernacular ceremonies and entertainments that involved what we might call 'playing'.

I want to stress here the importance of the word 'play'. In early modern England actors were called 'players' more often than they were called 'actors', as the places where they performed were playhouses rather than theatres. Playing, games and clowning were fundamental to early popular rituals, to mummings and morris dances, disguisings and masques. Playing was associated with festival: in an era when the majority of people lived harsh and uncertain lives working on the land, they made the fullest use of those occasions that allowed them holiday and relaxation, whether these were feast days associated with the anniversaries of the church year or festivals associated with seasonal cycles. It is important to remember that Shakespeare's theatre had its roots, however obscurely, in popular games, and that its origins were not primarily literary, as much scholarship might seem to imply; the primacy of the poetic text is something generated by subsequent history, and especially by the fact that today most of us are far more likely to encounter Shakespeare on the page than on the stage.

Early in the tenth century the Church itself began to develop a rudimentary form of drama within its own liturgy. Tropes, or musical phrases, were inserted into the Mass in the form of a brief exchange of questions and answers, creating a kind of rudimentary dialogue. The earliest known of these is the Easter *Quem quaeritis* of the church at St Gall in Switzerland, which, it appears, introduced a brief dramatization of the scene at Christ's sepulchre. There are enough remnants from various places in Europe to show that increasingly elaborate 'performances' began to build around Easter and Christmas worship, although it is impossible to construct a coherent history of the development of a full religious drama.

What we can say is that by the fourteenth century, in England and in other parts of Europe, an elaborate form of religious drama had developed. From about 1376 onwards there are records showing that, in a number of towns, annual performances were presented of groups of plays now variously called 'mystery', 'miracle', 'cycle' and 'Corpus Christi' plays. These plays were associated with the feast of Corpus Christi, which falls 60 days after Easter, though they were also performed at other spring and summer festivals. A complete cycle of plays represented the entire history of the world, both past and future, since it dramatized biblical stories (though often embroidered with legendary and imaginary material) from the Creation to the Last Judgement, with the events in the life of Christ at their centre. This was a vast undertaking, since a cycle consisted of many plays. The cycle performed at York, for example, was made up of 48, though it is possible that not all the plays in the cycle were performed in a given year.

The cycle plays were a form of outdoor civic or communal drama. They were not performed by professional actors; instead, each play in the cycle was the responsibility of a particular craft guild (this is where the word 'mystery' comes from: it is a now-archaic term for a 'trade'). Although we know these plays from the surviving written texts, most of the performers in them must have been illiterate. It is likely that the plays were originally composed communally and eventually written down by scribes, perhaps quite late in their history. The same actors would have performed their parts year after year, eventually passing them on to others by word of mouth. There could have been no absolute, fixed text, therefore, since like folk ballads the plays must have been modified from one performance to the next, either consciously to reflect topical interests, or accidentally through faulty memory. It is true that in certain cases scholars have identified individual styles: some of the better plays in the Wakefield cycle have been attributed to an anonymous 'Wakefield Master', and there are distinctive plays by a 'York Realist'. Both men must have been clergymen; we cannot know now whether they actually wrote the plays for the guild members to perform, or whether they simply imposed their individual styles on the dialogues they were recording. Either way, the 'literary' text was of secondary importance.

The plays were presented on horse-drawn pageant-wagons. Each wagon consisted of an enclosed lower area used as a dressing room and a covered upper platform for the stage. Exactly how the performances were presented is unclear. The little evidence that remains suggests that each play had its own wagon, and the wagons went one by one to a succession of public places or 'stations', each stopping at every station to allow its play to be performed before moving on to the next. Anyone who knows the medieval streets of York will realise, however, what problems a procession of 48 large wagons stopping and starting at frequent intervals would have caused. Various suggestions have been made as to how these problems were resolved: it is possible that not all the plays were performed at all stations, or that some were simply presented as tableaux, or that there were larger open areas that allowed a kind of multiple staging.[1]

The mystery plays survived well into Queen Elizabeth's reign, but they were eventually suppressed by reforming bishops for what was, in effect, a political reason: they were thought to contain too many pre-Reformation elements that associated them with popery. Shakespeare was probably familiar with the mystery plays, because the last recorded performance of a cycle at Coventry, a town close enough to Stratford for Shakespeare to have travelled there with ease, was in 1581. He would have seen the last manifestations of a form of popular drama rooted in the lives of the community; one, indeed, in which the community was both actor and spectator.

There was another major form of medieval religious drama that developed parallel to the mystery cycles but separate from them. The 'morality' plays might properly be called the forerunners of Elizabethan professional drama. Documentary evidence concerning the performance of morality plays first appears in the late fourteenth century at about the same time as that for mystery plays, although almost certainly both forms had been developing for a long time before this. Like the mystery plays, moralities were performed outdoors, but they were usually presented by travelling groups of actors who scratched out a living by performing at fairs and festivals where there were likely to be large crowds. They acted on temporary stages set up for the purpose.

The morality play seems to have developed out of medieval sermons, which frequently taught as their central lesson that for every individual repentance was necessary for the forgiveness of sin. Preachers of sermons were themselves notable for their oratorical skills, and the sins or virtues that formed the subject of their sermons often took on a life of their own. This allegorical method, in which the preacher personated vices and virtues, was essentially dramatic and easily adapted for the stage. Early morality plays had their focus on the representative individual; the central character was usually given a name that signified his representative status: Mankind, Everyman, Humanum Genus. His opponents and his protectors had allegorical names that signified their simple function: Greed, Envy, Wrath; Conscience, Good Deeds, Mercy. Since this was a drama of redemption, it developed a distinctive structure: the descent of the protagonist from innocence to sin, and his ascent from sin to salvation. Typically in these plays the Mankind-figure is tempted by various vicious characters until, after a cursory struggle against them, he falls into degradation and despair. Having learned the lesson that he must shun temptation he is raised up by figures representing either his own fundamental virtue or God's forgiveness. This is an essentially comic structure since, however weak the protagonist might be, however prone to temptation and the pleasures of the flesh, he always, either through repentance or through God's mercy, achieves heaven.

In the earlier moralities the Mankind-figure was usually tempted by a group of sins, but as the form evolved one figure gradually emerged as the leader of this group. He became known as the 'Vice', and eventually achieved an importance in the structure of the play equal to that of the human protagonist. As leader of the enemies of Mankind the Vice organized the tricks and traps that were set to tempt him into sin; as representative of the Devil, his function was to bring about the damnation of the protagonist. In later examples of the form, the plot of the play became structured around his actions. The Vice usually exhibited an irreverent wit and so he took on many of the attributes of the clown. He was the main source of laughter, but the audience was distanced from him by its awareness of the implications of his wit: to fall prey to his attractions was to commit the same error as the protagonist committed. Thus, in a very real sense, the audience's experience mirrored that of the protagonist.

We have little certain knowledge about the conditions of the performance of morality plays. A contemporary drawing representing the setting of *The Castle of Perseverance* (1400–25) is difficult to interpret but suggests that this play was performed in a circular arena in which were set up a number of scaffolds representing fixed locations (such as the castle itself), surrounding an open area which was unlocalized. The actors moved from one scaffold to another as the action changed location, and the audience, gathered in the playing area, probably moved with them, following them from scene to scene. This would have been a very awkward method of presentation and it is possible that most moralities, like the later *Mankind* (1465–70), were performed on platform stages set up in inn-yards. Certainly, the travelling companies who performed these plays (which consisted only of four or five men, and a boy to play the women's parts) had to be very flexible and undemanding in their staging needs, since they had to be ready to set up wherever they could find an audience, no matter how inadequate the facilities.

During the early Tudor period, the most aggressive years of the Reformation, the morality play offered a very useful theatrical pattern. Its structure dramatized a struggle between good and evil, and could be adapted for any number of political and ideological purposes; what, after all, do we mean by 'evil', if not the beliefs of our enemies? Both Catholics and Protestants used the form to discredit those who opposed them, and it became a vehicle for religious and political satire. For these purposes, much more consciously-crafted texts had to be produced.

Morality plays as such did not really die out, but by the 1570s they began to merge into what became Elizabethan popular drama. A variety of elements derived from both mystery plays and morality plays can be seen reflected in the work of the Elizabethan playwrights. The cyclical view of history that lies behind the structure of the mysteries also informs the belief that lessons can be learned from an examination of the past. This has a bearing on the assumptions made by the history plays of Shakespeare and others that plays could hold up a 'mirror for magistrates', that rulers could be taught a lesson from the stage. The allegorical structure of the moralities, in which good and evil characters struggled for the soul of the protagonist (a struggle known as '*psychomachia*'), survived as a pattern in numerous Elizabethan plays and can be seen in Shakespeare's earliest history plays. More crucially, the Vice of the morality plays, the evil tempter, appears in various guises on the Elizabethan and Jacobean stage, though modified by other elements, particularly popular misconceptions about the doctrines of Machiavelli: Richard III, Aaron the Moor, Iago all have something of the function of the Vice and use his methods of deceit, dissimulation and disguise.

These popular forerunners were not the only dramatic influence on Elizabethan theatre; there were also learned forms of drama that had developed for more aristocratic audiences. In the last years of the fifteenth century the humanist movement, already established in Italy and other parts of Europe, began to flourish in England around Erasmus and More. What began as an elitist attempt to revive Classical Greek and Latin literature developed into a great movement that profoundly modified Christian educational, social and political ideas. Convinced of the superiority of Classical literature, humanist thinkers stressed the need to imitate

Classical models, which included plays, and their ideas inevitably affected the understanding of dramatic structure. The sophisticated circles of the Tudor court already had a secular form of drama, generally known as 'interludes' and performed in specially-adapted banqueting halls. These interludes had borrowed from the popular forms discussed above, as well as from literary sources, and it was there that the humanists had their immediate influence. Plays that combined native with Classical constituents were written dealing with new ideas and reflecting the issues of the time. They included such works as Henry Medwall's *Nature* (1490–1500), which fuses a morality argument about reason and sensuality with a consideration of Aristotelian ethics. John Rastell's *The Nature of the Four Elements* (1517–19) discusses the latest scientific ideas, while John Heywood, in *The Play of the Weather* (1533), writes obliquely about the nature of the social order.

The Classical emphasis of the humanists had its fullest effect on another form of scholarly drama, written to be performed by the schoolboys of the grammar and choir schools. The most outstanding of these performers, and eventually the most enduring, were the boys of St Paul's school and the Children of the Chapel Royal, but there were other notable groups associated with Windsor Chapel, Eton College and the Merchant Taylors School. Latin texts were used in schools to teach grammar and rhetoric, and these included plays by Plautus, Terence and Seneca. The schoolmasters often produced their own imitations of Latin plays for the boys to perform. The boys were already performing for themselves and their masters by the latter part of the fifteenth century, and were eventually invited to perform for court audiences on festive occasions, especially at Christmas. Given the increasing demand for such court shows it is not surprising that the masters began to write plays in English in imitation of Classical models and neo-Classical continental plays, with a heavy reliance on witty dialogue, as appropriate for bright young boys aged between about ten and fifteen.

The boys developed their acting skills to a high degree, although because of their age they must have performed in a stylized manner. By the mid-1570s their court performances had brought them such prestige that they needed to devote more and more time to rehearsal. Around 1575 Paul's Boys, under their master Sebastian Westcott, established their own theatre in a hall somewhere near St Paul's, ostensibly to rehearse for their court appearances but admitting paying customers. In 1576 the Children of the Chapel Royal also began performing for paying audiences in a theatre in the Blackfriars district of London. They had, in effect, opened London's first commercial playhouses.

The theatres in which the boys' companies played were an elaboration of the Tudor banqueting halls where the interludes were performed. A hall screen with either two or three doorways was set up at one end of the rectangular hall; the space behind the screen was, in effect, the dressing room, from which two or three entrances led on to a stage which was constructed in front of the screen. The entire hall was lit with candles, so that the performance had to be interrupted at intervals for the candles to be trimmed. Bench seats were set in front of the stage and there were galleries along the side walls. The charge for admission was quite high: the lowest price was sixpence, which was the same as the highest price in the public playhouses, and some seats cost five times as much. The audience included the wealthy and the cultivated: the nobility, gallants, students and prosperous citizens. These indoor theatres were eventually known as 'private' theatres to distinguish them from the outdoor 'public' theatres of the adult companies which also began to develop in the 1570s. The distinction should not be misunderstood, however; the hall theatres were private only in the sense that admission was more expensive than at public theatres and therefore excluded those who could not afford to pay. Of course, the plays performed in private theatres were directed at a sophisticated audience, but many in that audience also attended public theatres. The two systems had more in common than their names might imply, and they coexisted in a relationship that was sometimes tense, but that nourished both.

## THE PROFESSIONAL PUBLIC THEATRE

1576 is a significant date in the history of English theatre, for in that year not only was the Blackfriars opened as a private playhouse, but also the first important permanent public playhouse was opened, at last providing a fixed place for what had been an itinerant profession. As we have seen, during the early Tudor period there were numerous groups of entertainers who travelled the country trying to make a living out of putting on shows wherever they could. These were 'players' in the broadest sense of the word, skilled at singing, dancing, playing drums and whistles, juggling, wrestling, sword-fighting, tumbling and low clowning, which they incorporated into the dramatic stories they presented.

As travellers, the players were essentially outlaws; in a rigidly stratified society, as England then was (and as powerful interests wanted it to remain), their position was not clearly defined but their mobility made them suspect. As early as 1531 they had fallen under the definition of 'Beggars & Vagabonds' as set out in an Act of Henry VIII of that year, and were liable to severe punishment as 'idle persons' (*ES* 4: 260–1). Forty years later official attitudes had not changed much; an Act of Parliament of 1572, in an attempt to curb the growing numbers of able-bodied masterless men who were wandering the land, listed 'Common Players in Interludes' along with fencers, bear-keepers, minstrels, jugglers, pedlars, tinkers and petty chapmen as 'Rogues Vagabonds and Sturdy Beggars', but it excluded players 'belonging to any Baron of this Realm or . . . any other honourable Personage of greater Degree' (*ES* 4: 270). People want to be entertained, even the rich and powerful, and some of the companies of players had avoided the stigma of being masterless by finding protection in the houses of nobles, where they were allowed to wear the lord's livery and call themselves his servants. No longer masterless, they were able to travel, when not needed by their employer, without threat from the law. Indeed, in 1574 this right was officially endorsed, at least for one company, when the Earl of Leicester's Men were given a patent 'to perform music, and plays seen and allowed by the Master of the Revels, both in London and elsewhere, except during the time of common prayer, or of plague in London' (*ES* 4: 272). According to this patent they were subject to certain obvious restrictions, but otherwise free to play where they wished.

It was a limited freedom, however, and it had disadvantages, for the players' fortunes depended on the fortunes of their noble patron. Once Queen Elizabeth acceded to the throne, ambitious aristocrats used the players to promote their own interests by entertaining important visitors, ultimately with an eye to being invited to present performances at court for the queen, who took a great interest in plays. The players thus became a valuable commodity, a kind of status-symbol. Their position also made demands and set limits on *what* they could perform, since they had to be wary of the political needs of their patron, and they were sometimes involved in presenting what was, in effect, subtle or even overt propaganda.

The Earl of Leicester's Men had been in existence since at least 1559 and performed at court for the Christmas festivities from 1560 to 1562, though they were still obliged to do much travelling and most of their performances were given in the provinces. The patent they were given in 1574 attests to their quality, however, and they included in their number James Burbage, one of the most important figures in the development of Elizabethan playhouses and the acting profession. Amongst other important protected companies during the early part of Elizabeth's reign were those employed by the Earl of Sussex, the Earl of Oxford, the Earl of Derby (Lord Strange) and the Earl of Pembroke.

When a company was invited to perform for the queen at court it was a matter of prestige for themselves and a sign of royal favour for their patron. Royal entertainments of all sorts were immensely important as an indication of wealth and power. There was a court office, the Office of the Revels, which had been set up under Henry VIII and had the function of overseeing entertainment for the monarch. Elizabeth herself created the position of Master of the Revels in 1581, which was given extensive powers, partly in an effort to ensure the quality of entertainments and partly to control any controversial content. In 1583 Edmund Tilney, the Master at the time, was set the task of bringing together some of the most outstanding players, including the great clown Richard Tarlton, who within the limited circumstances of his own day attained what we would now think of as superstar-status. While Queen Elizabeth's Men dominated the London stage until the end of the decade, the fortunes of the various companies inevitably rose and fell, sometimes because of their own fluctuating skills, and sometimes with the fortunes of their patrons.

Even as acting companies became of increasing importance to the political fortunes of their patrons, they still travelled the country and still had no fixed place to play. The status given to them by their livery did not mean that they could dispense with public performances, and in London, when they were not presenting plays for court circles, they had to work on makeshift stages, although some inns, notably the Bull, Cross Keys, Bel Savage and Bell, became regular acting places. Inevitably, as London became more and more a focus for the better companies, there was a need for purpose-built playhouses. Partly this was a matter of giving the companies places where they could rehearse the plays to be acted at court, but more than this, it made good commercial sense, for there was a need to control the audiences at public performances, making sure that those who saw the plays paid for the privilege, something that had not been possible in the more open inn-yards.

The earliest attempt at creating a permanent public playhouse appears to have been the construction in 1567 of the Red Lion at a farmhouse in Stepney, by John Brayne, brother-in-law of James Burbage. It was erected for performances of a play about Samson, but apparently it failed in the same year as it opened because of construction problems. As little is known about the Red Lion we have to accept as a more significant event the erection in 1576 by Burbage and Brayne of the playhouse which they called the Theatre in Shoreditch, a northern suburb of the city. They built it at a cost of £700 on land leased from Giles Alleyn. Probably most of us are familiar with the image of an Elizabethan playhouse: the circular open-air amphitheatre described as 'this wooden O' in the Prologue to *Henry V*. This was the shape of Burbage's playhouse, which he had built on the model of animal-baiting arenas. Bear- and bull-baiting were a popular form of entertainment throughout the period, and when we think of Shakespearean drama as an elevated art form we will do well to remember that, while many in his audience may have had refined tastes, there were many who were as happy to be amused by bear-baiting as by a play. In fact the Hope theatre, erected in 1614, was built to function as both an animal-baiting arena and a playhouse.

The Theatre was first used by Leicester's Men, the company in which Burbage performed, and later by the Lord Chamberlain's Men, which was Shakespeare's company. In 1577 a second playhouse, the Curtain, was opened close to the Theatre. It was used by a number of companies, the Lord Chamberlain's Men amongst them, and it may be the Curtain to which the phrase 'this wooden O' refers. It survived longer than any other of the playhouses, continuing to function for some 50 years. In 1580 a playhouse run by the entrepreneur Philip Henslowe was opened at Newington Butts, but although Lord Strange's Men used it for a time, and both the Lord Chamberlain's Men and the Admiral's Men played there briefly, it was not very popular and little is known of it. More successful was the Rose, which Henslowe built in 1587 in the Clink Liberty, Bankside, south of the Thames; it became the home of the Lord Admiral's Men, led by the great tragedian Edward Alleyn. The recent excavations of the Rose's foundations have provided valuable new evidence about these playhouses.

In locating the Rose in Bankside, Henslowe set up a second 'theatre district', and in 1595 Francis Langley built the Swan in the same quarter. This playhouse was used by a variety of companies, including the Lord Chamberlain's, and a sketch of it done by a traveller named Johannes de Witt remains the principal piece of information we have about the internal appearance of a public playhouse. In 1597 the lease on the land on which the Theatre was built expired and, as noted earlier, an acrimonious disagreement with Giles Alleyn forced the Lord Chamberlain's Men to move. On 28 December 1598 they began to dismantle the structure and carried it by night across the Thames, where they used its wood to build a splendid new playhouse only yards away from the Rose. This was the Globe, which became the permanent home of Shakespeare's company until it burned down in 1613, although from 1608 they also performed at the Blackfriars. Presumably the Admiral's Men could not take competition from so close at hand, because in 1600 Henslowe built the Fortune in the northern suburbs. The contract for the construction of the Fortune still survives; as far as we know, this was the only playhouse built as a square, presumably to combine features of the circular amphitheatres with those of inn-yard stages. In 1605 the Red Bull was built even further north; it presented defiantly lowbrow plays. By the time the Hope was built in 1614, the heyday of the open-air playhouses was over, and this one seems to have functioned more often as a bear-baiting arena than as a playhouse.

The locations in which the public theatres were built were not chosen randomly. The queen and her courtiers enjoyed the players, and it is probable that the court did not discourage the opening of the playhouses because they provided a permanent, convenient place for the rehearsal of plays for court performance. But the city government, supported by the Church, saw play performances as sources of riot and disease, undermining the moral strength of the people and subverting the influence of the Church. They had been instrumental in the suppression of the mystery cycles and their opposition to plays was unrelenting until the official closing of the theatres in 1642. An Act of the Common Council of the City of 6 December 1574 states, amongst other things:

sundry great disorders and inconveniences have been found to ensue to this City by the inordinate haunting of great multitudes of people, specially youth, to plays, interludes, and shows, namely occasion of frays and quarrels, evil practises of incontinence in great Inns, having chambers and secret places adjoining to their open stages and galleries, inveigling and alluring of maids, especially orphans and good Citizens' Children under Age, to privy and unmeet Contracts, the publishing of unchaste, uncomely and unshamefast speeches and doings, withdrawing of the Queen's Majesty's Subjects from divine service on Sundays and holidays, at which Times such plays were Chiefly used.

(*ES* 4: 273–4)

There is much more of this, but the point is clear: if the city authorities felt such strong antipathy towards plays, they would hardly have licensed permanent theatres in the city. The liberty of Holywell, in the suburb of Shoreditch, was outside the city's jurisdiction, and that is why the Theatre and the Curtain were built there.

The Rose, the Swan, the Globe and the Hope were all built in liberties in the area of Southwark known as Bankside, on the south bank of the Thames. 'Liberties' were areas which belonged or had belonged to a lord, and had not yet fallen under city control. The Fortune was built to the north of the city and west of Shoreditch, also outside the city boundaries. All the playhouses were located close to a large potential audience, and citizens had particularly easy access by ferry to those to the south. Southwark was already an established entertainment district in what was an essentially outlawed area. Alongside its inns and taverns, its gaming houses and its animal-baiting arenas were brothels, many of them on land owned by powerful people. Prostitutes were sometimes popularly called 'Winchester Geese' because they worked in brothels built on land leased from the Bishops of Winchester. The Lord Chancellor, Lord Hunsdon, the patron of Shakespeare's own company, owned Paris Gardens, notorious for its brothels. Henslowe built the Rose in the garden of a brothel that already went by that name ('rose' being another popular word for a prostitute), and probably maintained it as a source of income, for he certainly invested in other brothels. Inevitably, such places attracted the marginalized and the dispossessed: fugitives from the law or from political or religious persecution, unemployed soldiers, mountebanks and quacks, pedlars, beggars, migrants from the provinces who were fruitlessly seeking a better life, the masterless men of whom the authorities were in such fear.

That the playhouses should have been erected in these districts emphasized the ambiguity already inherent in the players, on the one hand considered to be vagabonds by their enemies and on the other hand at least nominally the employees of great men, for now they played both in the margins of the city and at its centre, in the outlaw liberties and at court. Liberties, playhouses and players were thus symbolically located at the centre of a struggle for authority amongst the court, the city and the Church. It is essential to remember this when considering the plays written by Shakespeare and his contemporaries. The geographical location of theatrical performance was both outside and inside the city, at court and in the marginal liberties, and its cultural location was also both outside and inside society. The image of the world that it presented to its audiences was thus complex and troubled, reflecting, commenting on and modifying both the official view of an ordered society and the reality of disorder and potential fragmentation.

The playhouses existed in a paradoxical relationship to London, and the men who performed in them, as we have seen, also had an ambiguous status. Over the 75 or so years that theatre flourished in the metropolis (from the 1570s to 1642) about 20 different professional companies performed in London, though at any one time there were at the most four or five. Besides these, over a hundred companies led a humbler existence touring the provinces. The best companies, those that made it in London, also had the most powerful patrons, and in spite of the disreputable nature of their activities they developed a high degree of celebrity and even, in some cases, of respectability.

The players achieved their success, then, by pleasing two quite different audiences. Their income came from their public performances, but their status derived from their patronage and, especially, from their ability to attract the attention of the court. The theatrical year itself was based on these two needs. It usually started around late August; the companies would have been touring the provinces during the summer, because the risk of plague in the London summer heat necessitated the temporary closing of the playhouses (in some years for more lengthy periods). From late summer to Christmas, however, they played six days a week, and do not seem to have been much hindered by inclement weather. Those were months of fierce artistic competition, for then the Office of the Revels chose the plays to be performed at court for the Christmas season, which ended on Twelfth Night. The companies played in the playhouses in January and February, and there were more court presentations in the first week of Lent. Playing was officially prohibited during Lent, but resumed in late spring.

For most of the 1580s the Queen's Men, hand-picked by Edmund Tilney, were the most successful of the London companies, giving more performances at court than any other, and drawing London crowds to the Theatre and various inns. The fortunes of the Queen's Men demonstrate how fragile success was, however, for the basis of theirs was the presence of the clown Richard Tarlton. Tarlton was the most famous and best-loved actor of the age. He developed the jig, a kind of comic song and dance often performed at the end of a play, and was known for an aggressive, often extemporized line of humour. It may be that Shakespeare had Tarlton in mind for Hamlet's account of the long-dead jester Yorick, 'a fellow of infinite jest, of most excellent fancy' (5.1.178–9), although since Tarlton died in 1588 it is not likely that Shakespeare had personal knowledge of him. After his death the company went into a decline. In the season of 1590–1 they performed at court five times, but in the following season they performed there only once. Thereafter they spent most of their time in the obscurity of the provinces, making their last court appearance on 6 January 1594.

The company that displaced the Queen's Men and was preeminent when Shakespeare arrived in London was the Lord Admiral's Men. They had started out as Lord Howard's Men, servants of Charles Howard who for a brief period was Lord Chancellor and then in 1585 was appointed Lord Admiral. Between 1587 and 1593 the Admiral's Men achieved their prominent position largely as the result of a series of plays written for them by Christopher Marlowe featuring roles for their leader, the tragic actor Edward Alleyn, notably the title roles of *The Jew of Malta*, *Tamburlaine* and *Doctor Faustus*. From 1594 they made their home at the Rose, and were backed and managed by Philip Henslowe; because of the account he kept of their financial activities in his *Diaries* we know more about this company than any other.

The Admiral's Men were not without competition. The son of the Earl of Derby, Ferdinando, Lord Strange, kept a company of actors who counted amongst them Will Kempe, Thomas Pope, John Heminges, Augustine Phillips and George Bryan. All of these were members of the company that emerged in 1594 as the Lord Chamberlain's Men, and it has been speculated that Shakespeare joined Lord Strange's Men when he first arrived in London, but there is no actual evidence of this. Strange's Men were very successful, as attested by the fact that they presented six of the nine plays performed at court in the 1591–2 season. Between 1589 and 1594 they worked in some sort of collaboration with the Admiral's Men, with Alleyn leading both companies. The 1592 outbreak of the plague devastated the theatrical profession, however, because it necessitated the prohibition of plays in London until the spring of 1594 and the companies were forced to take to the road. When the playhouses re-opened the Admiral's Men came together again and moved into the Rose, which previously had been open to various companies. Lord Strange died in that year, and with other actors the remnant of his men, apparently led by Richard Burbage and including as playwright William Shakespeare, moved into James Burbage's Theatre as the Lord Chamberlain's Men.

Although there were other companies performing in London, most notably the Earl of Pembroke's, the following years saw a struggle for dominance between the Admiral's Men and the Chamberlain's Men. The patron of Shakespeare's company, Henry Carey, 1st Lord Hunsdon, was a powerful figure; he was Queen Elizabeth's cousin and had been made Lord Chamberlain in 1585. His daughter was married to Charles Howard, the Lord Admiral, so the rivalry between these two men was friendly. However, the rivalry between the two acting companies was not, and it was intensified by the fact that from 1597 they had a monopoly on acting in London. This came about when in that year Pembroke's Men made the misguided decision to present a play by Thomas Nashe and Ben Jonson called *The Isle of Dogs*. The play no longer exists, so we can only speculate on its contents, but it presumably mocked powerful interests because it so offended the Privy Council that, on 28 July, they sent out an order prohibiting all plays in or around the city and demanding that all playhouses be pulled down. Three of Pembroke's Men, including Jonson, were imprisoned and the rest of the company fled to the provinces. Although the Privy Council order was not carried out (within three months the companies were performing again), it delivered a clear message about the limits of official tolerance. But perhaps it was never intended that it should be carried out, for in February 1598 the Privy Council confirmed licences to the Lord Admiral's Men and the Lord Chamberlain's Men 'to use and practise stage plays, whereby they might be the better enabled and prepared to show such plays before her Majesty as they shall be required at times meet and accustomed', and prohibited any other companies from playing unless given special permission (*ES* 4: 325).

With the Chamberlain's Men established at the Theatre in the northern suburbs and the Admiral's Men at the Rose south of the Thames it might be assumed that they developed different audiences and different kinds of repertoire. To a degree this was the case, but it did not lessen their rivalry. In this the Admiral's Men had the greater struggle, for much of their success had come from the collaboration between Marlowe and Alleyn, and after Marlowe's death Alleyn did not find a playwright who could provide him with such dynamic roles. Between 1594 and 1597 the Admiral's Men produced 55 new plays, sometimes at the rate of three a month; most of these plays have not survived, and their sheer number implies a desperate search for material. The Chamberlain's Men, on the other hand, had the advantage of a new team, the up-and-coming tragedian Richard Burbage and the playwright William Shakespeare.

It is impossible to say how much of the success of the Lord Chamberlain's Men can be attributed to Shakespeare. The popular audience was far more interested in actors than dramatists, and anyway the performance of plays was a collaborative effort. However, the Lord Chamberlain's Men did have good material as well as good actors, and from the season of 1595–6 they dominated court performances. They also began to achieve a degree of stability unusual for dramatic companies. Their move across the Thames in 1598–9 was a good one, for the Globe not only became their permanent home but also, and more importantly, was owned by the sharers, the main members of the company, of whom Shakespeare was one. It also put them in much closer proximity to their rivals at the Rose. In 1600 Henslowe opened another playhouse, the Fortune, in the northern suburbs, though at some distance from where the Theatre and the Curtain had been located, and Alleyn moved the Admiral's Men (by then known as the Earl of Nottingham's Company) from the Rose to the Fortune. This seems to have been a significant acknowledgement that they could not compete with the Chamberlain's Men.

James I, who succeeded Elizabeth in 1603, was also a great lover of theatre. He acknowledged the pre-eminence of Shakespeare's company by taking them into his service as the King's Men. The Admiral's Men had to be content with the patronage of Prince Henry. One other company, the Earl of Worcester's Men, had managed in 1602 to establish themselves in London despite the mighty opposition; they became Queen Anne's Men. But it was the King's Men who continued to dominate the theatrical world, both at court and in the public playhouses.

They did have rivals elsewhere, however. The boys' companies which had performed in private theatres from the 1570s, the Children of the Chapel Royal and the Children of St Paul's, had a troubled history, but there were times when they drew audiences away from the public playhouses. The age of the boys made it difficult for them to be taken seriously in plays demanding emotional depth and experience, so they specialized in plays dependent on verbal wit and in satirical plays, often with an overt and cynical sexual content, where the incongruity of their age sharpened the poignancy. Most of the leading writers of the time wrote for them, not only John Lyly, who had fostered their early development as professionals, but such dramatists and poets as George Chapman, Ben Jonson and John Marston. They had a long history of involvement in court entertainment and, because their entrance charges were so much higher than those of the public playhouses, they did not compete for the larger body of the public audiences but appealed particularly to the wealthier fashionable theatre-goers.

Presumably because they felt protected by their youth, the boys tended to perform risky material and sometimes went too far. After 1584, for reasons unknown, the Children of the Chapel Royal ceased to appear at court. Paul's Boys were apparently suppressed in 1589–90, probably because of their involvement in the Marprelate controversy: this was a battle of pamphlets which began in 1588 and continued into the following year, when a Puritan writing under the name 'Martin Marprelate' attacked certain Anglican practices. Some prominent writers, including Lyly, wrote anti-Martinist responses. The authorities, anxious to bring an end to the controversy, suppressed both sides, and Paul's Boys fell victim to their zeal. But in 1599 Paul's Boys were revived in their old playhouse, largely with their old repertoire, and in the following year the Children of the Chapel Royal returned to the

Blackfriars (the Chamberlain's Men had in 1596 attempted to take possession of the Blackfriars, which James Burbage had bought and converted with the intention of using it for his son's company, but as a result of a petition of local residents they had been prohibited from playing there). For the next seven or eight years the boys enjoyed a vogue, and Shakespeare was the only leading dramatist of the time who did not write for them.

The comments in *Hamlet* on the subject of the boy players presumably reflect the company's resentment, if not Shakespeare's own. When Hamlet asks why the adult Players are no longer held in as high esteem in the city as they used to be, Rosencrantz blames the change on 'an eyrie of children, little eyases, that cry out on the top of the question and are most tyrannically clapped for't'. These children, who 'are now the fashion', 'berattle the common stages' with their satirical attacks (2.2.337–40). Of course, the new fashion of 1600 soon went out of fashion and Paul's Boys were disbanded in 1607. The Children of the Chapel Royal lasted longer, but James I eventually tired of their frequent attacks on him and withdrew royal support, forcing them to change their name to the Children of the Revels. In 1608 they left the Blackfriars, which was taken over by the King's Men. The Children continued to perform for some years, but they never regained their earlier popularity.

The acquisition by the King's Men of the Blackfriars made their position as London's leading company unassailable. They could provide for every potential audience because they now had an outdoor and an indoor playhouse. The Blackfriars enabled them to try out different methods of presentation, since it allowed for spectacle and for more effective use of music. This does not mean that plays written for the two houses were very different, since plays for the Globe were performed at the Blackfriars and vice versa. But Shakespeare and his colleagues could please those who wanted the comfort and exclusiveness of a private playhouse as well as their long-time followers at the Globe. The King's Men maintained their pre-eminence beyond Shakespeare's retirement, until the closing of the theatres in 1642.

## THE PLAYHOUSES

Evidence concerning the structure of the Elizabethan public playhouses is remarkably slim and fragmentary, even with what has been gleaned from the recent discovery and excavation of the site of the Rose playhouse and the more limited exploration of the site of the Globe. Documentary evidence from Shakespeare's time includes brief accounts in the journals of foreign travellers who visited London, such as Johannes de Witt, Paul Hentzner and Thomas Platter; the most important of these is a transcription of de Witt's impressions of the four playhouses he saw there in about 1596, along with a sketch of the interior of the Swan. There are also in existence copies of the contracts for the construction of the Fortune (1599–1600) and the Hope (1614). The Fortune was built to emulate and outdo the Globe, except that it was square; this was unusual, according to contemporary panoramic etchings of London, which show public playhouses, including the Globe, to have been round or polygonal structures. Fragments of information can be gleaned from such sources as official documents of the Privy Council and the City of London authorities in their struggles for control over the theatres, as well as from Puritan preachers who attacked the theatres and dramatists who defended them. As for the plays themselves, they offer evidence about the conditions under which they were performed, but it is not always easy to interpret, which is why in the past mistaken assumptions have been made, for example, about the existence of an inner stage.

The discovery in 1988 of the foundations of the Rose playhouse provided new evidence, though its full implications are not yet clear. The Rose was built around 1587 by Philip Henslowe. In about 1592 he enlarged it by rebuilding the northern half of it; his reasons were probably twofold: to increase the audience-space (which attests to the success of his venture), and to upgrade the stage by increasing its size and adding a roof to it. The Rose fell into disuse in 1603. Scholars were surprised by a number of things brought to light by the excavation. They had envisaged a polygonal building of 20 to 24 sides with a diameter from its exterior walls of 100 feet, and they expected to find that a rectangular stage had been situated on the south side of the arena and had projected mid-way into it. In fact, the scale of the playhouse and the size of its stage were smaller than expected: measured from its external walls the building was about 80 feet in diameter, and the stage projected slightly more than a third of the way into the auditorium. The stage itself was situated on the north side of the arena, not to the south, so the actors would have performed not

in shadow, but with the sun directly overhead. The stage was much shallower than presumed and was hexagonal rather than rectangular in shape. The building itself had only 14 sides.[2]

The excavation of the Globe indicates that it did have 20 sides and was larger than the Rose, with a diameter of 105 feet. If the Globe's stage was proportionately as large as that of the Fortune, which according to its contract was modelled upon the Globe, it did project mid-way into the auditorium, providing a much larger acting area. The differences between the Rose and the Globe, set alongside differences in the accounts of the Swan and the Fortune, suggest that there was no single pattern for an Elizabethan playhouse. Any description of what the Globe might have been like, therefore, will have some details that are largely conjectural and some that may not be applicable to other playhouses.

The polygonal frame of the Globe was made of wood; this seems generally to have been the case, although the Swan was built out of flint, if we are to believe de Witt. The frame had an outer and an inner wall; according to the Fortune contract, the distance between the inner and outer walls of its frame was a little more than 12 feet, and the distance at the Globe was probably about the same. The stage, raised some five feet, extended from the inner wall to the centre of the arena, with the space beneath it concealed, perhaps by wooden boards or by curtains. The stage at the Fortune measured 43 feet by 27.5 feet and the Globe's stage was probably of similar dimensions. Although the excavations of the Rose show that in its earlier version there was no roof over the stage, it appears that in most playhouses there was such a roof, supported by two wooden columns, and decorated on the under-side with sun, moon and stars, and therefore called the 'heavens'. De Witt tells us that the columns were 'painted in such excellent imitation of marble that it is able to deceive even the most cunning',[3] and it is likely that the whole edifice was extravagantly decorated to give an impression of grandeur.

Within the walls of the frame on three sides of the stage were three tiers of galleries for spectators; according to the Fortune contract, the lowest was 12 feet high, the middle 11 feet high, and the upper gallery was nine feet high. Each of the two higher galleries overhung ten inches beyond the one below, with a thatched or tiled roof over the topmost. The arena itself, however, was not covered. It has been estimated that the Globe could have accommodated about two thousand people seated in its galleries and about eight hundred 'groundlings' standing in the arena around three sides of the stage, though the building would have been extremely crowded under such circumstances, and evidence from Henslowe's *Diaries* indicates that his playhouses at least were not full for all performances.

The cheapest rate of admission was one penny, charged to the groundlings who had to stand. Those who could afford to pay more could sit in the galleries, the highest level costing the most. Thomas Platter, a traveller from Basel, gave an account of his theatre-going experience in 1599:

> Every day at two o'clock in the afternoon in the city of London two and sometimes three comedies are performed at separate places, wherewith folk make merry together, and whichever does best gets the greatest audience. The places are so built, that they play on a raised platform, and every one can well see it all. There are, however, separate galleries and there one stands more comfortably and moreover can sit, but one pays more for it. Thus anyone who remains on the level standing pays only one English penny: but if he wants to sit, he is let in at a further door, and there he gives another penny. If he desires to sit on a cushion in the most comfortable place of all, where he not only sees everything well, but can also be seen, then he gives yet another English penny at another door.[4]

There was also a gallery above the stage at the rear, and those who went to be seen as well as to see might have been seated there. This gallery was apparently used as a musicians' gallery and for scenes played 'above', such as the balcony scene in *Romeo and Juliet*.

At the rear of the stage, beneath this gallery, was the 'tiring-house', with two or perhaps in some cases three curtained entrances to the stage. It used to be thought that at the centre of the back wall there was a curtained recess, an 'inner stage', because many plays contain discovery scenes, and so such a location seemed necessary. It is now generally accepted that there was no inner stage; more probably the doorways of the tiring-house were used for discovery scenes or for action taking place 'within'. The tiring-house was, as its name implies, a dressing-room, but it was much more than this. It performed all backstage functions, being used to store costumes and properties, to conceal actors waiting for their entrance, and to conceal the prompter, or 'book-holder'. The space beneath the stage was also put to use; it was concealed from the audience and a trap-door in the stage allowed for spectacular appearances or descents into hell. Above the heavens was a structure called the 'hut' which, it seems, contained machinery for special effects such as thunder, and was used to raise or lower objects and, possibly, actors. On the roof of the hut was a flagpole from which a flag was flown when a performance was in progress.

The staging itself was of the simplest: there were no sets and little attempt was made to create scenic illusion. As Platter's account indicates, plays were presented from two in the afternoon: this allowed these outdoor theatres to take the best advantage of daylight, so the entire action was illuminated by natural light, limiting the possibility of lighting effects. The midnight darkness, for example, of the opening scene of *Hamlet*, could be suggested by having the characters carry torches or lanterns, but any real sense of darkness had to be imposed upon the imagination of the audience through the power of the language. Similarly, location was indicated by the most rudimentary of properties: a couple of trees in pots might represent a forest, a table and a few benches could suggest the interior of a cottage or of a great hall. The passage of time was usually signalled by someone simply telling the audience that time had passed. The Prologue to *Henry V*, while apparently complaining about the inadequacies of this dumb, empty stage, cleverly indicates how the audience is to interpret it:

> But pardon, gentles all,
> The flat unraised spirits that hath dar'd
> On this unworthy scaffold to bring forth
> So great an object: Can this cockpit hold
> The vasty fields of France? or may we cram
> Within this wooden O the very casques
> That did affright the air at Agincourt?
> O, pardon! since a crooked figure may
> Attest in little place a million;
> And let us, ciphers to this great accompt,
> On your imaginary forces work.
>
> (Pro.8–18)

This is a remarkable piece of verse. A modern audience, accustomed to the explicit visualization that film and television allow (think of the Kenneth Branagh version of *Henry V*), is rarely asked to perform an act of imaginative collaboration akin to that routinely required of the Elizabethan audience.

The exiguity of the setting meant that it was up to the actors to present spectacle through dynamic stage groupings and splendid costumes. Elizabethan plays are full of processions and pageants, dumb-shows and plays-within-the-play, patterned conflicts of many sorts, including dancing, wrestling, fencing and warfare. The costumes were rich and elaborate. We know that the companies spent a great deal on their wardrobe; Henslowe's *Diary* for March 1598 lists 14 cloaks, 16 gowns plus an unspecified number of women's gowns, 17 jerkins and doublets, and 16 suits.[5] These were not cheap imitations either: the first cloak listed is scarlet with broad gold laces and gold buttons, and this at a time when a single cloak could cost as much as £19 and velvet cost £1 a yard. The actors were also often given the unwanted clothing of their patrons and other wealthy lords. Actors, therefore, were able to wear clothing of a quality that would not be available to the majority of those in the audience, perfectly reflecting an image of the rich and powerful of their own day, and no doubt giving ideas to their fashion-conscious middle-class spectators.

Because their costumes were of contemporary style and fashion, rank and station could be accurately reflected, but little effort was made to create historical or geographical authenticity in costuming. Rather, as with stage properties, such distinctions were indicated by simple signs added to the basic elaborate costume. The main exception to this appears to have been the depiction of Africans: Aaron the Moor's race would have been indicated through his wearing a black velvet mask and gloves. A very important effect of these contemporary costumes must have been that all locations, whether the Troy of *Troilus and Cressida*, the Rome of *Julius Caesar*, the Denmark of *Hamlet* or the Vienna of *Measure for Measure*, signalled themselves to be, at least on some level, contemporary England.

Since Shakespeare's final plays were written for the indoor playhouse at Blackfriars as well as for the Globe, it is necessary to say something about facilities at the private playhouses. They retained the basic structure of the banqueting halls I have already described, with all members of the audience seated. The capacity of the Blackfriars was about seven hundred. There was the potential for more elaborate scenic effects and, because the indoor playhouses were lit by candles, simple lighting effects were possible. Without the distractions of outdoor sounds, music could be put to better use. But it would be a mistake to exaggerate the differences between indoor and outdoor playhouses. The plays Shakespeare wrote for the Blackfriars had to be easily adaptable for the Globe, and indeed he had plenty of experience at adapting Globe plays for the court stages at Hampton Court and Whitehall. So, whatever superficial differences there were, it was the fundamental similarities that Shakespeare exploited.


## ACTORS AND ACTING

In these playhouses the relationship between actor and audience was much more intimate than we are accustomed to today, as there was so little distance between the groundlings and the stage (in some private theatres spectators who were willing to pay extra could actually rent a stool and sit on the stage), and the audience's sense that it was participating in the theatrical experience must have been very strong. Dramatists manipulated this closeness through the frequent use of asides and soliloquies. To a modern audience, accustomed to actors performing inside the frame of a proscenium arch, these may seem to be awkward devices, but if we think of them as being spoken to spectators who were only a few feet away, we can see that the actor was, in effect, acknowledging the presence of the audience and not simply talking to himself.

*Richard III*, for instance, opens with a soliloquy in which Richard defines himself and reveals his intentions to the audience. This is, in part, necessary exposition, but it is not merely that, because it draws the audience into a position of complicity with Richard, which is intensified by later soliloquies and a frequent use of asides. For example, after his seduction of Lady Anne he is left alone on the stage, and asks 'Was ever woman in this humour wooed? / Was ever woman in this humour won?' (1.2.227–8). He is not just congratulating himself here; he is inviting the audience to share his glee and also, implicitly, to acquiesce in his cynical exploitation of Anne. Another highly effective use of soliloquy occurs in *The Winter's Tale*. Leontes, for no good reason, has convinced himself that his wife has been unfaithful to him:

There have been,
(Or I am much deceiv'd) cuckolds ere now,
And many a man there is, (even at this present,
Now, while I speak this) holds his wife by th'arm,
That little thinks she has been sluic'd in's absence
And his pond fish'd by his next neighbour, by
Sir Smile, his neighbour.

(1.2.190–6)

This is an extraordinary moment, in which the intimate connections of 'this present' time and place allow the actor to project the character's tormenting doubt on to the audience. The soliloquy is not precisely a direct address to the audience (Leontes does not expect people to jump up and agree with him); rather, it creates an instant of recognition by acknowledging the artifice of the play.

These roles, separated by more than 15 years, were both played by Richard Burbage. He must have had a powerful presence and the rhetorical skill to make the playwright's words effective, for if the nature of this theatre was to throw emphasis upon the actor, what finally counted, as much as the eloquence of gesture and the ability to strut in fine clothing, must have been power and flexibility of voice. The traditional view of the difference between Burbage and his older rival Alleyn is that Alleyn was a ranting, melodramatic performer of the kind that today we would call a 'ham', and Burbage was a more sophisticated, realistic actor. To be sure, the evidence suggests that Alleyn was a large, very physical actor, and he is associated with the over-reaching energies of the villain–heroes of Marlowe's plays. Burbage triumphed in a series of less monochromatic roles, ranging from Richard III through the complex figures of Hamlet, Lear and Othello to Leontes and Prospero. However, the comparison may be unfair to Alleyn because contemporary accounts praise both actors in similar terms: both performed in a life-like manner, both had powerful, well-modulated voices and controlled gestures.

The fact is that we know very little about Elizabethan acting styles. For some 60 years a debate has raged about whether acting was formalistic, with much use of conventionalized gesture and a heightened delivery of speech, or whether it was realistic, with affinities to modern acting.[6] My own view is that it probably mixed the formalistic with the naturalistic, but even in taking this moderate position I have to note that it is complicated by the fact that what is understood as 'realistic' differs from time to time and place to place, and when the contemporaries of Alleyn and Burbage called their acting life-like this does not necessarily equate with what we today think of as life-like. Consider, for example, Sir Thomas Overbury's characterization of the actor's skill:

> He doth not strive to make nature monstrous; she is often seen in the same scene with him, but neither on stilts nor crutches. . . . By his action he fortifies moral precepts with examples; for what we see him personate, we think truly done before us. . . . All men have been of his occupation; and indeed, what he doth feignedly, that do others essentially: this day one acts a monarch, the next a private person. Here one acts a tyrant, on the morrow an exile: a parasite this man tonight, tomorrow a precisian, and so of divers others.[7]

Overbury here insists on the naturalness of the actor's performance while also noting the histrionic element in real life. Elizabethans and Jacobeans alike were fascinated by the idea that all men are players, and this being so it is impossible for us to know exactly how they understood and how actors represented 'nature'.

Still, some broad inferences can be drawn. The theatres used a repertory system and an actor might have had to learn a new part every two weeks while retaining in memory 40 or more others. Many plays have 30 or 40 parts, and since companies consisted of at most 15 actors, with three or four boy-apprentices, there had to be much doubling; the lead actors would usually have taken only one role in a play, but minor actors might have had to play up to six or seven.[8] From a modern perspective time given to rehearsal was very short; it could be as little as two weeks, and had to be fitted into the mornings, since the afternoons were given over to public performances of plays already in the company's repertoire. Plays had no 'director' as such, so decisions on how to perform were collaborative (perhaps in consultation with the playwright) and there must have been much improvisation; Hamlet's instruction to the Players to 'let those that play your clowns speak no more than is set down for them' (3.2.38–9) suggests that improvisation could at times get out of hand. Delivery must have been rather speedy; the reference in the Prologue of *Romeo and Juliet* to 'the two hours' traffic of our stage' apparently does not underestimate the length of performances by much, and even though they ran without a break, it would have been difficult to fit *Hamlet*, for example, into the time. Given these limitations, acting styles could hardly have been entirely naturalistic, at least in the sense that we understand the term today. There must have been a visual language of conventional signs and gestures.

The question of style is most interesting when asked in relation to the boy actors. Women did not act on the Elizabethan stage and women's parts were played by the companies' apprentices, boys who were taken on usually at some age between eight and fifteen and worked out their apprenticeship in seven years. What evidence there is suggests that once these boys became young men and ended their apprenticeship they acted in adult male roles. It is generally assumed that the boys must have been of small stature and with unbroken voices; when Hamlet greets the Players he says to the apprentice: 'What, my young lady and mistress: By'r lady, your ladyship is nearer to heaven than when I saw you last by the altitude of a chopine. Pray God, your voice, like a piece of uncurrent gold, be not crack'd within the ring' (2.2.420–5). But how naturalistically could these adolescent boys have acted? In the Induction to *The Taming of the Shrew* the page Barthol'mew is dressed as a woman and made to 'usurp the grace, / Voice, gait, and action of a gentlewoman' (Ind.1.129–30). We can imagine this boy easily enough in the roles of the young women of the comedies (Kate herself in this one), and Shakespeare made it easier for the boy or boys (there is almost no evidence pertaining to the identities of the apprentices) who played Portia, Rosalind and Viola by allowing these women to spend much of the play disguised as young men. We can imagine a 14-year-old boy in the tragic role of Juliet, who is about that age (although Juliet's sexual knowingness and readiness for marriage indicate that the Elizabethan idea of maturity was not the same as ours). But what about the roles of more genuinely mature women?

This is a more puzzling question. The powerful Burbage played Hamlet and we can imagine a young boy playing the fragile role of Ophelia alongside him. But what about the more demanding role of Gertrude? What about Lady Macbeth and Cleopatra? There is a weight of maturity and experience in these women that we cannot easily assume in a boy with an unbroken voice. It is possible, since some of the apprentices could have been approaching

20, that these roles were played by older boys – in fact, young men – but in that case the acting must have been stylized. How, for instance, would the role of Cleopatra have been played? This most alluring of Shakespeare's women has defeated many modern actresses, so what was the boy who played her like? Near the end of *Antony and Cleopatra*, with Antony already dead, Cleopatra thinks about the shame of public humiliation and imagines her own story dramatized on the public stage:

> I shall see
> Some squeaking Cleopatra boy my greatness
> I' the posture of a whore.
>
> (5.2.218–20)

If the actor playing this role was a squeaking boy, would Shakespeare have chosen this moment of high dramatic pressure to draw mocking attention to the fact? He might have; the Elizabethan audience had a high degree of tolerance for metadramatic or self-reflexive moments, as is abundantly indicated in his plays. Still, it would have been a very risky thing to do here.

The King's Men first performed *Antony and Cleopatra* around 1607, and their leading apprentice who played the role of Cleopatra might, in the two or three years prior to this, have originated the roles of Isabella in *Measure for Measure*, Lady Macbeth, Desdemona and Cordelia. Presumably the same boy performed at court in the Christmas season of 1604–5 when the King's Men put on ten plays in a period of a little over three months. He probably took the leading female roles in most of them, including those of Desdemona, Isabella and Portia, as well as demanding comic roles in *The Merry Wives of Windsor*, *The Comedy of Errors*, *Henry V*, *Love's Labour's Lost* and a couple of satirical comedies by Ben Jonson. It is an astonishing record. We have no answers to questions about the boys because the evidence is far too sparse. The best we can do is admire the high degree of skill that these anonymous youths, whatever their ages, must have possessed.

Apart from Burbage, the best-known members of Shakespeare's company were the comedians. Will Kempe was one of the original shareholders of the Lord Chamberlain's Men, a comic actor in the mode of Tarlton, and in his time almost as famous; indeed, he had a great reputation long before he joined the company. He specialized in clowning and dancing; his jigs, comic dance–dramas performed at the end of a play, contributed immensely to the company's success. His comedy was often physical and tended to depend on verbal confusion rather than on wit. He was probably the first to play the roles of Bottom and Falstaff, and certainly played Peter in *Romeo and Juliet* and Dogberry in *Much Ado about Nothing*. He left the Chamberlain's Men in 1599, apparently not wanting to make the move across the Thames, but perhaps he did not like the constraints of appearing in plays; Shakespeare may have had Kempe in mind when he had Hamlet criticize clowns who speak 'more than is set down for them, for there be them that will themselves laugh, to set on some quantity of barren spectators to laugh too, though in the meantime some necessary question of the play be then to be considered' (3.2.39–43). After he left the Chamberlain's Men, Kempe acted with the Earl of Worcester's Men, but his famous nine-day morris dance from London to Norwich, performed in 1600 as a kind of publicity stunt, suggests that he enjoyed the freedom to do as he wished or, perhaps, to be himself.

Kempe was replaced by Robert Armin, who was a comedian of a different sort. Armin's performances embodied the paradox of the tragic clown, and he was a comic actor with the ability to sustain a role rather than simply play himself, as Kempe seems usually to have done. He was the right man for the encroaching uncertainty of the Jacobean succession, and Shakespeare created for him a series of roles as an outsider who questions and mockingly undercuts the reality of social harmony. He was the licensed Fool, allowed the freedom to mock his superiors and thereby to question the underpinnings of authority. His first role was probably Feste in *Twelfth Night*, who promotes much of the comic action but remains outside it, insisting that however happy an ending may be 'the rain it raineth every day'. The part of Touchstone was probably written into the earlier *As You Like It* for him; the role of William would originally have been the main comic part in this play, acted by Kempe, and the juxtaposition shows precisely the differences between the two clowns.[9] Armin's later roles are characterized by their sense of alienation: Thersites, Lavatch, Autolycus. His most brilliant variation on this theme is Lear's Fool, a role that embraces and comes close to understanding universal chaos. Armin had true versatility, however, because he was also able to play the Kempe roles when the King's Men revived earlier plays.

What of the structure that kept these powerful talents under control? An acting company was a hierarchy made up of sharers, hired men and apprentices. The sharers were the leading players; they put money into the company, and owned it and its assets (mainly playscripts and the wardrobe) and took a share of the profits. In the case of the Lord Chamberlain's Men, their playwright Shakespeare was also a sharer, but this was an unusual situation: playwrights were usually paid by the script. Apart from Shakespeare himself the original sharers in his company appear to have been Burbage, Kempe, Heminges, Thomas Pope, George Bryan, William Sly and Augustine Phillips; there is evidence that Heminges was their financial manager and the one who handled licensing details with the Office of the Revels. When the company moved to the Globe, the sharers owned their playhouse as well. They were unique in this: usually a playhouse was owned by an entrepreneur, such as Henslowe, and the players paid him a part of their profits for the use of it. The sharers commissioned or chose new plays, and hired other actors and helpers when necessary. Judging from the numbers of parts in Shakespeare's plays, and allowing for doubling (it was not unusual for the less important sharers and the hired players to double up to six parts), the Chamberlain's Men/King's Men must have had a minimum of 12 sharers in their most successful years.

Hired men were paid by the week. Some of them were actors who were needed for minor roles, but the hired men included musicians (as many as six might be employed), book-holders, scribes or copiers, wardrobe-keepers, stage-hands, and money-gatherers. The most important of these was the book-holder, who not only acted as prompter and stage-manager, but also had the duty of looking after the scripts, including making any changes decided on during the rehearsal period. All of these hired men, including the money-gatherers, could be called upon to play minor roles, especially non-speaking roles and participants in crowd scenes.

Apprentices played the roles of children and of women. As with any trade, a boy was apprenticed to a particular master, in this case one of the company's sharers. The Lord Chamberlain's Men seem usually to have had four of them. An apprentice's pay was minimal, but he received food and clothing from his master and lodged in his house. Presumably the true reward was the training he received.

## PLAYWRIGHTS

When in 1605 a play-goer went to the Globe to see *King Lear*, he or she did not go because it was a play by Shakespeare, but because it was performed by the King's Men and featured Burbage and Armin. The vast number of anonymous plays from the period, and the fact that most editions of Shakespeare's plays that found their way into print during his lifetime did not identify him as author, indicate that playwrights had no special significance within the process of collaboration that produced a play. This was so even though dramatists earned more than other professional writers. In fact, while to be an amateur writer was respectable, to be a professional was not. Although a number of aristocrats wrote poetry and a rather smaller number wrote plays, most of them wrote out of vanity or (as did Sir Philip Sidney) to gain royal favour, and certainly not for money; they were amateurs before that word took on the pejorative implications of inept dabbling that it often has today. Some non-aristocratic writers tried to gain patronage for their writing and make it respectable in that way; Edmund Spenser and Ben Jonson spent most of their careers attempting to do this, because no professional writers of any sort were held in high esteem.

Indeed, there were very few outlets for professional writers. The closest thing to modern journalism was the pamphleteering of men like Greene and Nashe, and they certainly did not make a living out of it. There were no novels as we recognize them today, and the works of prose or verse fiction known as romances had a very small circulation. The most popular form of writing was printed sermons, and the men who published them were professional clerics rather than professional writers. A man who needed to sustain himself by writing had to turn to the stage, and if he hoped that by doing so he would gain social prestige, he was misguided. When in 1616 Jonson published some of his plays along with his poems as *Works*, he was consciously attempting to raise the status of plays. He saw himself as a poet and resented the fact that he had to work for what he called the 'loathed stage' to make a living; whenever he received patronage, and when he finally won the favour of James I as writer of court masques, he turned his back on the playhouses.

There is no evidence that Shakespeare shared Jonson's view of his profession, although his brief period of offering poems to a patron might suggest that he toyed with the idea of being a poet rather than a playwright. As sharer in his company, of course, he was in a different position from most other dramatists, and he made more money. But he seems to have been content to provide his two plays each year to his company, to perform in minor roles for them, and to invest his income wisely. Unlike Jonson, he appears to have had no interest in his plays beyond their life in the playhouse, and was certainly unconcerned about their publication.

In this it was Jonson who was unusual. A dramatist was paid by the acting company to provide a play, and once he had completed a script it became the company's property. Because he was a sharer, Shakespeare's position was a little different from that of other playwrights, but the status of his plays would have been the same. The play was a valuable commodity for the company, however, and except in emergency situations (as during the 1593–4 closings, when the need for money compelled companies to sell some of their plays) the actors protected their plays for as long as they retained a stage-life. There were no laws of copyright, and popular plays might be stolen by other companies or published in pirated editions, but only when a play was devalued in this way or when it ceased to draw audiences would a company sell it to a printer.

Shakespeare was not the only dramatist writing for his company, of course, but others would have been paid per play. The average payment for a play seems to have been about £6, but playwrights were expected to do other work as well, especially renovating old plays by adding new material, for which they would have received smaller amounts. When there was the need to provide a play in a hurry they often collaborated with other playwrights; G.E. Bentley estimates that half the plays by professional writers contain material by more than one hand.[10] Apparently Shakespeare himself had a hand, along with Dekker, Henry Chettle and Anthony Munday, in a play called *Sir Thomas More* (1601?), of which a manuscript fragment remains, possibly containing his handwriting. Near the end of his career he collaborated on *Henry VIII* and *The Two Noble Kinsmen* with John Fletcher, who succeeded him as resident playwright for the King's Men. For most of his career, however, it seems that he wrote his plays alone, although of course many of the extant texts show evidence of revision, sometimes extensive, and it is possible that some of this was done by other writers.

Shakespeare's output of around two plays a year throughout his career means that in general he must have had the time to produce a text that satisfied his own artistic needs as well as the demand of his company, although six months seems to be little enough time to write a *Hamlet* or a *King Lear*, especially considering his other playhouse duties. There was a constant demand for new plays, however, and other writers were more prolific. Thomas Dekker provided Henslowe's companies with 44 plays in five years, and Thomas Heywood, who worked for Queen Anne's Men and, like Shakespeare, was an actor as well as a playwright, claimed to have written or collaborated in 220 plays.

Most of Heywood's 220 plays no longer exist. It is difficult to estimate how many plays were written between 1576 and 1642 because it is impossible to know how many are now lost. We do know, from documents such as the Stationers' Register and Henslowe's *Diaries*, the titles of many plays that are no longer extant, and many more must have vanished without even that meagre trace. Henslowe's record names about 280 plays, of which only 40 or so still exist, a loss of six out of seven. Few Elizabethan or Jacobean playwrights, including Shakespeare, would have cared very much about this loss. Some of them were hacks, some were good craftsmen, some were minor artists, a few were great artists. Jonson knew he was an artist but few others would have given the question much thought. Their plays were, after all, an ephemeral form of writing, not even considered a branch of literature, and it is a matter of great good fortune that any at all are left to us.

## AUDIENCES

Plays are written for an audience, and to understand the original reception of Shakespeare's plays we need to know something of those who saw them. Since for much of the time the acting companies, like their patrons, were competing for the attention of the monarch, and since all playscripts had to be submitted to the Revels Office, it would be possible to claim that the primary audience for an Elizabethan play was Elizabeth herself and the courtiers, government officials, ambassadors and attendants who made up the audience for plays presented at court. However, the companies really depended for their living on the wider London audience, and the dramatists had to cater for the tastes of those who frequented the public playhouses. While Shakespeare and his fellow playwrights had to please a wide social spectrum from the queen to the groundlings, the fact that they could write plays that would serve as well at court as at the Rose or the Globe seems to suggest that the tastes at the two ends of the spectrum did not differ radically.

The private playhouses catered for a relatively affluent clientele, who could afford the minimum entry charge of sixpence: members of the aristocracy, the gentry and the newly rich merchant citizenry, and students at the Inns of Court. Many of the same clientele also patronized the public playhouses. Shakespeare's audience at the Globe embraced all classes except those immediately around the queen, and the very poor. A once-influential argument, proposed by Alfred Harbage, claimed that the private and the public playhouses catered for distinct 'rival traditions', with the boys' companies performing for a coterie, a wealthy elite group with sophisticated interests, and the adult companies performing simpler popular plays for middle- and lower-class audiences. This theory was countered more recently by Ann Jennalie Cook, who argued that the lower classes would not have been able to afford to go to the playhouses, or to obtain the leisure-time to attend afternoon performances, so that only a privileged elite could have afforded to go to any theatre, private or public.[11]

Neither of these views seems adequate. The 'rival traditions' have so much in common that it is difficult to believe that they were quite distinct. During the 1590s the private playhouses were closed but presumably their audiences did not stop attending plays. When Rosencrantz talks of the 'eyrie of children' who 'berattle the common stages' he is referring to the fact that the boys' companies had at the turn of the century become popular once again. He says that the boys were attracting custom away from the adult companies, which would make sense only if the boys' and the men's companies were competing for the same audience. And as we have seen, from 1608 Shakespeare's company, the King's Men, owned the public Globe and the private Blackfriars, and performed the same plays at both playhouses, so presumably the differences in expectations of the two audiences were not really very great.

As for the theory of the privileged play-goers, the city authorities would surely not have been so deeply hostile to a theatre that was patronized only by the rich; their opposition arose precisely because they perceived playhouses as gathering places of unruly members of the lower classes. The argument for exclusiveness depends on two main assumptions. The first is that the penny charged for the cheapest level of entry to a public playhouse was more than an Elizabethan working man could afford. Now while it might be true that this price excluded many of the lower classes, it would not have excluded all of them. The price of a quart of cheap beer was also one penny; a quart of good ale cost fourpence. Since most of us would accept that it is probable that working people drank beer, I think we have to accept that it is equally probable that some of them frequented the playhouses. The second argument is that the intellectual content of even the popular plays, the allusiveness and complexity of their language and ideas, implies a degree of sophistication in the audience that we could expect only of an elite group. There is indeed much in these plays that reflects the erudition of the dramatists and that might have been obscure to the ignorant or uneducated, but this does not mean that the uneducated were not present in the audience. Ben Jonson spent much of his dramatic career complaining about the failure of ignorant audiences to understand his plays.

It is true that, if plays were not restricted to an elite, then a large part of the audience must have been illiterate, although this does not mean that they were also unintelligent, and they would have been much more accustomed to listening than is a modern audience. No doubt much of the material in the plays did go over the heads of many, and not just the heads of the groundlings. Any student of Shakespeare will know how essential it is to have read a play before seeing it – we need to look up things in the notes, read and re-read passages to make full sense of them, and without such preparation (sometimes even with it) much in a performance goes over *our* heads. But even the literate members of Shakespeare's audience were not able to prepare in this way, since play-texts were not available. So some elements of the audience would have understood and appreciated more than others. But all of the audience would have been keenly interested in what the plays showed and what they said.

We cannot do much more than estimate the numbers of those who attended plays. It has been extrapolated from figures given in Henslowe's *Diary* that in 1595 the weekly attendance at plays was about 15 000, which represents some 13 per cent of the available

London population, estimated at 160 000.[12] Even assuming that many of those 15 000 attended more than one play in a week (and the playhouses certainly depended upon the support of a loyal audience), these figures must represent a good cross-section of London residents. But Henslowe's numbers do not present the full picture, for other figures suggest that at their peak the playhouses drew in between 8000 and 10 000 people per day. The comparatively small percentage of the population who made up the social elite could not possibly account for these numbers.

This was a time of great social flux and there were, of course, shifts in the make-up of the audience during the years between 1576 and 1642 that would have reflected this flux, as well as changes in fashion and taste. It is also probable that different playhouses attracted different audiences with a different social mix. For example, the audiences in the theatres in the northern suburbs seem to have been somewhat coarser than those at the Bankside theatres. They liked straightforward patriotic plays and a lot of rough comedy and spectacle, while their counterparts at the Bankside playhouses were able to accept more sceptical and thoughtful fare. This may be one of the reasons why Kempe did not make the move to the Globe with his fellow actors. However, it is reasonable to assume that prosperous middle-class citizens and tradesmen always constituted a majority at the public playhouses, whatever the location. Finally, after the private theatres re-opened there was a gradual shift of many of those who could afford it to these indoor theatres. After the accession of James I in 1603 the royal taste was for more sophisticated private entertainments, and this too might have affected the nature and tastes of the public play-goers.

The great interest that Elizabethan plays can still arouse in us arises, I think, from the fact that they had to be inclusive, that they had to embrace the concerns of such a wide social range. And we must not assume that there was a simple division in which the poetic and philosophical parts of the play were directed to the nobler element and the low comedy to the groundlings: the tastes of Elizabethans even at the highest levels allowed for a degree of crudity; it was not only the groundlings who attended animal-baitings. Conversely, the attempt of the 'rude mechanicals' in *A Midsummer Night's Dream* to put on a play for the aristocrats, even though Shakespeare may seem to mock it, demonstrates an aspiration in these working men to higher things. The theatre, by bringing together members of different social strata, adjusted the divisions in Elizabethan society at the same time as it reflected them.


## CONTROL AND CENSORSHIP

The playhouses operated in the space generated by the tension between court interests which were, with occasional exceptions, supportive, and the interests of city and Church authorities, which were generally hostile. Because the playhouses were located in areas that were technically outside the control of the city authorities, they were protected from too much interference, but there were times when, for practical or political reasons, the Privy Council was obliged to restrain playhouse performances. The most compelling practical reason was the presence of bubonic plague in the city. Another apparently practical reason that was sometimes actually political was the official fear of what was vaguely defined as 'riot and disorder'.

The plague certainly did provide legitimate cause for concern. It had been endemic in England since the fourteenth century, and by the late sixteenth century it was frequently epidemic, though mainly confined to urban areas (in 1563 about one fifth of the London population died of bubonic plague), where the most severe outbreaks occurred in the summer months. It was carried by rat fleas and was therefore particularly dangerous in crowded places that encouraged contagion. Whenever there were signs of an outbreak an official ban was placed on public gatherings, including those at playhouses. During Shakespeare's professional career there were two major eruptions, one from 1592 to 1594, and one in 1603, as well as numerous minor outbreaks that led to restraint on playing. As we have seen, the closing of the playhouses forced the companies into tours of the provinces where there was less danger from the disease, but these tours were a regressive step for the companies, which had to perform in uncomfortable conditions and for rather less than their customary profit.[13]

While I do not wish to minimize the horrifying effects of the plague, it does seem likely that the threat of the disease was sometimes used by the city authorities as an excuse rather than a reason to control the public playhouses, for the onset of plague did not have much effect on court performances. If this was the case, then official fear of plague blurred into official fear of disorder. Thus, on 23 June 1592 the Privy Council prohibited playhouse performances until Michaelmas because of 'unlawful assemblies' that 'draw together the baser sort of people' (*ES* 4: 310–11). At the urging of the city authorities the Council ordered a further prohibition in January of the following year because of the plague, and the lengthy disturbance of playing that followed this almost broke the acting companies.

As far as riot and disorder were concerned, the Privy Council seemed to fear them less than did the city authorities, and less than it did the plague. It did not take much notice of the frequent entreaties of the Lord Mayor and aldermen to control the playhouses in the name of order, presumably because it saw that their fears were exaggerated. On occasions when there actually were riots, as in July 1581 when a fight broke out between a group of actors and a 'disordered company of gentlemen', the playhouses were briefly closed (*ES* 4: 282–3). But the 1597 Privy Council order for the plucking down of the Curtain and the Theatre and 'any other common playhouse', that resulted from the Earl of Pembroke's Men's performance at the Swan of *The Isle of Dogs*, was unusual in its severity, and the 'very seditious and slanderous matter' contained in the play must have been uncommonly reckless (*ES* 4: 323). The affair, however, had no long-term effect on the profession, though both the Swan and Pembroke's Men went into a decline. Perhaps the fact that the order to pull down the playhouses was not carried out indicates that the Privy Council was less concerned than the order appears to suggest.

In fact, the punishment of players for performing seditious and slanderous matter was rare because there were numerous mechanisms designed to prevent such matter from being performed on the stage in the first place. As we have seen, the relationship between an acting company and its patron must have imposed a certain self-censorship upon the players, since they would have been foolish to risk performing material that would endanger the patron or bring him into disrepute. There were also more formal controls. In 1559, the year of her accession, Queen Elizabeth issued a proclamation putting into the hands of local authorities the power to license or forbid the performance of plays in their city or town, and further requiring of such authorities 'that they permit none to be played wherein either matters of religion or of the governance of the estate of the common weal shall be handled or treated' (*ES* 4: 263). Players who offended against this proclamation could be arrested and imprisoned.

The proclamation was effective in dealing with players while they were still travellers, but after the opening of the first public playhouses in London it left the Lord Mayor and aldermen with excessive freedom to interfere with them, and the queen initiated moves to bring the power of controlling the playhouses into court, through the Office of the Revels. In 1581 she issued a patent to Edmund Tilney, Master of the Revels since 1579, adding to his function of supervising court entertainments the power to license all plays. This appears at first to have been a means of protecting the players, but Tilney took his duties seriously. In 1589 his powers were augmented when the Privy Council ordered the institution of a body made up of the Master of the Revels and two others, one appointed by the Archbishop of Canterbury and one by the Lord Mayor. The Council instructed that any company that put on a play that had not been approved by this body should suffer severe punishment.

All manuscripts of plays had to be submitted to the Revels Office for licensing, which was usually done late in the rehearsal period when a play was taking on a definitive shape; for this service the acting companies had to pay a fee to the Master. The Master could pass a play without cuts, or demand that changes be made or, though this seems to have happened infrequently, refuse to allow it to be performed. Obviously he would be particularly vigilant in looking out for passages that contained matter relating to religious or political issues, but he also censored material that might give offence to foreign allies or that appeared to satirize influential interests. Tilney also apparently excised scenes that might raise awkward questions in the minds of an audience: the abdication scene from *Richard II* does not appear in any of the printed editions of the play that were published during Elizabeth's lifetime, and it is unlikely, though possible, that a scene suppressed in print would have been allowed on the stage. The whole issue of abdication was a sensitive one in relation to the aging and childless queen, but the scene was restored to editions printed during James's reign when the question of abdication was no longer relevant.

It is difficult to say how strict Tilney and George Buc, who succeeded him in 1603, were, because so little documentary evidence of their work remains. Janet Clare has argued that 'bad' quartos and other variant versions of plays by Shakespeare, as well as by others, might be texts that were altered for the censor, which would imply that plays were expurgated frequently.[14] This might be so, but it is probable that the rigour of the censor fluctuated, and that he would have pursued his duty with greater vigilance at times of anxiety. Even so it is impossible to control absolutely what is said on stage or how it is said. Lines can be interpolated into a play during performance, and words that seem harmless on the page can be made offensive in the delivery. So it is possible that the censor was not always very effective.

Still, there were real dangers. London was full of spies and informers, and some of them looked for seditious matter in plays. The most notorious of these, Richard Topcliffe, was involved in the affair of *The Isle of Dogs*. Ben Jonson, in the Induction to *Bartholomew Fair* (1614), mocks the 'state-decipherer, or politic pick-lock of the scene', the person who reads sinister meanings into plays (Ind.133–4).[15] He knew what he was talking about, not only from his experience with *The Isle of Dogs*. In 1605 he had collaborated with George Chapman and John Marston on a play called *Eastward Ho!* This play contained mocking references to the Scots which were taken as a reflection on King James, and Jonson was imprisoned once again, along with Chapman.

A dramatist who wanted to deal with controversial matter had to be circumspect and present it obliquely. In the first half of his career Shakespeare expended much energy on his English history plays, which certainly dealt with 'matters of the governance of the estate of the common weal', and sometimes with matters of religion. Shakespeare found in history plays a means of writing about current issues while obscuring the fact that he was doing so, and in the second half of his career he considered political questions through his tragedies. He has often been treated as a political conservative, an apologist for the Tudor (and later the Stuart) regime, but we have to bear in mind the fact that the play-texts we have were written, as Janet Clare puts it, 'in the shadow of the censor and . . . no dramatist could unchain his thoughts from the agent of that most arbitrary and punitive instrument of state control'.[16] If Shakespeare wanted to look sceptically at contentious questions, he obviously had to disguise his scepticism. But that does not mean it is not there.

# 3

# The Plays

The term applied to the body of work generally accepted as being entirely or largely by Shakespeare is 'canon'. The word has recently become controversial in its application to bodies of literature, however, because of its ecclesiastical connotation of 'sacred' writing, which suggests mystified reasons for including or excluding particular works. Even the more modest meaning of 'the recognized genuine works' of an author raises problems, for the evidence attaching Shakespeare's name to his plays is, when approached from a certain perspective, slight. The Shakespeare canon as it is generally recognized consists of 37 plays and a number of poems, the best-known of which are the sonnets. Existing in a kind of limbo is *The Two Noble Kinsmen* on which Shakespeare collaborated with John Fletcher around 1612–13; there is resistance against including it in the canon because it is not entirely or mostly Shakespeare's. This, however, opens up questions about some plays that have not been excluded; Fletcher almost certainly contributed work to *Henry VIII* and other hands have been detected, though not necessarily with certainty, in a number of other plays. Since we are dealing with a medium that was essentially collaborative in all its aspects, this clearly raises a number of tricky issues about the meaning of dramatic authorship to which we will come in due course.

The two major narrative poems, *Venus and Adonis* and *The Rape of Lucrece*, were published in 1593–94, the sonnets in 1609. For the plays, the canon was essentially established by the First Folio edition of 1623, published on the initiative of Heminges and Condell (a 'folio' was a large sheet of paper printed on both sides and folded once so as to form two leaves or four pages; a 'quarto' was a sheet of the same size but folded twice, to form four leaves or eight pages; a printed volume was identified by the size of its pages). This volume contained 14 comedies, 10 histories and 11 tragedies, plus *Troilus and Cressida*, which appears to have been included as an afterthought between the histories and the tragedies. These are all the plays now commonly agreed to be Shakespeare's, except for *Pericles* and the more doubtful *The Two Noble Kinsmen*. Of the 36 plays, 18 were printed for the first time, and for them the First Folio provides the closest that we can come to an 'authoritative' text: *The Comedy of Errors, The Two Gentlemen of Verona, The Taming of the Shrew, 1 Henry VI, King John, As You Like It, Twelfth Night, Julius Caesar, All's Well That Ends Well, Measure for Measure, Timon of Athens, Macbeth, Antony and Cleopatra, Coriolanus, Cymbeline, The Winter's Tale, The Tempest* and *Henry VIII*. The other 18 plays had already appeared in print in various quarto editions, and some have significant textual variations from the Folio, so it is much more difficult to establish an authoritative text for them. The question of what constitutes an 'authoritative' text is another tricky issue.

Heminges and Condell were amongst the earliest members of Shakespeare's company when it was still under the protection of the Lord Chamberlain. Since they were obviously respected and informed members of the company who had known Shakespeare for most of his working life, they must have known which of the company's repertoire he was responsible for, and they would have had little reason to pass off plays by other dramatists as Shakespeare's. There seems no cause to doubt their ascription of these plays to Shakespeare, yet over the years there have been scholars who have questioned the inclusion of some of the plays: for example, some have rejected *1 Henry VI* as too disordered and bombastic to be wholly or even mainly Shakespeare's, while others have tried to exclude *Titus Andronicus* and *Troilus and Cressida* as being too violent or unpleasant to be his work. These judgements are largely based on the scholars' tastes and their reluctance to believe that Shakespeare could have written such (in their opinion) weak or ugly plays. To justify the exclusion of any play we need better evidence than this.

More difficult to deal with are the arguments of scholars who have tried to ascribe other plays to Shakespeare. Over the years Shakespeare has been credited with writing a large number of otherwise anonymous plays; the most significant are *Edmund Ironside* (1588), *Arden of Faversham* (1592), *Locrine* (1594), *Mucedorus* (1598), *The First Part of Sir John Oldcastle* (1599), *The London Prodigal* (1605) and *A Yorkshire Tragedy* (1608). This is the so-called

'Shakespeare Apocrypha'.[1] As we have seen, the profession of dramatist was not held in high esteem at that time, and most playwrights apparently did not care whether or not they were identified as the author of their plays. This accounts for the extraordinarily large number of anonymous texts from the period. Shakespeare's name does not appear on the title pages of a number of the (possibly unauthorized) quarto editions of his plays that were published in his own lifetime; on the other hand, *A Yorkshire Tragedy* was entered in the Stationers' Register as 'written by William Shakespeare'. The obvious question to ask about these apocryphal plays is: why, if they were really written by Shakespeare, were they not included in the First Folio?

One conceivable answer to this question is that when they published Shakespeare's plays Heminges and Condell were, in effect, reconstructing his dramatic career, for no other record of his life's work existed. They would have wanted him to be remembered for his best work and they might well have excluded plays that they thought to be inferior, or that they knew that Shakespeare himself had considered to be inferior. Seven years earlier, in 1616, Ben Jonson had published the First Folio edition of *his* works and he certainly had excluded writings that he thought insignificant and no longer wished to acknowledge as his. However, Heminges and Condell did include such plays as *Two Gentlemen of Verona* and the three parts of *Henry VI*, considered by many critics to be Shakespeare's weakest work, so their concern with quality is not indisputable. It seems reasonable to conclude that the inclusion of these comparatively inferior plays, when a good apocryphal play such as *Arden of Faversham* is excluded, is in itself strong evidence that the excluded play is not Shakespeare's, and that the First Folio is a dependable record of Shakespeare's work.

Still, the fact that a play is not contained in the First Folio is not by any means conclusive proof that Shakespeare did not write it, or at least part of it. *Pericles* was not included in the volume, but it is now generally accepted that the play is in large part his work. Elizabethan playwrights were expected to provide inductions and additions to plays they had not themselves written, and most were expected to collaborate with other dramatists. Shakespeare collaborated with other playwrights at the beginning and at the end of his working life, though as far as we know he was able to avoid this for most of his career, but it would hardly be logical to claim that he could not under any circumstances have had a hand in other plays belonging to his company.

In the absence of anything else, the First Folio remains the best piece of evidence we have about what Shakespeare did and did not write. Scholars and critics who have claimed Shakespeare as the father of the various orphan-plays they have championed have in some cases mounted persuasive arguments, but none has been sufficiently persuasive to convince the academic establishment. However, we need to take note of the element of academic politics involved here. Many of those who are involved in the 'Shakespeare industry' have a vested interest in protecting the monolithic image of a universal genius that has developed historically, and resist the idea of compromising that image by assigning 'inferior' work to it. On the other hand, a scholar who could persuade the world that a hitherto-unassigned play was actually written by Shakespeare would be adding a great deal of glamour to his own reputation. The best that can be said is that, while there are not as yet sufficiently good reasons to modify the canon, neither are there absolute reasons to deny that Shakespeare might have had a hand in other plays.

Heminges and Condell's collection does, however, raise other, more complex questions. In a prefatory note to the reader the editors present their publication as being a labour of love for the late playwright:

> It had been a thing, we confess, worthy to have been wished, that the Author himself had liv'd to have set forth, and overseen his own writings; But since it hath been ordain'd otherwise, and he by death departed from that right, we pray you do not envy his Friends, the office of their care, and pain, to have collected & publish'd them; and so to have publish'd them, as where (before) you were abus'd with diverse stolen, and surreptitious copies, maimed, and deformed by the frauds and stealths of injurious imposters, that expos'd them: even those, are now offer'd to your view cur'd, and perfect of their limbs; and all the rest, absolute in their numbers, as he conceived them.[2]

While it would be mean-spirited to deny that Heminges and Condell intended their publication as a monument to their dead colleague, their own words indicate that they had other motives too. So long as a play was still able to attract audiences, it had commercial value for the company that owned it, and it was in the company's interest not to allow it to be printed. The fact that half the plays collected in the First Folio had not previously been printed indicates that they still had lucrative theatrical life in them. But it is clear from the reference to 'diverse stolen and surreptitious copies' that pirated versions of some of the other plays were in circulation. The publication of the 'authorized version' of the plays was therefore a sensible way for the King's Men to regain some control over what was, after all, their commercial property, and still a valuable one.

A problem arises, however, from the claim that the Folio texts perfectly represent Shakespeare's plays 'absolute in their numbers, as he conceived them'. In order to declare the superiority of their versions over the various pirated rivals the publishers had to make this claim, but we have to ask how far it can be taken literally. Not only are the Folio versions different from the pirated texts that were circulating, but they are often also different from the apparently authorized quarto editions printed during Shakespeare's lifetime, and in some cases the differences are extensive. Of course, even those versions that Shakespeare's company released to the printer probably had minimal supervision from the playwright, so we cannot argue that the quartos are more 'perfect of their limbs' than the Folio. Does this mean, then, that we have to accept the claims of Heminges and Condell for the authenticity of their edition? We can best answer this question by looking at a particular example.

*Richard III* was extremely popular from its first appearance, and six quarto editions were published between 1597 and 1622. The first quarto appears to be based on a memorial reconstruction: that is, it was constructed from what was remembered by actors who performed in it. Although it contains many errors it is sufficiently coherent for us to assume that it was put together by Shakespeare's own company, perhaps to replace the lost original manuscript. The five quarto editions which followed this imported more errors. The Folio editors seem to have used one or more of these quartos as their source, and to have made corrections derived from another, more reliable source, possibly, as they claim, Shakespeare's manuscript; their edition contains about two hundred additional lines. However, the Folio's compositors, the men who set the print, were themselves careless and introduced further errors into the text. If we are looking for what Shakespeare wrote we cannot say that any of these early texts is authoritative. Modern editors of *Richard III*, as of other plays, work out a compromise between the various sources, preparing what one recent editor calls 'a synthetic text'.[3] The synthetic text, although it is the product of the editor's wide experience and learning, has no more authority than the early texts from which it is derived.

What, then, can we mean when we talk about 'Shakespeare's *Richard III*', since early texts are so full of errors and modern texts so full of conjecture that none can be said to reproduce what Shakespeare wrote? This raises large and difficult questions about the nature of the Shakespearean text, and we will need to look in more detail at the conditions under which plays were written, what happened to them on their way to the stage, and the way in which they were finally given the permanent form of print.

First, when we think of Shakespeare sitting down to write a play we have to erase from our minds any post-Romantic idea we might have of the solitary genius sitting at his desk pouring out the dictates of his heart. Shakespeare was writing for his company, not for himself, and anything he composed had to be acceptable to them. Assuming that his methods of working were similar to those generally employed by dramatists of the time, the process would have been something like the following. When he had an idea for a play, he wrote an outline and took it to his colleagues before starting any serious work on it. Quite possibly the idea itself had been a product of consultation, in which the company had taken into consideration a variety of factors relating to the needs of the audience (what was fashionable), the needs of the company (what was likely to be competitive and commercially fruitful), the demands of the actors (that the main roles should offer sufficient scope and exposure for their particular talents) and the limitations of the acting space in which the play was to be performed. When he devised a plot, Shakespeare did not simply 'invent'. All of his plays have sources in earlier texts, some in works of history, some in works of verse and prose fiction, some in other plays, both classical and contemporary, some in sundry documents. There are passages in which Shakespeare did little more than paraphrase the texts he used: the Renaissance concept of imitation legitimized a good deal of what nowadays would be called plagiarism. Of course, Shakespeare transformed his sources, but we still have to acknowledge that his work was not 'original' in the modern sense.

We have no way of knowing how much input there was from Shakespeare's colleagues during the process of composition, but there were almost certainly additions and alterations that might or might not have pleased the dramatist. Once the manuscript (known as 'foul papers') was completed, it was handed over to the company and became its property. From this manuscript two further copies were made by scribes. One of these was kept intact to be used as a prompt-book; the company member in charge of it wrote on to the copy such matter as notes on performance or stage-business and costumes, as well as alterations to the text made for any reason, including those of censorship. The other copy was cut up into parts for the actors. The parts making up a role were pasted together into a scroll containing only the lines of the role and essential cues. Upon this the actor would make his own alterations; Hamlet's instruction to the Players to 'let those that play the clowns speak no more than is set down for them' (3.2.38–9) surely reflects something of Shakespeare's exasperation at the improvisations of members of his own company, but any improvisations that drew a good response from the audience would surely have been added to the text.

From all this it must be apparent that the play as performed might be at some distance from what Shakespeare originally wrote. Putting the play into print added further distance. There were three main reasons why a company would release a play to the printer: if a play was no longer drawing audiences publication might extract a little more money from it; if pirated versions of a play were already in circulation there would be no point in the company's continuing to protect its property, but publication of a more accurate version was a way to retrieve something of its value; if a company was under financial stress, for example after a period when the playhouses were closed because of the plague, it might be forced to sell its plays, but for obvious reasons this would be a final resort. Thus, there are what are called 'good' and 'bad' quartos, depending on the assumed closeness to the original manuscript, but how accurately any quarto text reflected the original manuscript is impossible to say. A quarto edition printed from a memorial reconstruction would obviously generate its own peculiarities. It is unlikely that pirated editions would have been made from authoritative texts, but even authorized quartos printed from manuscripts or good playhouse copies of the original often suffered from the haste or carelessness of the compositors.

One further problem arises. There are plays which exist in more than one version; most famously, the 1608 quarto version of *King Lear* has notable differences from the Folio edition. It was once generally thought that the revisions in the Folio were simply changes made for performance, but there is reason to believe that the revisions are Shakespeare's own, and that they change the meaning of the play. If this is so, then both texts are in some sense 'authoritative'. On the other hand, it is at least possible that the revision was carried out by someone other than Shakespeare. This raises unsettling but finally unanswerable questions about the extent to which all of Shakespeare's plays might have been revised, by himself or by others.

In the end these questions are of more concern to the editor than to the reader or play-goer. Still, we must at least remain aware of the problematic nature of any Shakespearean text as it exists for us today. Between the modern printed book and the originating mind of Shakespeare lie many layers of interference, and when we read *Hamlet* or see a performance of *Twelfth Night* or read works of criticism that claim to tell us about 'the mind and art' of Shakespeare, we need to remember that we are dealing with something that is not quite so firm and solid as the heavy volume of the Complete Works might suggest.

Another uncertain area of knowledge is the chronology of Shakespeare's plays. Heminges and Condell provide no assistance here, since they group the plays by genre, and even within their divisions they did not print them in the order of composition. For example, in grouping the comedies they give the prime position to *The Tempest*, one of the last plays to be written, and put the remainder in no apparent order. Dating the plays depends on three main kinds of evidence, one of them external, the other two internal.

The external evidence is documentary evidence, such as a record of performance, an entry in the Stationers' Register, or the publication of a quarto version of a play. Such evidence at least provides a date by which a play must have been in existence; but while this is helpful it does not allow us accurately to fix the date of composition of the play. To take one instance, there is evidence that *The Comedy of Errors* was acted at Gray's Inn on 28 December 1594, but it is widely believed that the play pre-dates this performance by some years. For reasons based largely on assumptions about Shakespeare's artistic development (assumptions which, as we shall see, are themselves open to question), the play is generally thought to have been written in 1592 or 1593, but there are those who believe that it could have been written as early as 1589. The date of publication of a play is not very helpful either, since plays were not usually released to the printer until they ceased to be commercially attractive on the stage, which might be some years after composition. A quarto edition of *Love's Labour's Lost* was printed in 1598, but the play was almost certainly written well before that date.

One of the most intriguing pieces of information that have come down to us is *Palladis Tamia*, a treatise by Francis Meres registered in 1598, which looks briefly at the activities of some contemporary poets and dramatists, and includes this statement about Shakespeare:

> As Plautus and Seneca are accounted the best for Comedy and Tragedy among the Latins: so Shakespeare among the English is the most excellent in both kinds for the stage. For Comedy, witness his *Gentlemen of Verona*, his *Errors*, his *Love's Labour's Lost*, his *Love's Labour's Won*, his *Midsummer Night's Dream*, and his *Merchant of Venice*; for Tragedy, his *Richard II, Richard III, Henry IV, King John, Titus Andronicus*, and his *Romeo and Juliet*.
>
> (*ES* 4: 246)

This is actually more frustrating than it is helpful. It does not give us the proper order of what Meres calls tragedies, since *Richard III* and *Titus Andronicus* almost certainly preceded *Richard II*. It does not mention any of the parts of *Henry VI*, thereby giving ammunition to those disintegrators who wanted to deny Shakespeare's authorship of them. It gives us the phantom play *Love's Labour's Won*, which might be a lost play, or it might be *The Taming of the Shrew* (or any other comedy written before 1598) under a different title.

Of the two kinds of internal evidence, the first has affinities with external evidence but in general is no more helpful. It consists of remarks within the plays that may be taken with more or less certainty as allusions to contemporary events. For example, a brief passage in *The Comedy of Errors* (3.2.120–2) has been understood to refer to the French civil war, which ended in 1593. We cannot, however, say whether the passage was in the original manuscript, or whether it was inserted at a later date for its topical value. Even if we insist that the allusion must have been in the original manuscript and was made while the war was going on, it still does not allow us to date the play more firmly than to say that it might have been written between 1589 and 1593. The reference in the Chorus preceding the final act of *Henry V* (30–2) to the Earl of Essex's expedition to Ireland, not yet completed, allows a little firmer dating of the composition of that play as early 1599, though we cannot give absolute weight even to this.

The other kind of internal evidence that has been used to try to establish an order of composition depends on assumptions that Shakespeare's style and thought underwent a constant process of evolution and maturation. If we look, for example, at the five comedies generally presumed to be his earliest (*The Comedy of Errors, The Taming of the Shrew, The Two Gentlemen of Verona, Love's Labour's Lost, A Midsummer Night's Dream*), we can see that they do have certain stylistic aspects in common. There is a degree of artificiality that sometimes seems to contribute to a lack of flexibility in much of the verse: a reliance on end-stopped lines, on rhymed couplets and more elaborate rhyme-schemes, on self-conscious devices that form part of a kind of verbal battle, such as stichomythia (line-for-line exchanges that repeat or vary preceding words or images), and the frequent use of puns and other would-be-clever wordplay. Poetic excesses of this sort have been attributed to Shakespeare's immaturity, but in some of the plays (for example *Love's Labour's Lost*) excess is part of the point: the dramatist is using it as an aspect of character, for parodic or satirical effect. This suggests assurance rather than immaturity. Stylistic measurement clearly has its insecurities, and any attempt to generate a chronology on mainly artistic grounds is bound to be controversial.

I do not have the space here to look in more detail at the arguments for dating specific plays, but I think it is necessary to know something of the problems that pertain to the established chronology, and how insecure its basis is. The list appended at the end of this book should be understood in that light. The dates are approximate, but the chronology is in accordance with that of most scholars. Some plays can be located more precisely than others, but for most of them the best that can be done is to indicate a flexible span of years during which they were probably composed.

## SOURCES AND MATERIALS

As I have noted, none of Shakespeare's plays is 'original', if by
that we mean that he generated the whole thing out of his imagination. He derived his plots from various sources, sometimes
combining a number of elements.[4] A full consideration of these
sources is beyond the scope of this book, but it is necessary to
say something of how the dramatist used them and of how this
contributes to an understanding of the plays. I think that it is
helpful to think of the materials of his plays not so much as sources,
but as elements in an intertextual relationship, in which the plays
have in a sense to be read in the context of the sources. This
does not mean that they cannot be understood without that context, but it does mean that their significance is enlarged and our
response to them is enriched by an awareness of it. *King Lear*
provides a good example of how Shakespeare synthesized a range
of materials into a structure that is at once greater than its sources
and partially dependent on them.

As the basis of *King Lear*'s main plot, dealing with the old king
and his three daughters, Shakespeare used an old play called *The
True Chronicle History of King Leir* and the story of Lear as told in
Holinshed's *Chronicles*. For the sub-plot concerning Gloucester and
his two sons he adapted the story of the Paphlagonian King from
Sidney's *Arcadia*. The Lear story is actually legendary; it appears
in Geoffrey of Monmouth's *Historia regum Britanniae*, where Lear
is one of the line of kings descended from Brutus. It was frequently re-told in Shakespeare's time: a version of it appears in
Book Two of Spenser's *The Faerie Queene*. In its early versions,
including Spenser's, the story of Lear has a happy ending, with
Lear restored to his throne and succeeded on his death by Cordelia.
The subsequent fate of his youngest daughter is not happy, however, for some years later she is imprisoned by the children of
her sisters and hangs herself in her cell. Shakespeare saw that a
happy ending was hardly appropriate to Lear's story, considering the extreme suffering he undergoes, and he turned it into a
tragedy, its implications and effects intensified by the parallel
action of the sub-plot. He also borrowed from other sources: Edgar's
pretended lunacy has close affinities with the accounts of demonic
possession in Samuel Harsnett's pamphlet *A Declaration of Egre-
gious Popish Impostures*, as does the thunder on the heath. Finally,
the social and moral scepticism that distinguishes this play reflects

the writing of Montaigne, which Shakespeare knew, probably in the original, but at least in the translation by John Florio.

Shakespeare found his plots in a few main groups of writings. Some, like *King Lear*, come from old plays, and it is possible that these are plays that Shakespeare was asked to refurbish for his company. There is evidence that *Hamlet* was based on an earlier play, no longer extant, known as the *Ur-Hamlet*, perhaps written by Thomas Kyd, perhaps by Shakespeare himself. For *King John* he made use of *The Troublesome Raigne of King John*, published in 1591, and he borrowed from a play published in 1598 but written some years before that, *The Famous Victories of Henry the Fifth*, for the two parts of *Henry IV* and *Henry V*.

For his ten English history plays, however, Shakespeare's primary sources were Edward Hall's account of the conflicts between the families of York and Lancaster (1548) and, more extensively, Raphael Holinshed's *Chronicles*, first published in 1578 and expanded into the second edition of 1587, which Shakespeare used. The growing sense of a national identity that marked the Tudor period had led to a widespread interest in English history. This was partly fostered by the desire of the Tudor monarchs to buttress their claim on the throne, but also there were those who looked to the past as a way to understand the present. The poem *The Mirror for Magistrates*, first published in 1559 but reprinted frequently, looked for examples from the past that would offer lessons to contemporary rulers; Shakespeare borrowed from this, too. The history plays carried this interest in the workings of power to a larger popular audience. Shakespeare also encountered the stories of *Macbeth* and *Cymbeline*, as well as *Lear*, in Holinshed. The Roman plays, for which Shakespeare found his material in Sir Thomas North's translation of Plutarch's *Lives* (1579), have related preoccupations. Shakespeare did not feel that he had to follow scrupulously the narratives of his sources, and indeed he was not overly concerned about what today we think of as historical accuracy, especially when he saw that judicious selection or even changes in the 'facts' might enhance the dramatic effect or give the material new relevance for his audience. Consequently, what he omits or reshapes has special significance, since it is there that he offers new insight into the meaning of historical (which is to say political) events.

The vast and growing body of verse and prose romances, for which there was a voracious popular appetite, also furnished him with many of his plots. These romances can be understood as forerunners of the novel; they were mainly written in French and Italian, but the market for them grew throughout Elizabeth's reign, and many were translated into English. The earliest collection in English was William Painter's *The Palace of Pleasure* (1566–7), which brought together 101 stories translated from such writers as Boccaccio and Bandello. This was followed by numerous other compilations. Many of Shakespeare's romantic comedies, including *The Two Gentlemen of Verona*, *Twelfth Night* and *The Merchant of Venice*, were based on these romances, either in the English translation or (since Shakespeare seems to have known Italian and French) from a reading of the original, as were the two more 'romantic' of his tragedies, *Romeo and Juliet* and *Othello*. Some English writers produced their own romances, amongst them, as we would expect, the University Wits. Robert Greene's *Pandosto* (1588) furnished much of the plot of *The Winter's Tale*, while Thomas Lodge's *Rosalynde* (1590) was the main source of *As You Like It*. These romances were characterized by sentimental feeling and sensational incident, and might seem to be escapist fare, but they provided Shakespeare with a viewpoint from which he could examine the struggles, sometimes subtle, often brutal, of personal relationships.

It is not only the plots of his plays that were borrowed, for the very fabric of his texts is filled with echoes of a wide range of other texts. Not all of these echoes can be attributed to his own reading; many are commonplaces. Taken together, however, they imply that he expected that his audience could respond to a broad field of allusion. The references to biblical events or Greek and Roman mythology that today have to be annotated would have had an immediate significance for at least the more sophisticated members of his audience. As I have noted, his plays allude to more than 40 books of the Bible; these would have been familiar to an audience that was expected to attend church weekly. Both the plays and his narrative poems indicate that Shakespeare's favourite poet was Ovid. They contain allusions to all the books of the *Metamorphoses* as well as to many of his other works. Ovid was the most erotic of the major Latin poets, considered for much of the Renaissance to be immoral (in his play *Poetaster* Ben Jonson, while clearly attracted by the figure of Ovid, has him banished from Rome, forced to give place to the lofty, pious figure of Virgil). Shakespeare goes against this moralistic grain, freeing Ovidian ideas about love, pain and transformation to pervade his plays, imparting to them a mythic resonance, for his own audience if not for us.

In this extensive use of other writers' work Shakespeare was no different from his contemporaries. Renaissance neo-Classical aesthetic theory understood the concept of artistic 'imitation' in a number of ways; the two most familiar might seem to be in opposition to one another. On the one hand imitation was taken to mean the copying of human nature or action, a kind of realistic representation of the world, as Hamlet suggests when he says that the purpose of acting 'was and is to hold as 'twere the mirror up to nature; to show virtue her own feature, scorn her own image, and the very age and body of the time his form and pressure' (3.2.21–4). This concept of imitation implies that the origins of art are in life. On the other hand was a concept of imitation that stressed the need for copying established models, and this could range from absorbing the spirit of the model to paraphrasing or translating it. This aspect of imitation implied that art had its origins in art rather than life. It did not imply restrictions or limitations, however, for the artist or writer was expected to re-create his models for himself and his own time, and was not prohibited from attempting to overcome them. John Dryden, in the preface to his own re-writing of Shakespeare's *Troilus and Cressida* (1679), put it this way:

> We ought not to regard a good imitation as theft; but as a beautiful Idea of him who undertakes to imitate, by forming himself on the invention and the work of another man; for he enters into the lists like a new wrestler, to dispute the prize with the former Champion.[5]

Shakespeare would not, perhaps, have thought of his use of his predecessors in quite such a competitive manner, but part of his purpose in using them was, paradoxically, to distance or distinguish himself from them, to turn his source material into 'beautiful ideas' of his own: not merely beautiful ideas, either, but useful ideas, critical, moral, historical or political ideas. Source studies have often been content to point out originals and parallels as if that in itself were sufficient, but the true interest in the relationship between Shakespeare and his sources is a matter of difference. A Shakespeare text resonates with the memories of all the texts he used, but that resonance is finally there to allow his text to proclaim its own identity.

What this means is that part of the significance of the plays lies in their intertextual connections. Their sources are a part of their context. When he was writing *Troilus and Cressida* Shakespeare was dealing with a story that was familiar to his audience. Nevertheless, he went to Chaucer's *Troilus and Criseyde* and its bleak continuation by Robert Henryson, *The Testament of Cresseid*. He consulted two other medieval accounts of the Trojan war, William Caxton's *Recuyell of the Historyes of Troye* and John Lydgate's *Troye Booke*. He also almost certainly used George Chapman's translation of the *Iliad* and Book Twelve of Ovid's *Metamorphoses*. His play needs to be understood in relation to the larger history of his materials as represented in these sources, and its harsh satiric effect, which makes it different from other versions of the story, depends at least in part on a knowledge of that history.

Of course, it is one thing to stress this intertextual richness when we are considering a printed text, especially if it has foot notes to point us to sources, influences or analogues. When we are in a theatre, however, and the spoken text is passing by us non-stop, allowing no possibility to consult notes or to go back and re-hear things we have missed or failed to understand, the significance of the documentary context may seem to diminish. A play's theatrical vitality is the most important thing about it, and I certainly do not want to suggest that the experience of reading a play is greater than that of seeing it performed just because reading can direct us to these sources. But I do think that a fuller response to Shakespeare's plays has to be worked for, and we lose nothing and may gain much by augmenting our knowledge of the wider literary context. It is important to note that most of the stories that Shakespeare re-told or re-shaped were familiar to his audiences. He was, in a sense, re-presenting to them what they already knew, but he was also enlarging and changing its meaning. Some familiarity with what Shakespeare's audiences knew can enlarge and change a play's meaning for us, too.

## LANGUAGE AND STYLE

One element of Shakespearean drama that modern readers or audiences often have difficulty with, accustomed as they are to what they think of as 'realistic' drama, is the use of verse. How can we accept as 'real' characters who speak in verse, which is a self-consciously unreal medium? A possible answer would be that characters in plays are not real; they are verbal constructs and we do not expect them to behave as people in real life do. We therefore suspend our disbelief and accept certain devices as if they were real, in order to enable the drama to take place. These devices are properly called 'dramatic conventions'. For example, in the final scene of *Love's Labour's Lost*, the Schoolmaster Holofernes puts on a play about the Nine Worthies to entertain the nobles. At the opening of this play Costard enters and says 'I Pompey am', but Boyet, a member of his audience, says 'You lie; you are not he' (5.2.541). Boyet is denying the fundamental convention without which drama cannot function at all: that we accept an actor to be who he says he is.

We have to understand verse as a convention like other dramatic conventions such as soliloquies and asides. An Elizabethan audience had to deal with rather more conventions than does a modern one, since it accepted boys playing the roles of women, and that a bare stage could contain armies or kingdoms. The Prologue to *Henry V* asks his audience to make an imaginative effort to respond to the language of the play: 'Think, when we talk of horses, that you see them / Printing their proud hoofs i'the receiving earth; / For 'tis your thoughts that now must deck our kings' (26–8). The play asks for a connection between 'our words' and 'your thoughts' in a collaborative effort, and as such is offering not just verse drama but poetic drama. There is a difference between verse and poetry. Verse can be unpoetic, and much of it is; prose can be poetic, and much of Shakespeare's is. I shall return to this issue, but for the moment I want to look at the dramatic possibilities that verse offers.

Sometimes, as a means of making a play more 'natural', a modern director has his or her actors play down the verse, speaking it as far as possible as if it were prose. This is a mistake not only because it blurs the distinction between verse and prose that is already there in the plays, but also because Elizabethan dramatic verse contains a range of expressive possibilities not easily available to prose. Blank verse is more artificial than most prose, but rhymed couplets are more artificial than blank verse, and elaborate rhyme schemes such as those of lyrics or of sonnets are more artificial than rhymed couplets. Blank verse is the standard verse form for all of Shakespeare's plays, but there are deviations from this standard in all of them, either towards the greater artificiality of rhymed forms, as in *Love's Labour's Lost* and *A Midsummer Night's Dream*, or towards the demotic relaxation of prose in, say, the tavern scenes in *1 Henry IV* or the Gravediggers' scene in *Hamlet*.

From its folk roots in song and dance and its ecclesiastical roots in liturgy, to the medieval miracle and morality plays, early English drama used verse of one sort or another, and it may be that verse was used precisely because it was not realistic; as a means that is, of distinguishing a play as a special event outside everyday experience. Blank verse, which became the staple form not just of Elizabethan drama, but of much of what we think of as the more elevated works of English poetry, such as Milton's *Paradise Lost* and Wordsworth's *Prelude*, did not appear in English until the middle of the sixteenth century.

Credit for the introduction of blank verse is usually given to the Earl of Surrey, who during the early 1540s used it for his translation of extracts from the *Aeneid*. The first play in which it was used was *Gorboduc* (1561) by Thomas Sackville and Thomas Norton, which can lay claim to being the first English dramatic tragedy; as Sidney wrote in *A Defence of Poetry*, it is full 'of stately speeches and well-sounding phrases, climbing to the height of Seneca's style' (113). Probably Surrey and Sackville and Norton were attempting to find a verse form that would approximate the loftiness of Latin verse; what they did find was a highly flexible line that *can* climb to stylistic heights, but that also, with its pattern of alternating stresses, comes close to the rhythms of ordinary English speech.

Blank verse is unrhymed iambic pentameter; each line has ten syllables, or five 'feet' each containing two syllables. An iambic foot has an unstressed first syllable and a stressed second syllable, which is the case with many English words: 'content', 'deceive', 'resolve', 'itself'. We can signify the stresses simply enough (as x = unstressed syllable, / = stressed syllable, ¦ = division between feet). Thus an iambic foot is rendered (x /) and a regular line of iambic pentameter as

$$\text{¦ x / ¦ x / ¦ x / ¦ x / ¦ x / ¦}$$

It is not difficult to imagine that a speech of, say, 20 lines, written entirely in regular iambic pentameter, would be quite monotonous.

The first major dramatist to use blank verse was Christopher Marlowe in *Tamburlaine* (1587). In the first line of the Prologue to that play he contemptuously dismisses the 'jigging veins of rhyming mother wits', what he saw as the laughably inadequate verses of his predecessors. He offers in their place blank verse full of pounding rhythms, its lines generally end-stopped and tending to form units which do not develop their sense beyond the line, and which depend much on rhetorical balance, repetition and parallelism. In his elegy on Shakespeare Jonson described this as 'Marlowe's mighty line' (30). Marlowe handled his inflated blank verse with ease when he was dealing with the heroic matter of Tamburlaine's boastful conquests, but he found difficulty in toning it down to deal with such subjects as Tamburlaine's wooing of Zenocrate, which emerges in the play as a variation of military conquest. The mighty line risked turning into what Thomas Nashe in 1589 called 'the swelling bombast of a bragging blank verse'.[6] In later plays, especially *Doctor Faustus*, Marlowe used the form with greater flexibility.

Shakespeare was well aware of the pitfalls of Marlowe's mighty line, which he mocked through the figure of Ancient Pistol in 2 *Henry IV*:

> Shall pack-horses,
> And hollow pamper'd jades of Asia,
> Which cannot go but thirty mile a day,
> Compare with Caesars and with Cannibals,
> And Troyant Greeks?
>
> (2.4.160–4)

This nonsense is a fool's misquotation of lines from the Second Part of *Tamburlaine*: 'Holla, ye pampered jades of Asia! / What, can ye draw but twenty miles a day?' (4.4.1–2). Pistol pushes into the realm of absurdity lines that were already inflated, but it is necessary to note that Shakespeare's play was written ten years after Marlowe's, and could only have a meaning for an audience still familiar with (and presumably still willing to pay to see) the earlier play. In fact Shakespeare had much to be grateful to Marlowe for, not least the epic posture of his own early history plays; consider, for example, these lines of Richard of Gloucester from 3 *Henry VI*:

Why, I can smile, and murder whiles I smile,
And cry 'Content!' to that which grieves my heart,
And wet my cheeks with artificial tears,
And frame my face to all occasions.
I'll drown more sailors than the Mermaid shall;
I'll slay more gazers than the basilisk;
I'll play the orator as well as Nestor,
Deceive more slily than Ulysses could,
And, like a Sinon, take another Troy.

                                          (3.2.182–90)

Notice here the comparative regularity of the meter with few deviations, the lines all end-stopped, the verbal repetitions, the parallel
structures, all deployed in the service of a larger-than-life rhetoric. It is a style suitable for such a grandiose purpose, but it is
not very flexible.

Shakespeare's later development of blank verse shows an astonishing range of possibilities. In particular, he moved beyond
the limiting restriction of the single line, developing his rhythms
as if he were building paragraphs, and resisting the monotonous
pull of the iambic pentameter. Consider this well-known passage,
from Hamlet's first soliloquy:

O that this too too sullied flesh would melt,
Thaw and resolve itself into a dew,
Or that the Everlasting had not fix'd
His canon 'gainst self-slaughter. O God! God!
How weary, stale, flat, and unprofitable
Seem to me all the uses of this world!

                                          (1.2.129–34)

The first thing to note about these lines is that none of them is
regular. In the first line the interjected 'O' must be stressed, consequently reversing the first foot. The insistently repeated 'too'
seems to demand a stress on each word, and the stress falls naturally on the first syllable of 'sullied', giving three stressed syllables in a row, but the two final feet are regular:

$$\text{¦ / x ¦ x / ¦ / / ¦ x / ¦ x / ¦}$$

Part of the effect of the lines comes from the use and repetition
of monosyllabic words that bring stresses together ('God, God'

echoes 'too too'; the juxtaposition in line 133 throws stress on 'stale' and 'flat'). The overall effect is to drag the rhythms, underlining precisely the weariness that is the subject of the passage. At the same time, monotony is avoided by moving the meaning through the lines, with 'thaw' in 130 restating 'melt' at the end of the previous line, thus drawing the sense forward. Line 131, with its opening 'Or' signifying an alternative direction, is not end-stopped, and the continuity of the phrase 'fixed His canon' carries the meaning on to the following line, but that meaning is completed before the line-unit is completed, with the emphasized pause ('caesura') after 'self-slaughter'. This throws extra stress on 'God, God'. The verse works not by conforming to the iambic-pentameter formula, not by remaining within the limits implied by the verse form, but through a tension between the expectations set up by our feeling of the rhythm of the regular iambic pentameter and the ways in which the verse modifies that meter.

Rhyme, especially rhyming couplets, but including more complex schemes, is more prevalent in Shakespeare's early plays. We cannot say, however, that this is simply a matter of his immature art, for it often serves a dramatic purpose. The intricate rhyme schemes used by the four young men in *Love's Labour's Lost* illuminate their characters, since part of the play's intention is to show how distant they are from the 'real' world. Consider, for instance, the speech of Berowne after his wooing of Rosaline has been discovered (5.2.394–415). The 22 lines consist of five quatrains and a final rhyming couplet, and indeed the last 14 lines of the speech constitute a sonnet. This formal affectation has been characteristic of Berowne throughout the play, and it has consistently undercut the apparent scepticism of his attitude. What is he saying in this speech?

> O! never will I trust to speeches penn'd,
> Nor to the motion of a school-boy's tongue,
> Nor never come in visor to my friend,
> Nor woo in rhyme, like a blind harper's song,
> Taffeta phrases, silken terms precise,
> Three-pil'd hyperboles, spruce affectation,
> Figures pedantical; these summer flies
> Have blown me full of maggot ostentation.

> (5.2.402–9)

He is rejecting ornate literary style at the same time as he is using it, caught in a contradiction between form and content. This disjunction is fundamental to his character. Compare these lines to the blank verse Berowne uses a few minutes later, after the death of the Princess's father has been announced:

> Honest plain words best pierce the ear of grief;
> And by these badges understand the king.
> For your fair sakes have we neglected time,
> Played foul play with our oaths. Your beauty, ladies,
> Hath much deformed us, fashioning our humours
> Even to the opposed end of our intents.
>
> (5.2.743–8)

The sudden irruption into the play of a message from the real world of death and decay sobers Berowne into an admission of the contradictions of his behaviour and that of his colleagues, and (though he cannot resist a little decoration in 'Played foul play with our oaths') the simpler form of the verse here underlines the force of that admission.

We can make a tentative hierarchical distinction between verse and prose in the plays: verse is used by aristocratic characters, whether serious or comic, who function in the main plot of a play; prose is given to lower-class characters, who are largely confined to the sub-plot. This is broadly true, but it needs to be modified, for while early in his career Shakespeare favoured verse over prose, in his later plays he used prose more frequently and with more flexibility. This is especially true of his comedies, in which he increasingly preferred prose for characters of any class; in *A Midsummer Night's Dream* the aristocratic young lovers speak in verse even though they are comic figures, while Bottom and his associates speak in prose, except when they are massacring the verse of their 'most lamentable comedy' about Pyramus and Thisbe. In the later *Much Ado About Nothing* and *As You Like It* the lovers, still aristocratic, frequently speak in prose. In the earliest history plays, the three parts of *Henry VI*, there is virtually no use of prose except for the scenes concerning Jack Cade. Of the two parts of the later *Henry IV*, about half of each is written in prose. Here, the pivotal figure of Hal links the two spheres in which he functions, speaking in verse when he is in the world of the court and politics, prose when he is with Falstaff and his cronies. His prose is part of his masquerade, however, as is indicated by the fact that in soliloquy he speaks in verse, clearly retaining a sense of who he 'really' is.

There is little prose in the early tragedies, but in the later ones it is used with great effectiveness. Hamlet, for example, as befits a prince and an intellectual, speaks in verse in court scenes as well as in soliloquy; his use of prose is dramatically associated with his feigned madness, but it is given further significance because he speaks in prose in those scenes where he functions as a malcontent or a satirist, that is with Rosencrantz and Guildenstern, with Polonius, with the Gravediggers and with Osric. Lear speaks in verse so long as he can hold on to a sense of his kingly dignity, but at the moment on the heath when he sees a reflection of his true self in the figure of Edgar/Poor Tom that sense breaks down, and he joins Poor Tom both by speaking in prose and by tearing off his clothing: 'thou art the thing itself; unaccommodated man is no more but such a poor, bare, forked animal as thou art. Off, off, you lendings!' (3.4.109–11). The division of prose from verse is particularly effective in *The Winter's Tale*. Except for the opening scene there is no use of prose at all in the first, tragic half of the play that ends with the pursuit of Antigonus by a bear; but immediately after that moment the old Shepherd's prose indicates a change of direction into comic pastoral.

It is not possible to make unproblematic distinctions between when Shakespeare uses verse and when he uses prose. If we follow the accepted chronology of Shakespeare's work we can see a broad but not consistent growth in flexibility and subtlety in the fashioning of both prose and verse as dramatic instruments (although we have to remember the uncertainty of the chronology). But even in his early plays the style and form are generally well-adapted to his needs. The early histories present epic events in a dramatic verse that might seem to us to be bombastic, but that was appropriate to the simple motives of most of the characters. It would hardly have been appropriate for Hamlet or Othello, to whom Shakespeare gave subtler verse rhythms, but there are echoes of the earlier manner in *Macbeth*.

I can hardly end a consideration of Shakespeare's verse and prose styles without considering the plays as poetic drama. This is a very thorny issue, for to many people Shakespeare is a poet rather than a dramatist, and the idea of 'poetic' or 'literary' language as being special and different from other language is a potent one. I think, however, that we have to see Shakespeare's poetry

as subservient to his drama, used in the service of characterization, or the setting of location and atmosphere, or the analysis of
emotional states or complex ideas. Dramatic poetry, one might
say, stretches language to its fullest, using all its resources of
sound and rhythm, of suggestion and allusion, of multiple meanings, of clarity and precision, of confusion and ambiguity. It is a
spoken, not a 'literary' poetry. Many, perhaps most, of the members of Shakespeare's original audiences were illiterate, and therefore far more accustomed to *listening* than we are today. Public
speakers, from entertainers to preachers and politicians, used
language in dynamic ways that we would now think of as poetic,
and spoke to audiences who could handle puns and wordplay as
well as complex analogical language. We have already seen that
this society shared rich metaphorical resources drawn from the
hierarchies of the great chain of being. They could understand
how a kingdom could be spoken of as if it were a garden or a
family, how ambition could be seen as a wolf, how a man's life
was really a kind of play. Shakespeare was able to exploit and
develop such correspondences better than any of his contemporaries, but what we call his poetry took its meaning from, while
giving meaning back to, this shared culture.

Because Shakespeare was unfailingly fascinated by language
and what it can do, so are his characters. They know the power
of language because they know that language is power. In the
first act of *Richard II* Richard sends Sir Thomas Mowbray into
permanent exile, and Mowbray responds with this:

A heavy sentence, my most sovereign liege,
And all unlook'd for from your Highness' mouth;
[. . .]
The language I have learnt these forty years,
My native English, now I must forgo,
And now my tongue's use is to me no more
Than an unstringed viol or a harp,
Or like a cunning instrument cas'd up –
Or being open, put into his hands
That knows no touch to tune the harmony.
[. . .]
What is thy sentence then but speechless death,
Which robs my tongue from breathing native breath.
                                    (1.3.154–5, 159–65, 172–3)

This is a brilliant revelation of the sources of power. The double meaning of 'sentence' creates an association between language and authority. Language is the source of national identity, which also informs personal identity ('I', 'native', 'English'). The similes, which relate the silenced tongue to a useless instrument, are not merely decorative because they connect language to music as a means of ordering experience. The disorder implied by the silenced instrument and the silenced tongue means death, since speech-lessness means the loss of national identity, which means the loss of meaningful life.

Even the most powerless can find some power, however perverse, in language. In *The Tempest* the slave Caliban mocks his master Prospero with 'You taught me language; and my profit on't / Is, I know how to curse' (1.2.365–6). In *King Lear* Gloucester's bastard son Edmund considers the power of the word 'legitimate', which has promoted his brother above himself; he uses his own words, in a letter, to undo that power (1.2.1–22). The powerful, on the other hand, do not always understand the sources of power. At the end of *A Midsummer Night's Dream* Theseus gives his famous account of what the poet does:

> The poet's eye, in a fine frenzy rolling,
> Doth glance from heaven to earth, from earth to heaven.
> And as imagination bodies forth
> The forms of things unknown, the poet's pen
> Turns them to shapes, and gives to airy nothing
> A local habitation and a name.
>
> (5.1.12–17)

He is here dismissing the poet as a marginal or a deluded figure, like the lunatic or the lover, with a power that is capricious and illusory. In claiming that the poet's language gives shape only to 'airy nothing', he is implying that poetic language is less 'real', less powerful than the statesman's (i.e. his own). But immediately before this he has shown himself no less capricious in the use of the power of his own word, when to allow the marriage of Hermia and Lysander he overturns the Athenian law that at the beginning of the play he has claimed 'by no means we may extenuate' (1.1.120).

I am saying here that we cannot compartmentalize the ways in which language is used quite so easily as Theseus or his modern disciples would claim. I do not want to deny that poetic language is beautiful, imaginative, complex, capable of moving us beyond ourselves. But the language of power can work the same effects upon us, and in much the same way. Shakespeare's poetry is a fundamental component of his plays, and his plays are about how things in human life and experience work, private or public, romantic or political, comic or tragic. This, I think, is what we must bear in mind when we think of Shakespeare's poetry: it is deeply engaged with all kinds of 'reality'.

## DRAMA AND METADRAMA

It is abundantly evident throughout Shakespeare's works, and not only from his concern with ambiguities of language, that he was fascinated by the relationship between theatre and world, between illusion and reality. This is not a simple matter of clear-cut distinctions, because what interested him was the ability of theatre to inhabit the border area where the difference between illusion and reality becomes problematic. He was intrigued by the mechanisms of theatre itself, by the ways in which illusions are created. Many of his plays have self-reflexive passages in which their subject-matter becomes the workings of theatre itself. There are plays-within-plays and masques-within-plays; identities are mistaken or exchanged through disguisings and cross-dressing; there are moments when a character steps outside the theatrical illusion, through soliloquy or asides, or even direct addresses to the audience; there are speeches that explore acting as an analogy of life. This kind of self-awareness in plays has come to be known as 'metadrama'. Metadrama is more than just a self-absorbed form of drama, playing with its own trickery. It looks out at the real world, recognizing that dramatic illusion has much to say about the more deceptive illusions that we define for ourselves as reality. 'All the world's a stage', says Jaques in *As You Like It*, 'And all the men and women merely players' (2.7.139–40). We might add that the stage is a world: Shakespeare's theatre was, after all, called the Globe.

Considering the tremendous social changes and the shifts in ideas and beliefs that were happening at that time, it is not surprising that a form of drama should have developed that was intensely concerned with the blurring or transgression of borderlines, the crossing of the barriers set up by rank or gender. The loss of social certainty that came about with the disintegration of feudalism created powerful needs. Feudalism had held men in their places, told them who they were. Its demise released a social fluidity and an uncertainty about place and function, and much Renaissance writing is concerned with asking new questions about personal identity. What were its foundations? How was is constructed? The useful term 'self-fashioning' has been employed to define acts and performances relating to 'the shaping of one's own identity, the experience of being molded by forces outside one's control, the attempt to fashion other selves'.[7] The whole concept is highly theatrical, and in suggesting that people fashion themselves it also suggests that they fashion reality. By scrutinizing itself and the mechanisms through which it mimicked reality, the stage could offer up through metadrama an image of the mechanisms of reality itself.

Let me consider the complex implications of the most conspicuous of metadramatic devices, the play-within-the-play. A primary purpose of this device is to re-stage the relationship between spectator and performance, or between reality and artifice. If I take as an example *Love's Labour's Lost*, the 'real' level of that play is the arena of courtship that involves the young aristocrats of Navarre and France. The characters who people this 'real' level become spectators of the 'artificial' level, the performance of the Play of the Nine Worthies. As such, they are a likeness of the actual spectators in the theatre watching *Love's Labour's Lost*. They mock the pretensions of Holofernes' play, but in doing so they are obliquely mocking their own pedantry, and by refusing to be taken in by his dramatic illusion they shed an ironic light on their own proneness to self-delusion. Most of all, they exhibit their own lack of generosity; the most human moment in the play is when Holofernes chides the young gentlemen for their mean-spirited response to his efforts: 'This is not generous, not gentle, not humble' (5.2.621). Through his theatrical metaphor Shakespeare is offering his own spectators a mirror up to their own behaviour, allowing them to align their reality with the play-reality. He is showing them how an audience ought not to behave, and he is also showing how insecure intellectual and emotional certainties may be. In *A Midsummer Night's Dream* the performance of the embedded play of Pyramus and Thisbe raises on a larger scale questions of how we can know what is real in our emotions and our experience, forcing the 'real' audience to examine its own understanding of 'reality'.

The issue of role-playing, the problem of the distinction between authentic and acted selves, underlies this metadramatic confrontation between real world and play world. When Jaques tells us that all the world's a stage he is not simply giving us a metaphor on which to hang a survey of the seven ages of man; his speech presents identity as a role. This idea is found everywhere in Shakespeare's plays. It is neatly and comically illustrated through the character of Christopher Sly in the Induction of *The Taming of the Shrew*. A Lord and his followers find the drunken tinker Sly asleep and decide to discover what will happen if he awakens to find himself dressed in fine clothing, with a loving wife (who is in fact the Lord's page decked out as a woman) and attended by servants. Sly's initial reaction is to assert his identity: 'I am Christophero Sly' (Ind.2.5), but his assertion quickly weakens into self-questioning and then turns into a recognition of the possibility that he is another self: 'Am not I Christopher Sly?' (17–18); 'Am I a lord?' (69); 'I am a lord indeed' (73). This progression from base to noble is accompanied by a switch from prose to verse, underlining the completeness of Sly's conviction of his new identity. Of course, Sly is not a lord, the transformation is not real, and we may assume that if the frame opened by the Induction had been closed he would have been returned ignominiously to himself. But the play does not give us this answer because the frame remains open, and we are left with the possibility that personal identity has no essence, that it is shaped by outside forces and we are only as others define us.

Other metadramatic devices offer different possibilities. The use of disguise suggests that identity can be expanded by allowing a character to explore the experience of a different self. Although Elizabethan playwrights employed disguise devices frequently, Shakespeare was sparing in his use of them. The disguise-situation he exploited most frequently was that of a young woman as a young man. No doubt he favoured it at least in part because it freed the boy actors to 'be themselves' (one fertile source of metadramatic double meanings that is lost to us today was generated by the fact that women's parts were played by boys; the result was a kind of metaphorical hermaphrodite that produced a constant interplay, especially in the dialogue, between the fictive level of the female role and the real level of the male actor). The dramatic effect of this disguise was to superimpose a male perspective on a female perspective within a single character. The disguised woman might satirize boastful male behaviour and the male idea of masculinity, like Portia when she says 'I have within my mind / A thousand raw tricks of these bragging Jacks, / Which I will practise' (3.4.76–8). But the full effect of these disguises is to enlarge experience rather than mock it by giving the woman the kind of freedom that was at this time generally limited to men. Rosalind disguised as Ganymede in *As You Like It* provides the richest exploration of this dichotomy of male and female experience.

There is a related effect in the disguises of Kent and Edgar in *King Lear*. Both are aristocratic characters who are forced into an alien experience of poverty, degradation and suffering, made to see life as the lowest know it. Both become reflections of Lear himself. Kent put in the stocks represents the denial of Lear's authority by the new regime to which Lear has given up his power. Edgar is an emblem of Lear's own experience, reflecting the tempest in the king's mind that begins to teach him sympathy for 'poor naked wretches'. Kent and Edgar thus represent the point of view of the privileged suddenly dislocated into the constricted experience of the decidedly unprivileged. This is the reverse of the effect of the female-to-male disguise. But both devices cast an ironic light on social hierarchies by illuminating the condition of their victims, those who are limited by them.

Most frequently, however, the central figures of metadrama are able to assert themselves through playing. Shakespeare's men and women of power are aware that power is generated by illusion, by theatre. The person who can manipulate illusion, the person who can control appearances has power. The actor on the stage is in some ways analogous to the ruler in real life, especially as analyzed by Machiavelli, who saw that the successful ruler needed the cunning of the fox: like the actor, the politician succeeds through histrionic control. Consider how Richard of Gloucester presents his programme for success in *3 Henry VI*:

> Why, I can smile, and murder whiles I smile,
> And cry 'Content!' to that which grieves my heart,
> And wet my cheeks with artificial tears,
> And frame my face to all occasions.

> (3.2.182–5)

In his own play, *Richard III*, he does precisely this, creating his own theatre, setting up 'plots' and 'inductions' (1.1.32), acting and murdering his way to power.

Like Richard, Claudius knows how to 'smile, and smile, and be a villain' (*Hamlet*, 1.5.108). In tragedy the problem of how to penetrate such illusion takes on sinister tones. To reveal the truth about his uncle Claudius, a consummate actor who has produced a world of shadows and surfaces where nothing can be trusted, Hamlet devises his own play with the multiple purpose of confronting Claudius with his guilt, giving himself the provocation to 'act', and revealing the illusion of power. When Hamlet is notified of the arrival in Denmark of the Players he says 'He that plays the king shall be welcome' (2.2.318). There is a degree of irony underlying his words, for from Hamlet's point of view Claudius, a regicide and usurper, is not a real king but only playing the king. There is a further level of meaning: the Player who will play the king is really a player playing the Player, and as such he exists on the same plane as the player who plays Claudius, exposing the illusory nature of both figures, but also implying something about real kings.

The idea of the player-king is a potent one throughout Shakespeare's histories and tragedies, and not simply confined to murderous usurpers like Richard III and Claudius. As we have seen, both Elizabeth I and James I saw themselves as figures set on a stage, their 'smallest actions and gestures' scrutinized by the world. Shakespeare's plays understand the implications of this very well: if it is true, then the monarch's actions and gestures are done not for themselves, but for their spectators. Where then lies the monarch's identity? Is there a real royal 'self', or is the monarch's identity imposed by the spectators, much as Sly's identity is imposed upon him? The concept of the king's (or queen's) two bodies implies that there is a royal essence; in *Richard II* Richard firmly believes in this:

Not all the water in the rough rude sea
Can wash the balm off from an anointed king.
The breath of worldly men cannot depose
The deputy elected by the Lord.

(3.2.54–7)

But when he is forced by Henry Bolingbroke to abdicate and hand over his crown he finds that he has no identity separate from the crown. He tries to locate a self by testing out other roles:

> Thus play I in one person many people,
> And none contented. Sometimes am I king,
> Then treasons make me wish myself a beggar,
> And so I am. Then crushing penury
> Persuades me I was better when a king.
> Then am I king'd again; and by and by
> Think that I am unking'd by Bolingbroke,
> And straight am nothing.
>
> (5.5.31–8)

A king or nothing. One role or nothing. Richard knows less about kingship and theatre than the man who took his throne, because he does not really understand that kingship *is* theatre. The Duke of York describes the scene when the triumphant Bolingbroke leads Richard into London. The populace, having cheered the winning player Bolingbroke, responds to Richard:

> As in a theatre the eyes of men,
> After a well-grac'd actor leaves the stage,
> Are idly bent on him that enters next,
> Thinking his prattle to be tedious;
> Even so, or with much more contempt, men's eyes
> Did scowl on gentle Richard.
>
> (5.2.23–8)

This is not simply a lament for the fall of the tragic actor; it also acknowledges the potential power of the audience, both in the theatre and in the state.

The self-reflexive potential of theatre functions in intricate ways in Shakespeare's plays. Often the playwright himself seems to be playing, immersing himself in the sheer pleasure of the 'theatrical'. But through metadrama his plays were able to register a complex relationship between stage and life, between actor and role, between appearance and reality, that was actually an exploration of the gaps and shifts, the divisions and realignments taking place in his society. Theatre was the most potent reflection of the realities of the culture of the time. Our own realities are in many ways different, but they still have their divisions and realignments, and Shakespeare's theatre can still provide us with a means of seeing and questioning them.

## CRITICISM AND 'MEANING'

For anyone making a serious approach to Shakespeare the most bewildering obstacle is not the plays and poems themselves, but the enormous amount of scholarship, criticism, polemic and other secondary writings that they have engendered. Each year thousands of books, chapters, articles and reviews appear. Much of this is valuable editorial work that sheds new light on the texts, or historical scholarship that expands our knowledge of the context in and for which they were written. But in many cases critics are offering new readings of plays or professing to set us straight on what the dramatist really meant, as if this had hitherto remained hidden. Before we can begin to consider how such work can be helpful to our own understanding of Shakespeare we need to establish what we mean when we talk about the 'meaning' of a work of art.

One of the founders of twentieth-century Shakespearean criticism was A.C. Bradley, whose *Shakespearean Tragedy*, published in 1904, still has many adherents. In his introduction to this book Bradley attempts to explain its purpose, which appears to have been to enter the mind of the playwright himself: 'to learn to apprehend the action and some of the personages of [the plays] with a somewhat greater truth and intensity, so that they may assume in our imaginations a shape a little less unlike the shape they wore in the imagination of their creator'.[8] That is, the play 'means' what the dramatist meant, and we have to try to recover this. Now there are numerous problems with this. One is that, given the collaborative nature of production of the dramatic text, the mind or imagination that lies behind the text is not simply Shakespeare's. A more fundamental problem arises with the question of whether, in fact, any text can lead us to the mind of its author. It is not inconceivable, after all, that a work might mean something different from what its author thought it meant. Furthermore, given a potential plurality of meanings, how are we to be sure which of them was the author's intended one? The only way we have to the author's mind is the texts themselves, and

we have no objective way to confirm that our reading coincides with the author's 'meaning'.

A more helpful definition of artistic 'meaning' is one that separates it from 'intention'. In a recent book, *Discovering Shakespeare's Meaning*, Leah Scragg locates a play's meaning in what she calls its 'design', the conscious organization of the play's various elements that may reasonably 'be thought of as Shakespeare's'.[9] This has the merit of assigning meaning to the plays rather than to an intention in a nebulous mind that lies behind them. Furthermore, it allows the meaning to change, or at least to appear to change: 'different aspects of that design may be foregrounded by different audiences and may acquire different meanings in different contexts'.[10] Scragg seems to be suggesting, however, that these differences in meaning are only apparent, since the play's real meaning, its design, remains constant.

Other recent work has denied that the plays themselves 'mean' at all. In *Meaning by Shakespeare* Terence Hawkes claims that meaning is something forced into the plays by the reader or spectator, who uses the text as a way of reflecting his or her own ideological position.[11] Now while it is clear that we do impose meaning on to a text, in that much of what we call its meaning must be what we think it means, to claim that a play does not mean opens the way to a kind of interpretative anarchy. To say all the meaning that a text has is what the reader imposes upon it implies that a text can be made to mean anything. But the meanings we impose upon a text are limited by what the text says, by the organized patterns of words. We may not be able to achieve certainty or agreement about what the words mean, but we can be sure that there are some things that they cannot mean. Some degree of potential meaning must, therefore, inhere in the text.

That meaning, while limited, is not fixed. The meaning of a text arises out of a collaboration between text and reader or play and spectator. How we understand a play depends on what we bring to it from our own time, place and experience, that is, our own context. Since this is necessarily different from the context in which the play was written, so must our understanding be different from that of the original audience. To know that the meaning we derive from a play is different from what its original audience understood, or even from what its author intended, does not invalidate our response, but rather enriches it. We need to be aware that a text does not have a meaning; rather it embraces multiple and even contradictory meanings, and it can gain or lose meanings.

Perhaps I can illustrate this by considering what might be the meaning of the character Shylock in *The Merchant of Venice*. The play appears to offer two radically opposed perspectives on Shylock. In his first appearance he explains why he hates Antonio:

> I hate him for he is a Christian;
> But more, for that in low simplicity
> He lends out money gratis, and brings down
> The rate of usance here with us in Venice.
> If I can catch him once upon the hip,
> I will feed fat the ancient grudge I bear him.
>
> (1.3.37–42)

The hatred between Jews and Christians is ancient and apparently inescapable, according to Shylock, and therefore he must hate Antonio. However, that reason for malice is secondary to his resentment towards Antonio for spoiling the money-lending business by giving interest-free loans. This figure of malevolence is what is perceived by other characters in the play, and it is how Shylock presents himself: as an offensive anti-Semitic stereotype, a caricature Jew who hates Christians and is as thirsty for blood as for money. Later, however, he is given the most moving speech in the play. He reverses the implications of this earlier speech by claiming that Antonio's persecution of him is entirely because he is a Jew, and goes on to assert the fundamental humanity of his race:

> Hath not a Jew eyes? hath not a Jew hands, organs, dimensions, senses, affections, passions? fed with the same food, hurt with the same weapons, subject to the same diseases, healed by the same means, warmed and cooled by the same winter and summer as a Christian is? – if you prick us do we not bleed? if you tickle us do we not laugh? if you poison us do we not die? and if you wrong us shall we not revenge?
>
> (3.1.52–60)

How are we to reconcile this with what we already know of Shylock?

One answer might be that we do not have to reconcile the two perspectives. Shylock is not, after all, a person, but merely a comic mechanism, a necessary villain whose plotting gets in the way of the play's happy resolution, and who must be removed before that can take place. Now while this is certainly true, it is of no use to the actor who has to attempt to make a coherent character out of discrepant pieces. The history of performance of the role of Shylock essentially indicates a pendulum movement between actors who perform the role as a gleeful piece of comic wickedness who gets what he deserves at the play's end, and those who try to find in the role a suffering human, a man of injured dignity who must endure the final humiliation of being forced to betray his faith and become a Christian.[12]

There is more to say. Many modern readers or spectators of the play find it anti-Semitic and therefore offensive. Shakespeare quite probably did not have any personal experience of Jews. Edward I expelled all Jews from England in 1290, and although by the late sixteenth century some had found their way to London, they were very few. Any anti-Semitism reflected in the figure of Shylock probably was not intended as a mockery of Jews as such, but arose from the fact that in the convention of the blood-thirsty Jew (which, after all, Shakespeare did not invent) the dramatist found a ready-made comic type to fit the needs of his plot. Furthermore, he does appear to have made an attempt to temper Shylock's unpleasantness by setting it in a context of Christian obnoxiousness; there is little Christian charity amongst these Venetians, notwithstanding Portia's speech on the quality of mercy, and there is a constant readiness to equate Shylock's unpleasantness with his Jewishness. The problems that Shylock raises for us were probably not problems for Shakespeare, and it is likely that nobody in his audience was offended by the portrayal of the Jew.

Knowing this does not make the problem go away, and in some ways it makes it worse. The willingness of Shakespeare's audience to accept uncritically an anti-Semitic stereotype indicates to a modern audience an endemic coarseness of sensibility that must have been shared by the playwright himself. We cannot congratulate ourselves on being more civilized; we have vicious stereotypes of our own. Still, our context includes in it a greater awareness than Shakespeare's of the history of Jewish persecution, and particularly it includes our knowledge of the Holocaust. Our experience of the play is inevitably coloured by this knowledge. Consequently it is not possible for us to perceive the same meaning in Shylock as did Shakespeare's audience, and most people would say that we are the better for it.

I have taken an extreme example here and, furthermore, I have been guilty of abstracting the character from the dramatic design or framework that is finally the necessary condition of his existence. Shylock does not mean anything in himself; he takes on a meaning in relation to the other parts of the play's structure. But that structure is not static; the relationships between its parts change as the play's relationship with its readers or spectators changes through time and space, and this is why the text resists any single 'meaning'. Perhaps we should not be concerned with what a play *means* so much as with what it *is* or what it *does*.

## GENRE

In the First Folio Heminges and Condell divided the plays into three categories: comedies, histories and tragedies. In doing so they were identifying differences in formal organization in order to separate the plays into different kinds, or 'genres'. The traditional dramatic genres, first distinguished by Aristotle, were tragedy and comedy, and it appears that the editors were identifying a new one when they grouped the histories separately. However, their efforts were somewhat arbitrary. They gave the title 'histories' only to the plays that deal with English history. *Julius Caesar*, *Coriolanus* and *Antony and Cleopatra*, which dramatize events from Roman history but have political concerns related to those of the English history plays, were treated as tragedies. So was *Macbeth*, which is concerned with Scottish history. Now of course all of these plays are tragic in form and we could argue that the editors simply chose to place them in the category that had the higher status. But at least two of the histories, *Richard II* and *Richard III*, are formally tragedies, and *Richard II* was identified as such on the title page of the first quarto edition. The consequence of these ambiguities in terminology is that either we have to consider the history play as being a hybrid genre, or we have to recognize that generic divisions are not watertight; genres, that is, can leak into one other.

Genre theory has its roots in Book III of Plato's *Republic* where he divides poetry into two kinds, one using direct speech, which represents its object by having the poet or speaker put himself in the place of the character supposedly speaking, the other using indirect speech, in which the poet stands outside what he describes to tell its story. The former is clearly 'dramatic', the latter 'narrative'. This broad division leaves little room for variation, and later Greek theorists developed much more elaborate classifications. Renaissance scholars, in proposing classical models for the writers of their own time, insisted on the distinctions between genres, as for example does Sir Philip Sidney in *The Defence of Poetry* (1579), where he lists eight of them and implies a few more: 'the heroic, lyric, tragic, comic, satiric, iambic, elegiac, pastoral, and certain others'.[13] Sidney believed that genres should *not* leak into one another; elsewhere in the *Defence* he examines the state of the drama of his own time and castigates dramatists who ignore the Aristotelian unities of time and place, particularly chastising them for generic impurity:

> But besides these gross absurdities, how all their plays be neither right tragedies, nor right comedies, mingling kings and clowns, not because the matter so carrieth it, but thrust in the clown by head and shoulders to play a part in majestical matters with neither decency nor discretion, so as neither the admiration and commiseration, nor the right sportfulness, is by their mongrel tragi-comedy obtained. (114)

It is interesting to speculate on how Sidney would have responded to Shakespeare's frequent mixing of kings and clowns, of the tragic and the comic. Even *King Lear* has its Fool, and many of his comedies mingle kings (or at least dukes) and clowns. The purity that Sidney seems to be demanding is unrealistic. In *Hamlet* Polonius catalogues dramatic genres thus: 'tragedy, comedy, history, pastoral, pastoral-comical, historical-pastoral, tragical-historical, tragical-comical-historical-pastoral' (2.2.392–5). Polonius is a tedious old fool and it might seem that he is being mocked for his generation of hybrid genres, but in fact most of Shakespeare's plays mix modes, and some of his last ones come pretty close to being 'tragical-comical-historical-pastoral'.

It is probable that most of the people working in the theatre in Shakespeare's time (with notable exceptions such as Ben Jonson) were rather less concerned about generic definition than was Sidney, and Shakespeare himself does not appear to have cared very much. If we take *Troilus and Cressida* as an example, we find that the original quarto title page (1609) calls it a history, as does an entry for the same year in the Stationers' Register. However, an epistle or advertisement attached to some copies of the quarto edition describes it as a comedy, while the editors of the Folio version of the play, placing it between the histories and the tragedies, entitled it 'The Tragedie of Troylus and Cressida'. The disagreement arises because the play hardly fits snugly into any of the three categories.

This is not to say that modern readers or viewers of Elizabethan plays do not need to be concerned about generic distinctions. It is, however, necessary to take great care not to bring inappropriate preconceptions, based on an uncritical understanding of genre, to the plays. John Dryden's treatment of *Troilus and Cressida*, already mentioned, provides an instructive example. In 1679 he produced a version of Shakespeare's play for the stage of his own day, and provided a lengthy critical preface to justify what he had done to it. His criteria were based on Aristotelian 'rules' and he began by defining Shakespeare's play as a tragedy, but then complained that it did not fulfil the requirements of tragedy: 'the latter part of the Tragedy is nothing but a confusion of Drums and Trumpets, Excursions and Alarms. The chief persons, who give name to the Tragedy, are left alive: Cressida is false, and is not punish'd.'[14] Dryden rewrote the play in accordance with Aristotelian prescriptions, having both Troilus and Cressida die. No one would dispute that Dryden's version is a formally more perfect tragedy than Shakespeare's, which may not be a tragedy at all, but even Dryden's strongest supporters have never denied that Shakespeare's remains the superior play. For Dryden, the need to fit *Troilus and Cressida* into a neat generic form got in the way of his understanding of how the play actually works, not by conforming to traditional generic standards, but by defying or even denying them.

It is more useful, perhaps, to try to see each play as an individual work with a special relation to generic convention. What is important is not how a particular play fits into a genre, as if generic conventions were a strait-jacket, but how the author stretches and re-shapes the genre to suit his own needs. One way of looking at *Measure for Measure*, for example, is to see it as an attempt by Shakespeare to fit tragic subject-matter into a comic structure. *Love's Labour's Lost* is clearly a comedy, yet it refuses the immediate satisfaction of a happy ending that we normally expect of comedy. There are ways in which *Troilus and Cressida* can be understood as a tragedy, but not if we insist on applying Aristotelian requirements to it. Perhaps we can summarize here by suggesting that the idea of genre sets up certain expectations about a play (though this is equally true of any literary text), but what is important is not so much how well the play conforms to those expectations, as how and why it teases and baffles them.

## COMEDIES

We tend to think of comedy in opposition to tragedy, and as primarily intended to generate laughter, an idea that might mislead us into thinking that comedy cannot deal with serious matter. While indeed laughter often is an aspect of comedy, it is not necessary to it, and certainly was not considered to be so by Renaissance theorists. In *The Defence of Poetry* Sir Philip Sidney wrote this about laughter in comedy:

> But our comedians think there is no delight without laughter; which is very wrong, for though laughter may come with delight, yet cometh it not of delight, as though delight should be the cause of laughter; but well may one thing breed both together. . . . Delight hath a joy in it, either permanent or present. Laughter hath only a scornful tickling.[15]

Ben Jonson, who spent almost all of his stage career writing comedies, went even further: 'the moving of laughter is a fault in comedy, a kind of turpitude, that depraves some part of a man's nature without a disease'.[16] Jonson did not follow this theory in his own comedies and we should not take the statement too literally; indeed, his plays depend for their effects on something like a 'scornful tickling'. But he clearly felt ill at ease with the potential for laughter to undermine the serious intentions of a comedy.

Although they were writing during the same period, Jonson and Shakespeare represent two different traditions of comedy. Jonson's kind, usually defined as satirical comedy, was serious in that it had (or at least claimed to have) a didactic purpose.

Jonson created a world that pretends to be real, a world of commercial exploitation presenting images of folly and vice for his audience to laugh at; he created characters who deviate from an implied social and moral norm, and his plays carry an underlying assumption that such aberrations can be corrected by mocking laughter. Shakespeare's comic world, on the other hand, does not pretend to be real; indeed, it insistently proclaims itself as theatrical. It is closer to the world of folklore and fairy-tale, concerned with the uniting of lovers or the reuniting of broken families, and even when it does not contain magic or fairies, it has improbable coincidences, deceptions and misapprehensions developed around identical twins, lost children, slandered women or women in disguise. This is generally known as romantic comedy, and the laughter it generates is usually (not always) gentler and more tolerant than the laughter of satire.

It would be wrong, however, to see these two traditions as mutually exclusive. Many of Shakespeare's plays contain characters who are the target of satire, such as Armado in *Love's Labour's Lost*, Malvolio in *Twelfth Night* and just about everybody in *Troilus and Cressida*. Indeed, the term 'romantic' is misleading, because it directs attention towards certain elements of these comedies at the expense of others. 'Romance' was originally used to refer to works written in Old French, often about knights and deeds of chivalry and tending towards the fantastic. The knights were usually in the service of an idealized Lady, but love as such was not necessarily at the centre of their adventures. Popular modern usage of the word 'romance' has diminished its meaning so that it refers primarily to erotic relationships; one widely used handbook to literature defines romantic comedy as 'comedy in which serious love is the chief concern and source of interest', and goes on to trace its sources in Elizabethan writers such as Greene and Shakespeare.[17] Now while Shakespeare's romantic comedies do deal with love, they are also about other issues. They are about human relationships and especially about the workings of power within relationships, whether this be sexual or generational, social, economic or political power.

In fact, once we look carefully at a Shakespearean comedy we may see that it reflects a good deal of darkness, and this is something that the label 'romantic' conceals. In a significant number of plays a character is under threat of death: Egeon in *The Comedy of Errors*, Antonio in *The Merchant of Venice*, Claudio in *Measure for Measure*. In the opening scene of *A Midsummer Night's Dream* Hermia is offered three fates to choose from: marriage to a man she does not love, a barren life shut away in a convent, or death. In *As You Like It* Rosalind has only two choices, banishment or death. Since these are comedies, the threatened characters are eventually saved, but the anxiety generated by the threat is a part of the pattern of the plays. The comedies, we might say, finally proclaim happiness and integration, life and fertility, but they also acknowledge loss and hold within them the potential for tragedy. Comedy is a way of delaying the pain and separation that cannot finally be prevented.

So the question of what constitutes a comedy is complicated. Even the most fundamental aspect of comedy, the happy ending, can raise problems. Who is happy at the end of a comedy? Not everybody, obviously. Shylock certainly is not happy at the end of *The Merchant of Venice*. Of course, Shylock is the 'villain' of this play, and we might say that it is sufficient for most of the characters, especially the main ones, to be happy. But at the end of *Love's Labour's Lost* the happy union of lovers is deferred for a year and a day, with a strong suggestion that the union might not indeed take place at all. At the end of *Measure for Measure* four marriages are announced, but the play itself has given us good reason to doubt that most of them will be happy. Is Katherina's capitulation to Petruchio in *The Taming of the Shrew* a happy ending for her? Shakespeare and the audience of his time might well have thought so, but many modern feminist critics do not. *The Winter's Tale* ends in reconciliation, certainly a happy ending, but it comes only after much pain and loss. We need, it is clear, to have a flexible understanding of what constitutes comedy.

Shakespeare's histories are confined to the first half of his career and the tragedies, with a couple of exceptions, to the second half, but he wrote comedies throughout, perhaps because comedy is the most adaptable of the three genres. About half of his plays are comedies. We can see from his earliest efforts a constant pressure to experiment, to recombine the comic conventions and push against the limits of the genre. This might be attributed as much to commercial as to artistic pressures, to Shakespeare's need to provide for an audience that was constantly demanding something new. Most of the time he knew how to respond to such pressure, though he may on occasion have misjudged what his audience would accept; *Troilus and Cressida* strays about as far as is possible from what most people would accept as comedy and, although the evidence is not conclusive, it appears not to have been performed during Shakespeare's lifetime.

Typically a comedy begins with a moment of social disruption: a daughter will not obey her father, a man banishes a brother, a man or woman rejects a lover, a man falsely suspects the woman he loves. This disruption opens the way for a series of plot complications that might include inversions in which women are given the power of men, or servants the power of masters. That is, the normal social hierarchical structure is turned upside-down. This sense of comedy as carnival liberation is often intensified by having the characters move from the threatening world of court or city to the green and magical world of nature, as the lovers of *A Midsummer Night's Dream* flee to the wood outside Athens, or the characters of *As You Like It* go out to the Forest of Arden. The comic experience often involves confusions of identity, a failure to distinguish appearance from reality that is underscored by confusions and slippages in language, the linguistic play of puns and malapropisms and the subversion of rhetorical and logical structure. The opening disruption is ultimately settled, often by magic or something that looks like magic, by a sudden revelation of identity or reversal of attitude, opening the way for a final harmonious resolution through marriage. Marriage implies natural harmony through fertility and the renewal of the cycle of life, and it also implies social harmony, being the fundamental pattern on which society is built. That is why these comedies are called 'romantic' comedies: they depend on the extravagant and wonderful which they connect with the workings of relationships between the sexes.

Shakespeare's concern with relationships has much to do with his interest in the nature of personal identity, which struggles to establish itself in the space that opens up between a character's sense of his or her essential selfhood, the roles the character plays, knowingly or otherwise, and the often inexplicable social identity that he or she is given by others. Any disturbance within this space leads a character to question not only his or her own identity, but the reality of the surrounding world. In *The Comedy of Errors* Antipholus of Syracuse is mistaken for his twin brother, and asks himself:

> Am I in earth, in heaven, or in hell?
> Sleeping or waking; mad or well advis'd?
> Known unto these, and to myself disguis'd.
>
> (2.2.212–14)

His sense of who he is has been disrupted. What is a 'self' if it can be known to others and disguised to itself? With this slippage of his sense of his own identity goes a loss of his certainty about the nature of reality: how is this suddenly questionable self to understand its relationship with what he seems to be experiencing? Such questions and doubts echo throughout Shakespeare's comedies, from Viola/Cesario's statement 'I am not that I play' (*Twelfth Night*, 1.5.185) and Troilus's 'This is, and is not, Cressid!' (*Troilus and Cressida*, 5.2.145) to Prospero's 'We are such stuff / As dreams are made on' (*The Tempest*, 4.1.156–7). This is one reason for Shakespeare's plays in general, but particularly the comedies, being full of self-reflexive, metadramatic moments.

To return to the cyclical structure of the comedies, this can be perceived in different ways. Northrop Frye, whose theories about the mythical structures of literature have been very influential, says: 'The mythical or primitive basis of comedy is toward the rebirth and renewal of the powers of nature. . . .' This renewal, brought about by the overthrowing of the anti-comic, is not social renewal, however, for it does not 'alter the actual hierarchy of society. Kings remain kings, and clowns clowns: only the personal relations within the society are altered.'[18] Thus Frye perceives comic structure as a conservative reinforcement of social hierarchies, and the renewal or rebirth amounts to little more than a new acceptance of the old ways. C.L. Barber, whose work has been as influential as Frye's, also provides an essentially conservative reading of the form, arguing that comedy aims for social stability, and that while it is healthy for subversive energies to be liberated, the ending of a play brings those energies back into control; disorder is licensed only to promote order the more firmly. Just as holiday or festival is always followed by business as usual, so comedy returns us to the way things were.[19]

I should like to suggest, however, that the plays also allow for a sceptical view of social harmony. Order may be restored at the end but the questions that comedies raise do not go away, and in fact the audience's experience during the play might well destabilize its response to the resolution. Relationships in plays inevitably exist in hierarchies that reflect the hierarchies of the world beyond the stage. Heroines like Kate, Hermia and Rosalind begin by attempting to escape from patriarchal domination, and each ends up in a marriage that replicates and confirms that domination. But the resistance that precipitates the comic action is important because it allows us to see an alternative to the way things are. For a brief moment, as she masquerades as Ganymede, Rosalind understands what masculine liberation is, and the audience experiences this with her. Once she returns to her own shape she submits herself to Orlando. This is necessitated by the demands of comic form, but there is something in what has been experienced during the play that resists the implications of the ending and complicates our response to it.

We might reasonably ask, for whom does marriage constitute a happy ending? At the conclusion of *Measure for Measure*, how does Isabella feel about Duke Vincentio's proposal? He is the play's ultimate source of authority as well as its most eligible bachelor, and one might think it would be difficult for Isabella to refuse him. On the other hand, considering the ordeal he has put her through, she has little reason to be grateful to him. The play, however, does not indicate her feelings. Vincentio twice proposes to her and each time she responds with silence. An actor playing the part will presumably contribute some gesture or stage business to indicate Isabella's response, but the fact remains that the text does not emphatically endorse a positive response, and indeed the silence, emphasized by its repetition, may be understood to imply the opposite. The ending of *The Taming of the Shrew*, with Kate's long speech of submission, raises even more problems, since it apparently is presented as a happy ending. G.B. Shaw considered this 'altogether disgusting to modern sensibility', and it is not only feminist critics who have agreed with him.[20] We do not know Shakespeare's intentions in this; most likely, as a child of his time he saw Kate's acceptance of her inferior position in the domestic hierarchy as laudable, but he has also been understood as a kind of proto-feminist who questioned the attitudes of his time by loading his play with irony. Whatever his intentions might have been, however, the play does bring its own ending into question.

Even in those plays where there appear to be no ironies in the romantic ending, such as *The Merchant of Venice*, *Much Ado about Nothing* or *Twelfth Night*, we might wish to ask whether what we have seen of Bassanio, Claudio and Orsino suggests that they will be adequate husbands for the respective heroines. The obvious response to this is that it is a long-standing comic convention to forget at the end of a play a character's faults and weaknesses and the pain they may have caused if the character shows signs of reformation (the most spectacular reversal of this sort is that of Oliver in *As You Like It*). It is certainly true that comic form depends on such 'forgetting'; like fairy-tales, it assumes that marriage means living happily ever after. But if we set these marriages beside the enforced marriage of Angelo to Mariana that is a part of the 'happy' ending of *Measure for Measure*, the sour questions that are inevitably raised about the possibility of the reformation of Angelo must have their resonances in these apparently less ambiguous plays.

Indeed, although the happy resolution of almost all of the romantic comedies involves marriage, there are *within* the plays few signs that marriage can be happy. Jealousy or selfishness undermine the relationships of Adriana and Antipholus of Ephesus in *The Comedy of Errors*, Oberon and Titania in *A Midsummer Night's Dream*, Leontes and Hermione in *The Winter's Tale*, explosively in the latter two cases. In this context the remarkable number of single-parent families in the plays is worth commenting on, for they are all families in which the single parent is a father. In this they reflect a grim social reality of the time, which was that a distressingly high number of women died in childbirth, something that could hardly have made marriage a more alluring prospect for women. More to the point here, in most cases the father exerts authoritarian power in a troubled relationship with a daughter: Baptista in *The Taming of the Shrew*, Egeus in *A Midsummer Night's Dream*, Frederick in *As You Like It*, even Prospero in *The Tempest*. This disturbance in father–daughter relationships might affect our response to husband–wife relationships, which share the same assumptions about domestic hierarchy. At the end of *The Taming of the Shrew*, Bianca refuses to obey her husband much as, at the beginning, Kate had refused to obey her father. The play treats this as farce, but it acknowledges that the causes of strife have not gone away.

This complication of response to comic endings is in many cases underscored by other disturbing elements. We might add to the marriages within the sub-plot of *The Taming of the Shrew* the deferring of the happy ending in *Love's Labour's Lost*, or the

self-exclusion of Jaques from the 'dancing measures' of social harmony in *As You Like It*, or the song at the end of *Twelfth Night*
sung by the weary Feste, surely the play's embodiment of the
comic spirit, about the rain raining every day. The happy ending
is as fragile and insecure as the marriage of Touchstone which,
as Jaques cynically but probably truthfully points out, is 'but for
two months victualled'. I would conclude here that comic form
contains within itself elements that tend to its own destabilization.
This is not a fault; it is both a source of comic energy and a way
in which comedy can embrace serious meanings, for it allows for
conflicting responses and a resistance to reductive moral readings.

Most of Shakespeare's comedies are versions of the 'romantic',
but often with radical variations and anti-romantic or parodic
elements. The ten comedies he wrote before 1600 experiment in
different ways with romantic conventions, but there is a marked
change of direction after 1600 when sceptical ingredients that
were always a part of his comedies became their main feature.
Between 1601 and 1605 he wrote three plays that have earned
the label 'problem comedies'. After 1607 he wrote four plays (five
if we include *The Two Noble Kinsmen*, which I think is largely
Fletcher's work) that diverge sufficiently from his earlier forms
to require a designation of their own and are called 'tragicomedies'
or 'romances'.

One reason for Shakespeare's interest in the comedy of romantic
love must have been that it offered rich material for the exploration
of illusion and delusion. Often we perceive the object of our love
only from the viewpoint of our own desire: we construct what
we wish to see upon the surface of what is there, and there may
be a great divergence between what we see and what is real. As
Helena says in *A Midsummer Night's Dream*, 'Things base and vile,
holding no quantity, / Love can transpose to form and dignity'
(1.1.232–3). Romantic comedy is thus highly 'theatrical' in its
preoccupations, and open to theatrical playfulness. Theatrical
illusion and the transpositions of love overlap, and drama can
explore the metadramatic territory where experience itself is illusion.
However, illusion can fall away into disillusionment, and again
we see that on the borders of comedy there is always the potential
for tragedy.

In *The Comedy of Errors* Shakespeare used Classical models (two
plays by the Latin dramatist Plautus, the *Menaechmi* and the
*Amphitruo*) for a play that is entirely about illusion. In his study

of the sources of the play Kenneth Muir suggested that Shakespeare was challenging and defeating Plautus on his own ground,[21] but it is probable that Shakespeare was concerned to challenge more immediate rivals. In the late 1580s or early 1590s, when this play must have been written, Shakespeare was attempting to break into a profession dominated (for comedy) by John Lyly, who for ten years had been writing plays for the children's companies, and by the so-called University Wits (Thomas Lodge, George Peele, Robert Greene and Thomas Nashe) who in their plays and other writings made a great parade of their Classical learning. It is hardly surprising, therefore, that Shakespeare should have started out by writing his own 'Classical' play in which, with great energy, he exhibited his mastery of plot-construction as well as his ability to generate a range of styles, mixing prose with blank verse, rhymed couplets, even near-sonnets.

We come to the play expecting a comedy, and we are immediately dislocated by the frame-story because its tone is tragic. In the opening scene the Syracusian merchant Egeon has been arrested and condemned to death because of an unreasonable Ephesian law. Two disquieting issues are raised here that will resurface in many plays: the first is the relation of authority and mercy; the second is the equation between material goods and human life (later in the play an equation is made between the commercial and the erotic). I think that Shakespeare intended the sombre tones of this scene, with its emphasis on loss, to resonate through the body of the play and complicate our responses to its undoubtedly hilarious events – the farcical results of the confusion generated by two sets of twins who delude everyone, and who themselves become victims of the general disorder.

Since the play ends with one of the most complete moments of restoration anywhere in Shakespeare, we might ask what effect is created by its insistence on reminding us of loss and especially of the pain, even terror, of loss of self. I think that much of Shakespeare's drama forces us to question the very responses that it raises in us. After all, in one sense the difference between comedy and tragedy is no more than a difference of perspective. We all know, if we have seen silent film comedies or television slapstick, that the sight of a fat man slipping on a banana skin is comic. But it is only comic if we do not see it from the fat man's point of view, and while I should not wish to go so far as to claim that from his point of view the fall is tragic, I certainly have to acknowledge that it is painful. Comedy can control us and distance us from events so that we see only what is laughable, and for the most part this is what *The Comedy of Errors* does. But it does also trouble our response to it by reminding us of alternative perspectives.

There is more to be said about the play's self-questioning. Here is the account that Antipholus of Syracuse gives of Ephesus, a city long associated with witchcraft:

They say this town is full of cozenage,
As nimble jugglers that deceive the eye,
Dark-working sorcerers that change the mind,
Soul-killing witches that deform the body,
Disguised cheaters, prating mountebanks,
And many such-like liberties of sin:

(1.2.97–102)

Consider these lines in relation to the following attack on the theatre by the Puritan preacher Philip Stubbes in 1583:

if you will learn cozenage; if you will learn to deceive; if you will learn to play the hypocrite, to cog, to lie and falsify . . . if you will learn to play the Vice, to swear, tear and blaspheme both heaven and earth . . . all these good examples may you see painted before your eyes in interludes and plays.[22]

Shakespeare's echoes may be accidental but the implications surely are not. This account of cozeners, deceivers of the eye, mind-changers and disguised cheaters is an account of theatrical illusion as it was perceived by its enemies. This does not mean that Shakespeare agreed with the Puritans, but it suggests that he was acknowledging and asking his audience to acknowledge ambivalent feelings about the seductions of the theatre, which can be as dangerous as they are pleasurable.

*The Comedy of Errors* asks what identity is: if I think I am Antipholus but everyone else denies it, then who am I? *The Taming of the Shrew*, a play with realistic, essentially anti-romantic elements, asks questions about the possibility of transforming identity. Its perspective is coloured by the Sly Induction in which the drunken tinker, like Antipholus of Syracuse, undergoes an experience so strange that he questions its reality: 'Or do I dream? Or have I dream'd till now?' (Ind.2.70). The answer to both questions is, of course, 'No'; he is simply the victim of a theatrical trick. But the Induction makes problematic a whole complex of ideas related to identity, because the frame opened by the Induction is never closed, and we are left with questions about the meaning and stability of identity that have an important bearing on the transformations of the play proper.

Kate is at the outset an angry, verbally violent woman, perhaps because she feels trapped in a world of patriarchal authority, forced to live by her father's rules until she is sold as a wife to the highest bidder like an object in a market-place (it is worth noting here that Tranio and Gremio do indeed bid for Bianca). We cannot know if this shrew is the 'real' Kate who has to be changed by Petruchio, or if the 'real' Kate is a gentler person who plays the role of shrew in self-protection. Petruchio woos her by playing the shrew himself, crude in temper and language, tormenting her with an extreme version of the kind of behaviour she has inflicted on her family. This is a controversial aspect of the play. Petruchio has been seen as callous and brutal, taming his wife by breaking her spirit, but he takes her away from a paternal home where she has been constrained and unhappy, and offers her an opportunity to be not so much a better self as a happier self. Does this end justify the means? Perhaps one way to look at it is as a process through which Petruchio finds Kate's true value and demonstrates it to her. He begins, after all, by coming to Padua to 'wive it wealthily' (1.2.74), and when he hears about Kate it is the gold of her dowry that attracts him. When he meets her, however, he clearly sees something in her spirit that is of a different order of value, and in his treatment of her he moves both himself and her away from materialistic judgements. When they return to Padua, Kate and Petruchio stand outside the mercenary middle-class values of Baptista and those who see marriage as a commercial transaction.

This question of value and how it is perceived is probed also in the sub-plot. As soon as Lucentio sees Bianca, he falls in love with her, and expresses his love in a style that would have been very familiar to the play's first audiences:

> Tranio, I burn, I pine, I perish, Tranio,
> If I achieve not this young modest girl.
> Counsel me, Tranio, for I know thou canst.
> Assist me, Tranio, for I know thou wilt.

(1.1.155–8)

The language of pain and death, the artifice of the parallelism, are echoes of the Petrarchan conventions that were fashionable in the sonnet sequences of the decade or so before the play was written and that Shakespeare both used and mocked in his own sonnets. Lucentio describes his emotions in terms of literary convention, suggesting that his knowledge of women comes from books. Love at first sight, however, may well be misperception, and Bianca certainly turns out to be something other than Lucentio expected.

In so far as it is about love, the play tells us that a love that has to be struggled for is worth more than one based on the superficial and the material. However, there are problems with the way this is presented, and they come into focus in the final scene. Kate's speech of submission clearly accepts the inferior position of women within the domestic hierarchy: 'Such duty as the subject owes the prince / Even such a woman oweth to her husband' (5.2.156–7).

But how seriously does she mean this? It is, of course, a statement of the status of women in Elizabethan England, and as such reflects the realities of the world beyond the stage, but it is hard to believe that the spirited Kate could have been as humbled as this implies. We can read the speech as a continuation of the game she and her husband have been playing, intended to mock Bianca and the Widow who have just revealed themselves as shrews. Or we can read it as ironic, denying its own apparent meaning.

Many of Shakespeare's comedies begin with an arbitrary act of authoritarian will. In *The Comedy of Errors* it is an act of state authority, in which Solinus feels forced to condemn the old man Egeon to death, but more usually this act is a sign of the disjunction between generations, as when Baptista makes conditions about the marriage of his daughters. The collision between the rigidity of age and the passions of youth had of course been a staple of comic plotting since Greek times, and one could argue that much of what we call 'history' has been the outcome of the struggle of the oppressed young (whether as individuals or as a community) to define themselves by freeing themselves from the rules and the power of an older or entrenched generation. In turning this pattern to his own uses Shakespeare showed a particular interest in the experience of women, sometimes as victims of paternal will, sometimes as beings attempting to assert themselves in a love-relationship. Kate opposes both her father and Petruchio by rejecting the kind of feminine passivity apparently represented by her sister and taking the 'masculine' prerogative of violent language.

By permitting Kate to exhibit what were generally thought of as masculine characteristics, *The Taming of the Shrew* brings into question the Elizabethan understanding of the division of the sexes. In *The Two Gentlemen of Verona* Shakespeare went further with this interrogation by allowing a female character, through the use of disguise, to take on a male role. It is difficult for a modern reader or viewer to understand all the original metatheatrical implications of this device, but as female parts were played by boys there is clearly a level of resonance in the idea of a boy actor playing the part of a girl who disguises herself as a boy that is no longer available to us. Julia's disguise frees her to learn truths about the man she loves as well as about masculine experience. The play deals with ideas about masculine friendship and erotic love and their relative value that would have been of great interest to the more sophisticated members of the audience. It is difficult to tell how seriously the main plot was meant to be taken; Proteus attempts to betray both his best friend and the woman he is committed to but is so ineffectual as to appear ridiculous. The ending is quite arbitrary: Proteus's treachery in attempting to steal Silvia from Valentine is discovered; Proteus professes shame; Valentine, in true friendly fashion, forgives him and offers to give Silvia to him, as if she were an object with no will of her own. The happy resolution, unlike that of *The Taming of the Shrew*, is quite unearned. It is tempting to take all of this as parody but it is very thin, and the play's main comic interest comes in the scenes containing the servants Speed and, especially, Launce (and his shoes and his dog).

Julia is the only character in the play's main plot with whom the audience can have much sympathy because her experiences generate real anxiety. When she takes on her disguise she is isolated within the play, her identity known only to the audience. While herself remaining an embodiment of constancy (and an ironic emblem of the 'truth' of dramatic illusion), she becomes the observer of her own betrayal, but this partially detaches her from the play; she inhabits a kind of middle ground between the other characters and the audience, making ambiguous comments or speaking in asides that have a meaning fully available only to the audience. Thus, after Proteus sings 'Who is Silvia' Julia says to the Host

'He plays false, father' (4.2.57). Her comment has three levels of meaning. The Host naturally assumes that she is referring to the music, when, as the audience is aware, she is referring to Proteus's betrayal of her. Her use of the word 'play' in this context also serves as a reminder of where we are. Shakespeare himself, in playing with the idea of playing, has also found a means of manipulating the audience's responses by aligning them with a particular perspective.

Both this play and *The Taming of the Shrew* seem to exhibit some uneasiness in their concern with romantic love. What real substance can there be in the quick-change love of Proteus, or the regard that Valentine has for Silvia that allows him to donate her to Proteus? Lucentio falls in love with Bianca's beauty without knowing anything about her, and the play's conclusion hardly holds out much optimism for his future happiness. Love for him has been based upon delusion, a false image of the beloved generated out of Petrarchan attitudes and Ovidian stories. In *Love's Labour's Lost* Shakespeare examines in much more detail questions of the value of romantic love and its relation to literary convention.

How can love be expressed? If it is expressed through words, how is one to demonstrate the superiority of one's own love over that of others who use the same words? How is the beauty of the loved one to be described if words have become conventional through over-use? What, indeed, is the relationship between a word and its meaning? Love has to be expressed through words, but words keep slipping away from their meanings. On her first appearance the Princess of France responds to Boyet's praise of her beauty:

> Good Lord Boyet, my beauty, though but mean,
> Needs not the painted flourish of your praise.
> Beauty is bought by judgment of the eye,
> Not utter'd by base sale of chapmen's tongues.
>
> (2.1.13–16)

She rejects the language of praise, perceiving it as artificial adornment, and further links it to the materialistic concerns of buying and selling. As it happens, Boyet is not a lover but a kind of professional wit and flatterer, and his words *are* 'painted' in that their sincerity is open to question. But what is a true lover to do, since he too must use language that can be dismissed as 'painted'? (King Lear raises the same dangerous question, with far more terrifying results, when he demands that each of his daughters 'tell' her love.)

The play's aristocratic young men begin by attempting to deny love altogether, along with time and its injuries, by retreating from the world into an academy given over to the life of the mind. Confronted by a group of women they swing to the opposite extreme of erotic self-submission. The women have the advantage of a much more realistic view of erotic desire, and the contest that develops between the two groups is really about the ability of language, and especially language elaborated by convention and affectation, to express truth. In the sub-plot comic characters try to pin down the meanings of words in a range of ways, from the euphuistic affectation of Armado, through the pedantic rephrasings of Holofernes, to the puns and malapropisms of Costard and Dull. 'Truth is truth', says Costard, but he hits on the truth only by accident and what we see is the disturbing slipperiness of language, its potential to become dislocated from truth. The young aristocrats are involved in a kind of dance, and when 'real life' intrudes with the announcement of the death of the Princess's father, the dance ends without resolution: the men have taken it for reality, the women as a game. The customary happy ending is deferred for a year, during which the men will have to prove their sincerity by performing various tasks in the real world. There is no reassurance that Jack will have Jill at the end of the year, however; as Berowne says, 'That's too long for a play' (5.2.868).

*A Midsummer Night's Dream* is Shakespeare's most complex and most comprehensive account of romantic illusion. Love is seen, in effect, as fantasy, an inexplicable and irrational preference. In the opening scene there is division between Hermia, who wishes to marry Lysander, and her father Egeus, who wishes her to marry Demetrius, which precipitates a move out from the oppressive court world to the healing green world of the forest. Egeus's demand seems arbitrary given that, as Lysander says, the two young men are alike in most things (1.1.99–102); however, the play shows that the choices of love are also arbitrary, a matter of 'dotage'. The irrationality of love is represented by the actions of the fairies, particularly Puck, whose manipulation of the affections of the four young lovers from one object to another suggests that love has no grounding in anything real. When the lovers are restored to one another at the end of the play it is poetically but uneasily satisfying.

The unease comes from a sense that behind the apparent selflessness of romantic love there lies only appetite, the desire to impose one's own needs upon the object of love. This appears to be the case with Oberon and Titania, the play's married couple. Their quarrel over the changeling boy is explosive enough to cause disorder in nature, and there is something ugly and violent in Oberon's willingness to humiliate his wife in order to get his way. This violence echoes that of Theseus in his winning of Hippolyta: 'I woo'd thee with my sword, / And won thy love doing thee injuries' (1.1.16–17), he says to her, and indeed Theseus's history of relationships with women is a history of violence and betrayal, as indicated by Oberon:

> Didst thou not lead him through the glimmering night
> From Perigouna, whom he ravished,
> And make him with fair Aegles break his faith,
> With Ariadne, and Antiopa?
>
> (2.1.77–80)

The civilizing influence of an ordered society holds appetite in check, but it is there in the play as an alarming presence.

It is ironic, given his history, that Theseus should be the play's figure of authority. His central role does not mean that the audience should unquestioningly accept his point of view, however, for like *Love's Labour's Lost* the play exposes the complacency of aristocratic culture and values. Bottom and his friends may not have much of a grasp either of the ethos of romantic love or of the principles of theatre, insisting as they do on making illusion impossible (they do not need a Boyet to deny it for them). Theseus does purport to be an expert on these things, but his condescension towards the mechanicals has far less of human warmth and generosity in it than do their 'tongue-tied' offerings. At the least the play opens itself up to opposed interpretations, and we could read the final act as an allegory of what popular theatre could offer to official court culture.

The disturbing idea that love is appetite, or a sublimated form of materialism, casts a shadow in all these plays. An overt statement of it could upset the delicate balance of romance. In *The Merchant of Venice* the play's two worlds, romantic Belmont and commercial

Venice, collide, and although Portia's aristocratic wealth is an inherited fortune that seems uncontaminated by Venetian business, the commercial values of Venice pervade romantic Belmont also. Bassanio, having wasted his own estate, uses the credit of his friend Antonio to pursue Portia's 'golden fleece' (1.1.170). The phrase is double, combining the romantic overtones of mythical quest with the materialist recognition that Portia is 'a lady richly left' (161), and though Bassanio acknowledges that she is fair and virtuous, it is her commercial value that first comes to his mind.

Shylock, likewise unsure whether he values his daughter more than his ducats, is the representative figure of Venice because his venality and malice are replicated in his Christian enemies. The self-sacrificing merchant Antonio, who hates him for his business practices and his Jewishness, nevertheless agrees to a bond that equates his own flesh with money. Evaluation, the difference between appearance and reality here, is firmly tied to commercial matters. 'O what a goodly outside falsehood hath' (1.3.97) Antonio says of Shylock, implying that hypocrisy is the key to Shylock's commercial success. This is the wisdom of Venice: don't be taken in by appearances. But it is also the wisdom that underlies Bassanio's success in winning Portia. 'So may the outward shows be least themselves' (3.2.73) are the first lines of a lengthy speech that states and re-states the one idea. Bassanio chooses the right casket not because he is above material considerations (he clearly is not) but because he practises Venetian shrewdness.

It is often said that Portia is the only one who can resolve Antonio's problem because she is outside the sordid affairs of Venice, but she defeats Shylock not by the law but by a trick. No doubt Shylock deserves this, and no doubt he deserves no mercy, but how are we to understand the vengefulness of the woman who has spoken so eloquently on the subject of mercy? This is one reason why many people are disturbed by the treatment of Shylock: he receives justice but it is tainted by the fact that it comes from characters whose motives are twisted. The sourness of this is projected into the final act, which begins with Shylock's daughter Jessica, his representative and betrayer, who remains as a constant reminder of the discords through which the musical harmonies of the happy ending have been achieved.

In Portia we see Shakespeare beginning to endow his female characters with an increasing amount of power, and he continued in this direction in the comedies that followed. In the history plays women exist mainly on the margins of masculine, public activity, but comedy has the potential to focus on domestic and private worlds. In *The Merry Wives of Windsor* the two wives, Mistress Page and Mistress Ford, are given most of the comic authority in the play, which is particularly interesting in a play that contains Sir John Falstaff. There is a legend that Shakespeare wrote this play on the orders of Queen Elizabeth, who wanted to see Falstaff in love. Whether or not this is true, Shakespeare had other reasons for his attempt in this play to break new ground. The Admiral's Men, rivals to Shakespeare's company, had enjoyed considerable success with new comic sub-genres. In 1596 they presented George Chapman's *The Blind Beggar of Alexandria*, the first extant 'humours comedy', which satirized the affectations or excesses of characters understood to be suffering from an imbalance of the elements known as humours. Two years later the Admiral's Men performed William Haughton's *Englishmen for My Money*, the earliest known 'citizen comedy'. Citizen comedies had local and contemporary settings and dealt with the material and moral values of the developing middle class. *The Merry Wives of Windsor* has affinities with both these kinds.

Shakespeare transported the characters of the comic sub-plot of the *Henry IV* plays into the bourgeois Windsor world and set them into an intrigue involving jealousy and an attempt to avoid enforced marriage. Falstaff is the play's comic centre but not its comic intelligence. Self-intoxicated, he sees himself, without irony, as a lover and becomes entangled in a complicated attempt at seduction that turns him into a clown. He is the victim not only of his former London companions, but also of the wives, who are endowed with comic power as well as good sense. Although the play has a satirical element its tone is genial, and at the play's end Falstaff is punished for his ludicrous excesses but is not excluded from the social healing of the Pages' feast. What is particularly notable about *The Merry Wives of Windsor* is that, in spite of the unfounded jealousy that partially drives the plot, it contains the established, more-or-less stable marriages that are absent from other Shakespearean plays.

*Much Ado about Nothing*, like *As You Like It* and *Twelfth Night; or, What You Will* that followed it, proclaims itself by its title as a thing of light pleasure, but this play offers a potentially disturbing experience. The story of a soldier who is tricked by a malicious colleague into believing the woman he loves has betrayed him is

reworked as tragedy in the later *Othello*; and indeed in this play
the plot mimics tragedy, for Claudio's accusation and rejection
of Hero causes her to swoon, allowing her friends to make public
the claim that she is dead. The slander against Hero even convinces
her father, who thinks it better for her to die than live in shame,
revealing even in him a male materialist valuation of women:
loss of virginity means loss of worth.

The play, of course, works towards a comic resolution of the
situation and we need not take all this too seriously. The villain
Don John is little more than a device who disappears from the
play after his work is done, and we know even before the accusation
is made that the characters in the comic sub-plot have in Borachio
the evidence to exonerate Hero. But there is something more to
it than this. Much in the play happens in an oblique way that
has to do with theatricality, with disguises and shows. A masked
Don Pedro woos Hero on Claudio's behalf, Don John sets up
Hero's servant to pose as Hero, Hero acts her own death and
then pretends to be her cousin to marry Claudio. This obliqueness
has its effect on the relationship that most interests the audience,
that between Beatrice and Benedick. These two share a genuine
friendship that the audience recognizes as love, though the
characters do not. They disguise their feelings, from others and
from themselves, by a show of mockery, and only embrace the
truth and one another after yet another theatrical manipulation
by Don Pedro. We seem to be in a world where what is true can
never be certainly known, and where the manipulation of illusion
is one of the mechanisms of power. In this *Much Ado about Nothing*
has affinities with the 'problem' play *Measure for Measure*.

The true centre of *Much Ado* is Beatrice. In his romantic comedies
Shakespeare had increasingly given the most comic intelligence
and human warmth to his main female character, and in the two
comedies that followed, *As You Like It* and *Twelfth Night*, he found
a way to expand the theatrical power of this character by exploiting
to its fullest the use of transvestite disguise. In his two earlier
experiments with the device he had confined its use to a small
part of the play: Julia's disguise in *The Two Gentlemen of Verona*
mainly exploits the pathos of a situation in which she observes
her own betrayal, and the chief function of Portia's in *The Merchant
of Venice* is to allow her to perform in the masculine domain of
the law court. In these later plays Shakespeare gets his characters
into disguise as early as possible and then allows most of the

dramatic complication to arise out of the disguise. The two plays differ from each other in that Rosalind is freed by her disguise and becomes a kind of dramatist-figure in her manipulation of the plot, while Viola is trapped in her disguise and can be released only by the appearance of her twin brother.

*As You Like It* has elements of pastoral comedy; it begins when a number of characters flee the repressions of city life for what they take to be the freedom of the forest. Within this framework the play gently mocks a number of literary conventions, including Robin Hood-style illusions of liberty and the main focus of pastoral, the desirability of the shepherd's life. The mockery is finely calibrated, for the satirical mode itself is mocked in the figure of Jaques. The play has a splendid fool in Touchstone who demonstrates, at least to his own satisfaction, the inferiority of pastoral life, and at its end most of the city characters return to the court, perhaps renewed, but acknowledging that pastoral holiday is only a temporary escape from reality.

It is Rosalind, however, who most absorbs our interest. Her freedom to test out masculine experience allows her to function both inside and outside her role. 'I'll prove a busy actor in their play' (3.4.55) she says as she decides to interfere in the affairs of Silvius and Phebe, and she could also be referring to her function in the play itself. The deeply theatrical trick of allowing her, disguised as the youth Ganymede, to play herself for Orlando permits a complex examination of male and female erotic and emotional experience. She gains an empathy with masculine feelings that equips her to educate Orlando out of his Petrarchan excess into an understanding of love that is as realistic as her own, and no less profound for that. 'Men have died from time to time', she says, 'and worms have eaten them, but not for love' (4.1.101–3). Love has an important place, but it must be kept in perspective. Rosalind's metadramatic self-consciousness is the catalyst for all healing revelations in this play. If the attitude to theatricality in *Much Ado about Nothing* was ambivalent, we seem here to have a complete endorsement of the integrative power of theatre, for when she presents the masque that resolves all the play's confusions Rosalind becomes a figure of the playwright and vindicates his art.

As its title implies, *Twelfth Night* is about festive misrule. At opposite extremes are Malvolio who, Puritan-like, wishes for a kind of order that would preclude most kinds of pleasure, and Sir Toby Belch, who would embrace complete lawlessness if he could get away with it. Their competition for power provides one locus of the play's comic action. At the play's end Malvolio is humiliated and excludes himself from the final reordering, while Sir Toby gets a wife, the conventional reward of romantic comedy. This is, to say the least, a disturbing resolution, but it is appropriate for a play that is at once very entertaining and shot through with a deep melancholy.

The other locus of the comic action is provided by Viola's disguise and the confusions it generates. Whereas Rosalind's secret is shared by Celia and Touchstone, Viola's isolates her and traps her in a situation that gives her a degree of anxiety: she is made to woo Olivia on behalf of Orsino, with whom she has fallen in love herself, and she becomes the object of Sir Andrew's threatened violence. This is, of course, comic stuff, but the poetry that it generates reaffirms the melancholy, as when Viola indirectly reveals her feelings to Orsino:

> she never told her love,
> But let concealment like a worm i' the bud
> Feed on her damask cheek: she pin'd in thought,
> And with a green and yellow melancholy
> She sat like Patience on a monument,
> Smiling at grief.

(2.4.111–16)

There is deep emotion, in spite of the playfulness, behind these words, and they provide a sharp contrast to the self-indulgent pose of melancholy struck by Orsino in the play's opening speech.

In her disguise Viola finds herself at the centre of a set of mis-understandings that she is powerless to clear up: 'O time, thou must untangle this, not I! / It is too hard a knot for me t'untie' (2.2.40–1). The rueful way in which she gives herself up to time may be the key to this play, for although time will resolve her problems it is also the enemy of the comic. We might consider that *Twelfth Night* is the last night of Christmas festivities, and in Elizabethan England in early January people had little to look forward to but hard work, to winter and rough weather. The play's fool, Feste, is perhaps ironically-named, for he is the saddest of Shakespeare's comic fools, and as the play ends he is left alone on the stage to sing a song about failure, time, age and the rain raining every day. The song is appropriate considering that beside the happy pairing of the two young couples we have experienced the parody-marriage of Sir Toby and Maria, the unresolved torment of Malvolio, the harsh casting-off of Sir Andrew and the peculiar segregation of Antonio. There is enough 'sportful malice' here to darken the conclusion considerably. *Twelfth Night* perhaps signals that the romantic comic form no longer satisfied the dramatist's needs.

*Troilus and Cressida, All's Well That Ends Well* and *Measure for Measure*, written between 1601 and 1605, raise further questions about comic form and tone. They have been variously termed 'dark' and 'bitter' comedies, 'problem comedies', and even 'problem plays', avoiding the word 'comedy' altogether. Any real problems seem to lie as much in the critical need for definition as in the plays themselves, however. The ending of *Twelfth Night*, with so many characters excluded from the celebration, suggests that Shakespeare felt dissatisfied with the manner in which romantic comedy resolved the real tensions and issues that it raised. Even the happy coupling of Viola and Orsino raises questions: Viola goes off to marry a man who a few minutes before had threatened to kill her, and even though he was not aware of her real nature his threats leave a taint of unpleasantness in the atmosphere. Romantic resolution depends on illusion, on magical or arbitrary transformations, or on an assumption that unpleasantness can be forgotten, that Julia will still want to marry the man who attempted to betray her or that Hero can forgive Claudio's outrageous treatment of her. The problem plays openly acknowledge the unpleasant elements of the appetites and urges that drive their plots, and they work in terms of a conflict between form and content, which is why their endings seem unsatisfying to many.

*Troilus and Cressida* might not indeed be a comedy, although it is termed such in an epistle attached to the 1609 quarto edition. The 1623 Folio version offers two endings, with Pandarus dismissed by Troilus at the end of 5.3 and again at the play's end. One of these must be cut for performance. If Pandarus is dismissed at 5.3 the play will end with Troilus's agonized speech about Hector's death and his vow of revenge, which is tragic in tone. However, if Pandarus is not dismissed at this point the play ends with his comic epilogue, sending the audience away in a different frame of mind. The same material, that is, can be seen as either tragic or comic in emphasis, but the play's form resists any true closure, insisting on its indeterminacy.

In so far as it is a love story *Troilus and Cressida* mocks the romantic. Troilus is like many of the young lovers of the earlier comedies or like Romeo, constructing out of Cressida before he has even met her an ideal image of immutable virtue and love. When she betrays him he is emotionally and mentally shattered, unable to grasp what is real. At the same time, however, it is suggested that his attempt to idealize his own love is really no more than a sublimation of his appetites, as Pandarus suggests in the opening scene when he compares Troilus's attempt to win Cressida to baking a cake. Cressida is hardly an ideal woman, but she is not a bad one either. She does indeed betray Troilus, but she herself has been betrayed both by her father and her uncle, her supposed protectors, and has been used by the Trojans as a piece of currency, exchanged for the captured Antenor. She is the victim of a masculine world of materialist and military intrigue.

This decidedly unromantic handling of romantic material runs parallel to a plot in which the great leaders and heroes of the Trojan War are deflated by a corrosive satirical treatment that, in Shakespeare's canon, is approached only by *Timon of Athens*. The mythical figures are diminished into petty fools and braggarts, especially as they fall victim to the satirical scorn of Thersites, who knows well the destructive power of language. The stage itself becomes the means by which the pettiness of their motivation is revealed. In few of Shakespeare's plays is the theatrical metaphor so pervasive; characters are constantly playing roles, or directing others in roles, or being made into spectators. The clear implication is that identity is no more than a role, that these puny figures are merely playing at being heroes and lovers.[23] What is real? When Pandarus tries to describe Troilus to Cressida she mocks his description with 'true and not true' (1.2.98). Having observed Cressida's betrayal of him Troilus says 'This is, and is not, Cressid' (5.2.145). The play constantly acknowledges opposing possibilities, and that is reflected in its ending, which resists closure, and resists formal definition.

*All's Well That Ends Well* is less problematic in form, but its ending too is unsettled. It has all the trappings of romantic comedy, including Helena's near-magical curing of the dying King of France (she presents herself as an instrument of divine will, and this has led to Christian readings of the play, but her skills can be seen as reflecting generic convention). Helena is unshakably in love with Bertram, who is unshakably not in love with her. The King rewards her by making Bertram marry her, but the young man immediately abandons her and embarks on a military career that also includes seduction, hypocrisy and a good deal of straightforward lying. Helena wins him back through an elaborate set of illusions that involve disguise and a bed-trick (she goes to bed with Bertram who thinks she is someone else).

What can we say of Helena's triumph? The fact is that she is far too good for Bertram and yet is unable to stop loving a totally unworthy object. Although Bertram asks for pardon once his lies are revealed, he has done his best to weasel out of all his responsibilities and there is no reason to believe that his feelings for his wife have changed. The play's title must be understood ironically; its words are modified in the closing lines spoken by the King: 'All yet seems well, and if it end so meet, / The bitter past, more welcome is the sweet' (5.3.327–8). The 'seems' and the 'if' here leave closure insecure; after what we have seen there is not much reason to believe in the happy ending.

Of course, one could argue that the source of the problem is the King himself. His use of his authority to force an unwanted marriage on Bertram is no less questionable than Egeus's attempt to force Hermia to marry a man she does not love, and yet the play seems to present as reasonable what *A Midsummer Night's Dream* presents as unreasonable. The use of authority or political power to enforce comic resolution is a disturbing element of *Measure for Measure*, where the figure of authority, Duke Vincentio, is the source of most of the uneasiness. At the beginning of the play the Duke withdraws from Vienna because it has become necessary to enforce laws against unruly sexual behaviour and the Duke is unwilling to associate himself with the required repression, even though, presumably, it was his laxness that allowed behaviour to become excessive. His deputy, the Puritan Angelo, is a man apparently in control of his feelings and only too happy to be the repressor. Inevitably, Angelo finds his self-control tested by the chastity as well as the beauty of the novice nun Isabella, and reveals himself as a predatory hypocrite because of his desire to seduce her and his refusal to grant mercy to her brother Claudio, who is under sentence of death for precisely the act that Angelo wishes to commit.

Whether any law can control human desire is open to question, but having created the problems, the Duke, disguised as a friar, spends much of the play trying to solve them. In doing so he subjects Claudio and, more particularly, Isabella to a great deal of unnecessary anxiety, and he has to resort to a lot of dubious theatrical trickery before he can bring about a semblance of order through the four marriages he organizes. As the symbol of social integration marriage is the conventional resolution of romantic comedy, but here it is clear that the Duke is using marriage as an instrument of social control and repression. Of the four marriages two at least are punitive. The marriage of Angelo to Mariana, a woman he had previously abandoned, has affinities with that of Helena and Bertram. Mariana, in spite of the treatment she has received from Angelo, continues to love him, but there is nothing to indicate that Angelo marries her willingly. Lucio, the cynical lecher and liar (whose loyalty to Claudio is paradoxically one of the most human aspects of this play) certainly does not wish to marry a whore, and nobody asks the whore what she wants. The Duke's own proposal to Isabella is the most problematic. She responds to it with silence, and although given the social attitudes of the time it is improbable that she would refuse such an offer, it is also unthinkable, given the pain and humiliation she has suffered, that she would willingly accept it.

This ending suggests that Shakespeare was sceptical of the ability of theatre, of convention or of political authority to order the consequences of human desire. *Measure for Measure* looks back on the romantic comedies and presents a 'happy' ending so troubled that it challenges the endings of all those sunnier plays. Isabella's silence is, perhaps, an eloquent statement of how far Shakespeare had moved, by 1604, away from the sunny implications of romantic comedy along a path whose darker outlines can, however, be perceived even in his earliest plays.

When in 1608 the King's Men moved into the Blackfriars Theatre they must have inherited at least some of its more sophisticated audience, and this might be part of the reason for Shakespeare's development, in the last years of his career, of a new kind of hybrid play. Around 1607 John Fletcher had written *The Faithful Shepherdess*, a pastoral tragicomedy. Tragicomedy subjects its main characters to the anxieties of tragedy but ends happily, usually as a result of a surprising turn of events. Shakespeare might have been influenced by Fletcher, who also wrote for the King's Men and collaborated with Shakespeare on two or more plays. Shakespeare's last plays are more often called 'romances' than 'tragicomedies', but both words identify them as developments from a fundamentally comic structure. What the romances have in common is a willingness to take extreme liberties with dramatic conventions. *Pericles*, *Cymbeline* and *The Winter's Tale* all involve untidy plots and large dislocations in time and place; *The Tempest* does the opposite, concentrating its minimal action with complete regard for the unities of time and space. All make use of sensational or magical incidents of the kind associated with fairy-tales, within a plot that has at its centre a story of loss and restoration.

*Pericles* was not included in the 1623 folio, perhaps because much of it was not Shakespeare's work. Its plot subjects Pericles to the loss of both his wife Thaisa and his daughter Marina whom he believes to be dead, but directed by dreams he recovers both of them. In the major tragedies the death of an innocent woman is the most terrible part of the protagonist's suffering: Ophelia, Desdemona, Cordelia – 'gone for ever', as Lear says. The final romances defy this irreversible fact of tragedy by allowing re-birth and restoration; in each play either the loss or the recovery is in some way associated with the sea, which takes on mystical transformative powers, as in Ariel's song in *The Tempest*: 'Nothing of him that doth fade, / But doth suffer a sea-change / Into something rich and strange' (1.2.402–4).

The plot of *Cymbeline* has much in common with *Othello* in that the loss of Imogen comes about through falsely-aroused jealousy. In this case Shakespeare returned also to the device he had used in earlier comedies of having his heroine disguise herself as a boy. Imogen's experience in this guise is different from that of the earlier heroines, however, for her situation generates pathos and she is constantly vulnerable, at the edge of mental and emotional torment, which at its most extreme has her believing that the headless Cloten is her husband Leonatus. The resolution involves ghosts and the descent of Jupiter on an eagle, as if defiantly insisting that only the miraculous can bring about closure. What we are seeing here is the yoking together of reality and artifice: however preposterous the events in which the characters find themselves entangled, the pain they feel and the harm they do are real enough. The pattern of guilt, expiation and restoration has led many critics to read these plays as Christian allegories, but they might better be seen as exploring the possibilities and limitations of art. Perhaps Shakespeare's main concern in these last plays is with the claims of art to transcend time and shape reality.

*The Winter's Tale* most poignantly represents the healing power of art as well as the limits of that power. Once again Shakespeare turned to the problem of misdirected jealousy, but Leontes' suspicion is more disturbing than Othello's or Claudio's because it does not have the excuse of false evidence generated by a villain. Leontes is his own villain and the isolating ferocity of his self-inflicted suffering is terrifying in itself, but it also causes the death of his son, the apparent death of his wife and the loss of his daughter. At its mid-point the play reverses its direction from the winter of tragedy to the summer of pastoral comedy. The change is announced by the allegorical figure of Time 'that makes and unfolds error' and who claims the power 'To o'erthrow law, and in one self-born hour / To plant and o'erwhelm custom' (4.1.2, 8–9). The powers Time is claiming are clearly the powers of the play itself, and the remainder of the play repairs the damage done by Leontes. However not all things can be repaired. Paulina's magic trick with the apparent statue of Hermione is an analogue of what theatrical art can do. As she reveals the statue to Leontes she demonstrates an art so like reality that Leontes says of it 'The fixture of her eye has motion in't, / As we are mock'd with art' (5.3.67–8). In bringing the statue to life Paulina heals the broken family and enables the harmonious ending. Her illusion cannot evade its own limitations, however. Hermione is not a statue and Paulina has presented the illusion of an illusion. She cannot make it overcome time: she cannot erase Hermione's wrinkles any more than she can restore Mamillius and Antigonus to life. The play is a marvellous work of art but it seems to suggest that art does indeed only mock us.

The authority of art and the relationship of art to authority preoccupied Shakespeare throughout his career. In setting into play competing voices, competing perspectives, competing ideologies, Shakespeare's art both reflected and gave shape to the energies that informed his culture. Whether or not we see *The Tempest* as Shakespeare's farewell to the stage, we can hardly avoid seeing how the illusion-maker Prospero exemplifies the self-contradictions of artistic authority. What is discovered in him is that theatrical authority is like political authority in that it generates illusions that are intended to liberate but that might actually repress, like Gonzalo's self-contradictory utopia. Prospero's power heals, in its way, but its healing power cannot be separated from its power to dominate. To make his magic work he needs the enslaved

Ariel and Caliban, and even his daughter's growth is carefully controlled by him. The benevolent enchanter and the tyrant are inseparable one from the other, just as the liberating and the manipulative powers of theatre are inseparable.

*The Tempest* explicitly connects theatre to oppression. Caliban is seen as a savage, even a monster, by the other characters, yet his comforting words to Stephano that 'the isle is full of noises, / Sounds and sweet airs, that give delight, and hurt not' (3.2.133–4) indicate in him the tattered remnants of a poetic innocence. From his own perspective he is Prospero's victim, bent out of shape when the usurper stole from him the island that was his by right of inheritance from his mother. If we see Prospero as both creator of illusions and authoritarian ruler it is difficult to avoid identifying theatrical power with political power.

If we remember Shakespeare's concern with the disquieting ambiguities of theatre in such early plays as *The Comedy of Errors* and *Richard III* it may appear that he has come full circle. The ambiguities of Elizabethan and Jacobean theatre, however, were both intrinsic and extrinsic, there both in the medium itself and in the culture it observed. The plays reflect and project a monarchy that cloaked itself in the mysteries of myth and paradox, a court that had an intensely theatrical conception of power, and a populace that was faced with constantly shifting surfaces and meanings. Even at their most self-reflexive, when they seem most preoccupied with theatricality and the trickery of illusion, Shakespeare's plays, like those of his contemporaries, are powerfully concerned with the instability of the 'real' world they reflect.

## HISTORIES

During the last decade of the sixteenth century Shakespeare wrote a series of plays about English kings, which examined such issues as the nature of leadership and especially the sanctity and duties of kingship, the value of nationalism, the causes of civil unrest and the dangers of rebellion. These plays fall into two groups of four, called 'tetralogies'. The first tetralogy, probably written between 1589 and 1594, consists of the three parts of *Henry VI* and *Richard III*; the second, probably written between 1595 and 1599 includes *Richard II*, the two parts of *Henry IV* and *Henry V*. There is also a play called *King John*, perhaps written between

1594 and 1596 between the two tetralogies. *Henry VIII*, written at the end of Shakespeare's career, fits only very loosely into the category. As well as these plays about English history Shakespeare wrote three plays about Roman history: *Julius Caesar* around 1599 and *Antony and Cleopatra* and *Coriolanus* between 1606 and 1608. These plays were included by Heminges and Condell amongst the tragedies, but they deal with issues related to those of the English histories, of leadership and the state.

Before going any further, we need to ask what Shakespeare's audience would have understood by 'history' as a body of knowledge, and we need to consider the implications of the term 'history' as defining a dramatic genre. Holinshed's *Chronicles of England, Scotlande and Irelande* is the source of much of the material that went into all of these history plays. Holinshed apparently did not make a great distinction between 'real' history and pseudo-history, for his *Chronicles* mixed the legendary with the real, including the stories of King Lear and Cymbeline alongside those of the medieval English kings. Even his accounts of historical figures embrace unsubstantiated rumour and frankly improbable incidents. For the Elizabethan historian it was not so much the literal truth of history that mattered, as the didactic uses to which it could be put. History provided a vast array of examples and models through which contemporary events could be understood.

However crude it may seem to us today, Holinshed's work represents Elizabethan historiography at its most rigorous scholarly level. Many of those who attended Shakespeare's plays, being illiterate, would have gained their knowledge from even less reliable sources: from ballads and sermons. Ballads stressed the romantic and the sensational in the stories they told, while sermons were more concerned to exploit the moralistic possibilities of their stories. The history plays were themselves a source of historical knowledge of a sort, and may have been, for many in the audience, the only source. This is suggested in the remark by Thomas Heywood, a dramatist contemporary with Shakespeare, in his *Apology for Actors* (1612), that 'plays have made the ignorant more apprehensive, taught the unlearned the knowledge of many famous histories, instructed such as cannot read in the discovery of all our English chronicles'.[24]

History, as Shakespeare's audience would have understood it, was about the lives of the powerful, about kings and queens, emperors and tyrants. It was cyclical in form and fundamentally tragic. This concept of history can be perceived in the work of the Italian poet Giovanni Boccaccio who around 1363–4 published his *De Casibus Virorum Illustrium*, a collection of stories about great men falling from apparently secure power and happiness to catastrophic misfortune. Boccaccio provided a pattern for the careers of illustrious men which, put simply, saw them as fixed to Fortune's wheel; success was inevitably followed by disaster because the wheel never stopped turning. The '*de casibus*' concept of tragedy set out in Boccaccio's book had an influence throughout medieval Europe and retained its potency in Elizabethan England, informing such popular compilations as *The Mirror for Magistrates*, first published in 1559. As its title implies, *The Mirror for Magistrates* presents its tragic stories of figures from history as a lesson for contemporary rulers, but it moves away from the *de casibus* pattern by assuming in rulers the moral freedom to imitate or to reject the models it offers them: 'For here as in a looking glass, you shall see (if any vice be in you) how the like hath been punished in other heretofore, whereby admonished, I trust it will be a good occasion to move you to the sooner amendment.'[25]

The idea that history moved in patterns and had a moral meaning obviously had its uses as propaganda. We have seen that Henry VII and Henry VIII wanted to make English history prove the right of the Tudors to the English throne, and to that end they had employed historians. Throughout the Tudor period there was a concern to understand the shape and meaning of historical events, and a number of books were published that contributed much to Shakespeare's own explorations of English history. In 1548 Edward Hall's *The Union of the two Noble and Illustre Famelies of Lancastre and Yorke* appeared posthumously; this book fed into Holinshed's massive *Chronicles*. The second edition of Holinshed's work (1587) is the source of most of Shakespeare's historical material, although he made use of many other sources, including going directly to Hall.[26]

In the sweep of history, from the dethronement of Richard II and his murder in 1400 to the triumphant ascent to the throne of Henry Tudor, Earl of Richmond, as Henry VII in 1485, the Tudor historians found a providential pattern. The civil unrest that marked the reign of Henry IV was punishment of his regicide of Richard, a punishment of both king and country. His son Henry V saw a few brief years of triumph but they ended with his death, and the reigns of Henry VI, Edward IV and Richard III saw the greater civil turmoil of the Wars of the Roses. The agony of a divided England was seen as divine retribution, with the reign of Richard III as its bloody climax. The triumph of Richmond and the foundation of the Tudor dynasty could thus be seen as God's will made manifest. This is a conservative myth of great power. The legacy of bloodshed that came of the dethronement of Richard II stands as a terrible warning to those who would revolt against a monarch, and this is reinforced by the Tudor claim to rule by divine appointment.

As we know, it has been argued that all Elizabethans believed in this Tudor myth of order, and that Shakespeare's plays reflect this.[27] The final speech of *Richard III*, certainly, may seem to show that Shakespeare held the providential view of Tudor divine right. Richmond, having defeated the monstrous Richard and triumphantly wearing the crown, foresees the country reunited through his marriage to Elizabeth of York, and their descendants ruling over an ordered land:

> O, now let Richmond and Elizabeth,
> The true succeeders of each royal house,
> By God's fair ordinance conjoin together!
> And let their heirs, God, if Thy will be so,
> Enrich the time to come with smooth-faced peace,
> With smiling plenty, and fair prosperous days!
>
> (5.5.29–34)

The words are a prayer, but they are prophetic too, pointing forward to the moment at which Shakespeare is writing, when Richmond's granddaughter, another Elizabeth, rules over a land of peace, plenty and prosperity.

We know, as Shakespeare did, that this vision of Elizabethan England was not entirely an accurate one, but the realities of the English political situation and the constant threat of censorship made it impossible for him to deal directly with issues that he knew to be sensitive. It can hardly be doubted, however, that the issue that most deeply concerned the English was the future of their country. When Shakespeare began writing for the stage (that is, when he wrote his first history plays) the childless Elizabeth, approaching 60, steadfastly refused to name a successor and kept her subjects in a state of doubt about what would happen to the country after her death. During her reign she had defeated enemies abroad and had brought a degree of internal stability to England. But while the defeat of the Spanish Armada of 1588 had generated immense nationalistic pride, it had also reminded the English that their country was vulnerable; and there was no shortage of plots and rumours of plots against the throne. It is hardly surprising, then, that Shakespeare should have used the theatre to stage civil unrest and division, and to examine the workings of power.

Shakespeare was not the only author of history plays. The *Annals of English Drama* records more than 80 plays apparently dealing with English history for the period between 1586 and 1606, with the majority appearing during the 1590s, and we can be sure that there were many more examples of the genre that are now lost to us.[28] We cannot entirely explain away this enthusiasm as a sudden popular interest in history as such, although that certainly was a component of it. As a theatrical subject history offered rich material: pageant and spectacle, tense scenes of combat and violence, and stirring and bombastic speeches given by larger-than-life heroes. However, we have to see history plays also as political texts which dealt obliquely with pressing contemporary issues by displacing consideration of them into the past.

Seen in this way, Shakespeare's histories look somewhat less whole-heartedly patriotic than Richmond's speech might suggest. By staging conflicts of power, the plays offer competing perspectives, setting the sceptical alongside the patriotic. They examine the workings of authority and they subject aristocratic values to ironic scrutiny. A school of historicist criticism more recent than Tillyard's has argued that Shakespeare's theatre was only allowed to exist so long as it supported official ideology, and that whenever Renaissance drama allows subversive voices to speak it always finally contains and silences them; as Stephen Greenblatt puts it, 'the form [of drama] itself, as a primary expression of Renaissance power, helps to contain the radical doubts it continually provokes'.[29] I should say, however, that if once a drama has provoked 'radical doubts', those doubts will continue to resonate simply as the result of having been voiced. Whatever Shakespeare's personal views might have been, his history plays do give voice to the potentially subversive.

The four plays of the first tetralogy deal with the period between the death of Henry V in 1422 and the defeat of Richard III by Henry Tudor in 1485. This is a great deal of history to be compressed into some 12 hours on the stage, and Shakespeare felt at liberty to telescope time and to manipulate the recorded details that he found in his sources in order to give dramatic shape and political meaning to the material. For example, Part One of *Henry VI* spans the period from the death of Henry V in 1422 to the Truce of Tours in 1444. Its climax is the death of Talbot at the hands of French forces led by Joan La Pucelle. In fact, Joan was executed in 1431 and Talbot's death did not take place until 1453, but by bringing the two into close proximity Shakespeare is able to clarify in a fine dramatic moment the issues of nationalism and betrayal that are at the centre of this play. Again, Part Two ends with York's victory at the Battle of St Albans, and has his son Richard, who in fact was only two years old at the time, as a powerful figure. This allows for Richard's eventual emergence as the fullest and most potent of a series of machiavellian figures that begins with Winchester and includes Suffolk and York.

Each of the four plays must be seen as an independent unit because it is improbable, given what is known about how the acting companies worked, that they were ever presented all together. They have, nevertheless, an overall coherence that indicates that Shakespeare either conceived them as a whole or revised them into one. The three parts of *Henry VI* move from the initiation of disorder in the quarrel between Gloucester and Winchester over control of the infant-king Henry VI, into increasing chaos fuelled by ambition and betrayal that leads to the loss of English possessions in France, through division within England itself and the dangerous rebellion of York and its populist parody in the Cade rebellion. The complete and tragic loss of control that accompanies the struggle between the houses of Lancaster and York is summed up in the emblematic scene in Part Three in which Henry VI meets a father who has killed his son and a son who has killed his father. This collapse of all natural human ties clears the way for the monster-tyrant Richard III. To hold all this together Shakespeare provides a complex arrangement of parallel scenes and figures, making one event echo another, one action comment on another as, for example, the scene between Talbot and his son finds an ironic echo in the scene between Joan and her father, and the murder of Rutland has its counterpart in the murder of Prince Edward; and these hints of inter-connection are underlined by the frequent use of prophecy. Shakespeare also develops a kind of dramatic shorthand to present battle scenes, giving a sense of the flux and urgency of the struggle for power. This was an ambitious undertaking for any dramatist in the early stages of his career, and Shakespeare had no precedents from which he could borrow.

Because of supposed deficiencies in the language, style and structure of the three parts of *Henry VI*, some scholars have tried to deny, or at least to limit, Shakespeare's authorship of the plays. Certainly, there is little subtlety in the characterization, and the verse is often very crude and bombastic, as if the dramatist were trying to respond to the 'mighty line' that Marlowe had developed for his *Tamburlaine*. On the other hand, the dramatic structure is quite remarkable, considering the vastness of the task taken on in these plays. But why should we blame some other dramatist for work that Shakespeare had reason to be proud of? Aesthetic snobbery should not obscure the fact that Shakespeare had to learn his craft, that he was writing for a popular audience, and that he did, apparently, give them what they wanted. In his pamphlet *Pierce Penniless*, Thomas Nashe describes what must have been the popular reaction to the heroic English figure of Talbot:

How would it have joyed brave Talbot, the terror of the French, to think that after he had lain two hundred years in his tomb, he should triumph again on the stage and have his bones new embalmed with the tears of ten thousand spectators at least (at several times), who, in the tragedian that represents his person, imagine they behold him fresh bleeding![30]

The opening of *1 Henry VI* is a highly effective dramatic moment, implying an ending rather than a beginning: a group of noblemen enter for the funeral of Henry V, the stage shrouded in black as if for a tragedy. To an Elizabethan audience, Henry V was the greatest English monarch before their own day, a king who united warring factions in England and extended English power over France. Henry is described by his brother Gloucester in almost mythical terms:

England ne'er had a king until his time.
Virtue he had, deserving to command:
His brandish'd sword did blind men with his beams:
His arms spread wider than a dragon's wings:
His sparkling eyes, replete with wrathful fire,

More dazzled and drove back his enemies
Than mid-day sun fierce bent against their faces.

(1.1.8–14)

Through hyperbole 'English Henry' is turned into a symbol of English heroic virtue, and his memory dominates the play. It is a memory, however, that represents loss.

The loss of selfless heroic idealism symbolized by the death of Henry V clears the way for a new breed of politician, for machiavellian 'realists' like the Bishop of Winchester. The figure who, in Part One, stands opposed to what Winchester represents and carries on Henry's values is Talbot. Talbot may seem to be the play's hero; like Henry, he identifies himself with England, seen in terms of honour and noble blood, 'God and Saint George, Talbot and England's right' (4.2.55). The scenes in which he and his son struggle to outdo one another as representatives of family love and national honour cast an ironic light on the earlier scenes of factional struggle, and we have to recognize the nobility in their doomed stand against the French. But what is it worth? At Talbot's death Joan La Pucelle points out the banal reality: 'Him that thou magnifiest with all these titles, / Stinking and fly-blown lies here at our feet' (4.7.75–6). The dead hero is turned into garbage both in fact and in an act of La Pucelle's cynical wit, and although he was killed by the French the play insists that his death is the result of faction amongst the English who failed to provide him with support; Talbot, and by implication the body of England, is a victim of the ambitions of men who elevate their personal desires over the good of the country: 'The fraud of England, not the force of France, / Hath now entrapp'd the noble-minded Talbot' (4.4.36–7). Lucy here marks the passing of an heroic ideal, displaced in a new world of ruthless cunning.

To admit that Talbot was defeated by Joan La Pucelle would be problematic, for she is a figure of some ambiguity. Her military success is attributed to supernatural aid which is at first presented as divine, but after her defeat the play provides Joan with familiar spirits, implying that her aid is diabolic. This does not mean that Shakespeare saw her as such, or felt that he had to resolve the question of whether she was 'Puzzel or Pucelle', whore or virgin; he is simply providing contrasting perspectives upon her. Most of what she does can be seen as being in line with good military strategy, and it is only because she is a woman that her success is assigned to supernatural causes. In fact, it is Joan's sex that makes her problematic. It is significant that the play contains only three women and that all of them are, in some sense, enchanters. Furthermore, the play relates the seductive power of women to the seductive power of language. Joan persuades Burgundy to 'turn' through a remarkable display of rhetoric, and at her first appearance we are told 'These women are shrewd tempters with their tongues' (1.2.123). The Countess of Auvergne attempts to capture Talbot using a 'woman's kindness', while at the end of the play, Margaret's beauty 'confounds the tongue' (5.3.71), depriving Suffolk of words. Thus the play raises, but does not explore, the question of the place of women in this very masculine world.

It might be as well here to note that in the history plays women are mainly marginal figures. Dealing as they do with public action these plays reflect Elizabethan reality, and most female characters function as victims of masculine brutality (like Anne in *Richard III*), as pathetic figures whose suffering is a kind of by-product of masculine suffering (like Isabel in *Richard II*) or as semi-comic reflections of the domestic ineptitude of men, like Lady Percy in *1 Henry IV*. Those women who do attain a measure of success are usually demonized, like Joan, or like Margaret of Anjou in the remaining parts of *Henry VI*. Joan's success comes about because as a soldier she takes a role meant for a man (it is interesting to speculate on how Shakespeare's audience must have responded to this oblique representation of the queen herself). This might be why many readers have found her final scenes offensive. She begins by denying her father and proclaiming her superior birth and absolute chastity. When this fails to move her English captors she reverses herself and claims to be pregnant, naming different figures as the father. This too fails and her final words are a curse upon her enemies. This is all very unpleasant, but we have to note that she is simply doing what most men in the world of this play do (and we will find this increasingly in the plays that are to follow): attempting to save herself through evasion and trickery.

In a sense, the nominal protagonist of these three plays, Henry VI, is the reverse of Joan. Mild and self-effacing, he possesses 'feminine' characteristics. At his first appearance (3.1) he tries to reconcile his uncles through prayers and with 'sighs and tears' – not, one might think, the best instruments of a strong king, and indeed, his reign is a disaster for the country. Nevertheless, his mildness has a high moral component, as is made clear in his chastisement of his bishop-uncle:

> Fie, uncle Beaufort! I have heard you preach
> That malice was a great and grievous sin;
> And will you not maintain the thing you teach,
> And prove a chief offender in the same?

(3.1.127–30)

Is goodness weakness? Henry is certainly not politically astute, as he shows when he chooses the red rose while claiming not to favour Somerset over York, thus confirming York as his own enemy. Perhaps this can be understood in terms of Talbot's distinction between shadow and substance. Talbot himself would be merely a shadow without his 'substance, sinews, arms, and strength' (2.3.62), the power of his supporters. This is one of the realities of political success: goodness without strength is impotent.

Shakespeare here explores a situation that would have seemed very close to the Elizabethans' own. A shrewd politician, Elizabeth had created a degree of stability in the state, but her failure to name a successor left open the possibility of precisely the kind of factional division represented here. Furthermore, although the play contains a clear nationalist message, it is also deeply critical of aristocratic irresponsibility. To Elizabethan authority the threat of faction was all the more troubling because it could encourage popular uprising – what we see, in fact, in *2 Henry VI*. Jack Cade, who leads the popular rebellion, is not presented as a genuine populist leader since he is York's instrument, a dupe with courage but small intellect and essentially a hypocrite, a comic devil from the morality tradition. The play nevertheless acknowledges that there were genuine popular grievances, such as the Second Petitioner's complaint against the enclosure of common land (1.3.21–2), and the grotesque emptiness of Cade and his followers does not negate the reality or validity of popular dissatisfaction.

Parts Two and Three of *Henry VI* are closely inter-related. The visual image that dominates them is that of the severed head: there are four of them in Part Two, and Part Three begins with Richard throwing the head of his family's enemy, Somerset, at York's feet; York's own severed head will figure prominently later in the play. The head severed from the body is a potent graphic image of the savagery unleashed by aristocratic irresponsibility, but it also represents the failure of authority in a more subtle way. It is ironic that Shakespeare should have named three plays for Henry VI, for we might expect the eponymous character to be protagonist, but as head of state Henry is an absence rather a presence, a head who is not there. At the end of Part Three, when Warwick insists to Edward, who has claimed the crown, that Henry is truly king, Edward points out that Henry is his prisoner and asks, 'What is the body when the head is off?' (5.1.41). England, having a king who is no king, is a body without a head.

With no leadership, no coherence, all England can produce is a number of player-kings. Cade, who in Part Two claims to be 'rightful heir unto the crown' (4.2.128), parodies York, who with his attractive energy seems to have the makings of a 'true' king. A machiavellian, he knows the virtues of manipulation, but he depends upon the support of others and this is a world in which no one can be trusted. He too is made into a player-king, enthroned upon a molehill and crowned with a paper crown, before he is diminished into yet another severed head. The man who emerges from the carnage of these plays to fill the void understands perfectly the relationship between playing and power, as he understands that he can trust no one but himself. 'I am myself alone' (3:5.6.83) says Richard Crookback, defining himself as the logical and horrific authority over an apparently irredeemable land.

After the sprawling energies of the *Henry VI* trilogy *Richard III* is a remarkably concentrated play, its form created by its protagonist. For most of the play Richard's plots are the play's plots, as he works to destroy his enemies and strengthen his own control. His enemies are themselves guilty of terrible crimes, and he is in a sense a figure of retribution; the play, through its frequent use of prophecies, omens and dreams (many of them associated with Queen Margaret, the figure of bloody and powerful passions in *2 & 3 Henry VI*), insistently links past and present, past crime with present punishment. Richard's motives are certainly not moral, and much of the time they are not even political, for he is concerned with the playful exercise of his manipulative wit. The first two scenes allow him to present virtuoso performances in taking over the will or emotions of his victims, first his brother Clarence whom he tricks to death, and then the Lady Anne, widow of one of his victims, whom he seduces over the coffin of her father-in-law. He understands the power of playing and he understands that it has its sources in the shiftiness of language. Commenting on his own double meanings, he says 'Thus, like the formal Vice, Iniquity, / I moralize two meanings in one word' (3.1.82–3).

His manipulations include the audience too. His opening soliloquy, in which he defines his character and states his intentions, is partly exposition but partly an invitation to the audience to take his side, and he consolidates this relationship with frequent asides and soliloquies that are in effect asking us to applaud his genius. And we do indeed witness an astonishing performance and might easily find ourselves taken in by his comic energies. Nevertheless, the play is a tragedy in form and the true victim of his malevolence is the body of England. Those he tricks are to a degree responsible for what happens to them, most being guilty of acts of betrayal or murder; even Anne falls for what is really an appeal to her pride – the Petrarchan idea that she has the power of life and death over him. In effect, Richard is an extreme embodiment of the guilt in his own society.

What is it that brings Richard down? Tudor orthodoxy saw Richard's crimes as the culmination of a history of strife and bloodshed that would be ended through the retributive figure of Henry Richmond, the future Henry VII. Thus the foundation of the Tudor dynasty was presented as a providential event. Certainly, there is a strong element of this in Shakespeare's version of Richmond, who on the eve of the Battle of Bosworth Field experiences the positive obverse of Richard's nightmares. There seems, however, to be something within Richard's own identity that dooms him. When he orders the murder of the young Princes he is for the first time committing a crime against someone who cannot be said to be guilty. This act estranges him from Buckingham, his strongest supporter, leaving him truly isolated, and perhaps it also estranges him from himself. 'I am myself alone' has terrifying implications for the man who says it. Once Richard has achieved the throne, he has nothing left to do but look into his own emptiness. He loses his grip on his acting genius; when he approaches Queen Elizabeth to ask for the hand of her daughter, he thinks he has achieved a repeat of his performance with Anne, when in fact Elizabeth is playing him at his own game.

In the final act a total understanding of his emptiness forces itself upon Richard. He awakens from his nightmare feeling for the first time the sting of conscience:

> I shall despair. There is no creature loves me;
> And if I die, no soul will pity me.
> Nay, wherefore should they, since that I myself
> Find in myself no pity to myself?

> (5.3.201–4)

It is probably too little and too late for us to feel any tragic emotion for him. Yet he goes to his death with courage, and at the end of the play what we remember is not the avenging hero Richmond, who is a rather pallid figure, but the outrageous power, comic and anarchic, of Richard Crookback.

Although *Richard III* ends with an assertion of the Tudor myth through the glorification of Richmond, the tetralogy offers a sceptical view of the workings of power. Over and over again we see the heroic ideal crushed by egoism and ruthless ambition. The plays have much more to say about loss and betrayal and the conditions that allow the assertion of control by the tyrannical appetite than they do about order and stability. Furthermore, the fact that many of the aspirers and betrayers of the plays were the ancestors of members of Elizabeth's court, that the same family names were there competing for favour and position, was in itself an alarming sign of the continuity of history and the ever-present possibility of faction and its terrible results.

*King John* was probably written between the two tetralogies, around 1596, though possibly earlier. It is unusual amongst the English history plays in that it takes its material from the early thirteenth rather than the fifteenth century. It has related (and topical) political preoccupations, however, being concerned with a monarch who has an uncertain claim to the throne. What, indeed, is the significance of the idea of the divine or absolute right of kings if no one has secure title? In terms of primogeniture, John's right to the English throne is less than that of his nephew Arthur, but John claims it as his by 'Our strong possession and our right' (1.1.39). There is here a conflict between theoretical right and practical need, complicated by the fact that Arthur, a gentle, loving child, does not want to rule. He becomes the instrument of the ambition of others, much as Henry VI had done, and his claim endangers England, since it involves French military support. The play explores the compromises that all are forced to make. John eventually turns villain when he orders Arthur's death; he differs from Richard in that he has misgivings about killing a noble kinsman, but he knows he cannot be secure while Arthur lives (surely an echo of the situation that had existed between Elizabeth and Mary, Queen of Scots).

To provide a perspective on the play's political machinations, Shakespeare introduced a character who had no historical existence and yet takes an active part in the play's historical events. Philip the Bastard is, by definition, a figure from the margins who can mock and judge the hypocrisies of political power. He is the most interesting figure in the play, having something of the wit of Richard III without his destructive purpose. He tries to retain a stance of detachment from what he observes, but he cannot do so as he perceives the need for patriotic dedication. When the play's upheavals are ended and Henry III introduced as the youthful king who will restore peace, it is Philip who is given the final words about how England can have no successful enemy unless it turns upon itself: 'This England never did, nor never shall, / Lie at the proud foot of a conqueror, / But when it first did help to wound itself' (5.7.112–14). It is an idea that echoes throughout the *Henry VI* plays. Here, the shaping and judgement of historical events by a fictitious character raise intriguing questions about what Shakespeare thought he could do through his art. The play ends with order restored, but it is the illusory order of fiction imposed on history.

In the second tetralogy, probably begun in 1595, Shakespeare sought the causes of the disorder he presented so graphically in the first. Richard II had unquestionable title to the throne, but he was a weak and indecisive king. His arbitrary acts provoked the rebellion of his cousin Henry Bolingbroke that led to Richard's forced abdication. Bolingbroke certainly had qualities that made him potentially better material for kingship than Richard, but he was nevertheless a usurper. This situation allowed Shakespeare to consider the rights and limitations of kingship. The reign of Bolingbroke as Henry IV was plagued by rebellion and civil dissention, but his son, Henry V, united the country in a brief period of national glory before his early death opened the way for the chaos of the Wars of the Roses. Orthodox Tudor doctrine presented all these civil upheavals as divine retribution exacted upon England as punishment for Henry's act of usurpation and as a warning against rebellion. The doctrine of divine right is explicitly stated on a number of occasions in *Richard II*, most notably in speeches by Gaunt (1.2.37–41) and the Bishop of Carlisle (4.1.115–49). In *Henry IV*, the troubles of the king's reign are linked to his feelings of guilt. Nevertheless, these plays do not simply follow the official line.

On one level *Richard II* dramatizes the impracticability of a doctrine that depends on the idea of absolute right rather than on military and popular strength allied to a concern for the good of the state. In the first half of the play Richard is intoxicated by the power of the word 'king' and the power of a king's words. He wants security without responsibility and believes that his title protects him. He allows his public actions to appear arbitrary, treats the dying Gaunt with callous disregard, surrounds himself with flatterers and seizes the possessions of his cousin Bolingbroke without any consideration for the hostility that he generates. This creates a degree of sympathy for Bolingbroke, who has legitimate cause to resent Richard. As the play progresses, however, questions arise about whether Bolingbroke is motivated by a desire for justice or whether he is driven by ambition.

After Richard's loss of the crown we see him begin to change. He is matured by suffering and reveals a genuine sensitivity (he is sometimes described as being a poet but we have to remember that, as with all Shakespeare's characters, the poetry comes from his creator). Having been stripped of the title 'king' he seeks the meaning of that title and looks within himself for some essential being with an existence separate from it. In his torment, ironically, he develops a degree of majesty that, for all his success, the humourless pragmatist Bolingbroke never shows. Richard's new stature is augmented by his capacity to generate love. His followers, the supposed flatterers Bushy and Green, are described by Bolingbroke as 'The caterpillars of the commonwealth' (2.3.165), but they go to their deaths with courage and dignity, showing a loyalty to Richard that belies Bolingbroke's words. His wife Isabel is also important in this respect, for her love leads us to the private qualities of the public figure.

This perhaps is why, on the quarto title-page, the play is called a tragedy. Richard is far more admirable out of power than in it and is a victim of the realities of kingship. Suffering develops in him strength, a capacity for change and a desire to understand. In the earlier history plays the focus was on external, political struggle rather than on its effects on any individual. In *Richard III*, to be sure, it is the character of Richard III that interests us, but only in so far as we are amused and led on by his black wit. He is essentially static, with no real capacity for suffering, and there is unlikely to be any pity or sympathy in our response to his death. This is not, I think, the case with Richard II, who generates genuine tragic feeling, if only in a minor key.

*Richard II* has one scene (3.4) that is essentially emblematic. A gardener gives his assistants advice that is ostensibly about gardening but really about government. England is like a garden overrun with weeds and parasites, with uncontrolled and excessive growth, that is in need of a good gardener. This scene could be taken to represent all the history plays. The garden of England as we have seen it is always overgrown. Who should be its gardener? Some, such as Richard III, are themselves 'noisome weeds' that must be eradicated. Bolingbroke is certainly a good politician but this may not make him a good keeper of the garden-state. At the end of the play he is worried about his 'unthrifty son' who will inherit the garden, and this anxiety leaves the play to end on a sour note.

The remaining plays in this tetralogy are about the growth and education of this unthrifty son into Henry V, a figure, as much myth as man, whom many Elizabethans considered the greatest English monarch prior to their own. In the two parts of *Henry IV* Prince Hal is the pivotal character, moving (often in alternating scenes) between the grim world of history and duty in the court and the pleasing world of comedy and license in the scenes with Falstaff and his companions. He negotiates the division between these two worlds by presenting a false version of himself to both. He allows his father to see him as a failure, unconcerned with duty or honour, and he allows Falstaff and his friends to believe that they have captivated him to their shady desires. The audience is reassured early in *1 Henry IV*, however, when he reveals his game to them: he is like the sun, hiding its splendour behind clouds so that it will be all the more amazing when it is revealed (1.2.190–212). He, too, knows how important it is for a prince to be a player.

The political world in these two plays is glum and exhausted. King Henry, who had energy in *Richard II*, has failed to unite the country behind him and faces constant civil upheavals because he has made the political error of failing to deal well with former supporters. In 1 *Henry IV* he is faced with uprisings of the Scots and the Welsh, and the Percy family, who are fighting these uprisings on his behalf, turn against him for what they see as his ingratitude (though their motives are mixed with ambition). The most prominent and most attractive of these rebels is Harry Percy, or Hotspur. Henry is fascinated by Hotspur who seems to have all the princely qualities that Hal apparently lacks, and in Hotspur's defiance and satirical energy and in his heartfelt embracing of honour there is an undeniable allure. As the play progresses, however, it becomes clear that honour is all he cares about, and a narrow concept of honour at that, which makes him incapable of recognizing the virtues of others. He is wilful and lacking in political judgement, and becomes the simple dupe of his machiavellian father and uncle.

Hotspur is a foil for Hal, and Falstaff is another. He is the embodiment of carnival or theatricality, the fleshly comic spirit opposed to the cold peevishness of Henry; he is a walking denial that the irresponsibility of youth must come to an end, and we cannot blame Hal for the pleasure he takes in this perverse father-figure. Falstaff's famous speech mocking honour (5.1.127–41) is not so much an admission of cowardice as a down-to-earth corrective of the excess of Hotspur, a statement of the comic instinct for survival. He also represents a dangerous temptation to lawlessness, the opposite of what Hal must represent if he is to become king, and as such he presents Hal with his most serious test. However, there are indications in the play that Hal will pass the test (his reply to Falstaff's mock plea not to banish him, at the end of the scene in which he and Falstaff pre-parody Hal's interview with his father, is 'I do, I will' (2.4.475), their game suddenly sliding into reality).

At the end of the play Hal proves himself at Shrewsbury by saving his father's life and defeating Hotspur, resolving the main conflicts, but in 2 *Henry IV* there is distance between father and son once again, and further rebellion in the north, beginning a cyclical reiteration of the structure of its predecessor. The repeated form is essentially ironic, as suggested by the play's use of Rumour as a prologue. Rumour is report of doubtful accuracy, here the story that Hotspur has defeated Hal. However, Rumour suggests more broadly the play's general concern with misread appearances. In Part One Hal was the commander of false appearances, but in this play he has become the victim of what he created, trapped by his reputation of profligacy; the clouds will not reveal the sun. His father, still stern and forbidding, is convinced that Hal is anxious for his death, an anxiety that is apparently justified when Hal, believing him to be dead, takes the crown. The confrontation that develops at this point allows the father finally to see the true nature of his son and to put away the guilt of his usurpation of Richard's throne by passing on the crown.

The misreading of Hal carries over into the comic scenes of the play. Falstaff also believes Hal is the unthrifty son who will allow him to subvert the system of justice and usher in a 'golden' age of comic disorder. The Falstaff scenes have a distinctly less genial tone than those of Part One; Falstaff is feeling his age and is associated with images of disease and decay, providing a parallel to the King. While his collusion with Shallow and Silence and his treatment of the Lord Chief Justice are funny, they set him outside the stable world that Hal wants to govern and obviously he has to be cast off. We can see Hal firmly distancing himself from his old companion, though Falstaff does not see it, and when the time comes for the new king to speak the terrible words 'I know thee not, old man' (5.5.47) it is a wrenching moment both for Falstaff, who does not expect it, and for the spectator, who does – and, perhaps, for Hal himself. He has seen clearly where his duty lies but in dismissing Falstaff he is also dismissing a part of himself, becoming a tighter, colder man; or perhaps, since he predicted this moment at the beginning of *1 Henry IV*, he is only revealing what he has always been.

The two plays could be seen as an experiment that explores the border between history and fiction, with history finally casting out fiction. Falstaff threatens to take over the play, as he would like to take over the administration of justice, and he has to be defeated both by Hal and by the playwright. The play is concerned with history and the comic subverter cannot have his way; perhaps Shakespeare is acknowledging the limitations of his own art. At the same time, he has created in Falstaff one of the greatest, most memorable pieces of comic art, who has managed to deny those limitations, to become history himself.

Hal emerges into his own play as the hero-king Henry V. The structure of *Henry V*, with its Chorus framing each act, insists on the epic nature of the play's events, pretending frustration at the inadequacy of theatre to do justice to the magnitude of its materials. In the play we see Henry deal firmly with domestic rebellion, unite his country behind him (this is the significance of the representative English, Scottish, Welsh and Irish captains who follow him), and lead his armies to victory against what ought to have been overwhelming French opposition. Throughout, the Chorus points out the patriotic momentousness of the events, as in these lines before the second act:

Now all the youth of England are on fire,
And silken dalliance in the wardrobe lies:
Now thrive the armourers, and honour's thought
Reigns solely in the breast of every man.

(2 Chorus, 1–4)

The play has the happy ending of comic structure in a marriage that will bring French territory under English control. We are surely being presented with what the Chorus calls 'the mirror of all Christian Kings' (2 Chorus, 6).

There is a counter-movement of interrogation within this affirmative structure, however. What does successful leadership require? The play opens, after all, with cunning churchmen plotting ways to divert Henry's attention to foreign adventures and away from their own material affairs, and convincing him (he does not need much persuasion) that his will and God's will coincide. What do we make of Henry's threats before Harfleur that unless the town surrenders he will not restrain his men from raping its women and murdering its infants? Perhaps this is no more than a threat, justified because it succeeds, but if we set it alongside other of Henry's actions, such as his order to his soldiers to kill all the French prisoners, there certainly seems to be an indication that effective use of power entails some dehumanization of its user. In the famous scene (4.1) in which Henry goes in disguise amongst his armies on the eve of Agincourt, the King's intention is to hear about the closeness and loyalty to him of the common soldiers, but what he actually hears raises questions, which he evades answering, about the justice of the cause for which they are all fighting.

We might say that in the *Henry IV* plays Henry was, from the outset, learning how to be a king, well aware that kingship is a role. Part of his education was to move amongst the common people, but in becoming king he made a decisive withdrawal from this common humanity, epitomized by his dismissal of Falstaff.

This is why his disguised walk amongst his men ends in sourness, which is reinforced by the exhaustion of the Falstaff subplot in *Henry V*. This is not even the play's main comic sub-plot, which is taken up by Fluellen; Falstaff appears only indirectly, through the Hostess's touching account of his death, and his central position in this diminished sub-sub-plot is appropriated by the increasingly bizarre and querulous Pistol. Henry's order to execute his one-time companion Bardolph in the same play marks the distance that kingship has brought him from London tavern life.

We cannot blame Henry for this distance because he too is its victim. He understands kingship as a public role and we now see almost nothing of the private Hal. Even his courtship has to be a public affair, carried on for political motives. His claim to love Katherine is somewhat questionable, since he had earlier rejected marriage to her because her accompanying dowry was insufficient, but at such a level marriage is a matter of the public good rather than of private desire. So even though the play has the structure of comedy there is a certain unease at its end, and this is recognized in the final Chorus, which brings us full circle to the beginning of the earliest of Shakespeare's history plays, when the death of Henry left his infant son as king, 'Whose state so many had the managing, / That they lost France and made his England bleed: / Which oft our stage hath shown' (11–13). It is a moment of deep irony that at the end of his long series of history plays the dramatist should leave us with the one successful king he has been able to show us, cultivator of 'the world's best garden' (7), and should insist on reminding us of how sadly brief the hard-won peace and harmony would be.

Elizabethan history plays developed out of the patriotic mood that was England's response to the defeat of the Armada, but Shakespeare's history plays are more complex than this, embracing sceptical and even radical positions. By the end of the century the national mood had changed, was less secure and much darker. It is possible that this change led Shakespeare to look elsewhere for political models – to the republican Roman state. His three Roman plays were treated by his first editors as tragedies, but they are at least as much concerned with political issues as are the English histories; indeed, one critic has written of *Coriolanus* that 'political theory is its *raison d'être*'.[31] Like the English histories, the Roman plays are concerned with crisis within the state. *Julius Caesar*, staged in the autumn of 1599, examines the declining moments of the Roman republic before it was swept through popular unrest into civil war and transformed into empire. It presents a negative view of republicanism, wary of the factionalism that such a form of government encourages. Its horrifying vision of civil war was all too close to the fears of many English people in the declining years of Elizabeth's reign:

> Blood and destruction shall be so in use,
> And dreadful objects so familiar,
> That mothers shall but smile when they behold
> Their infants quartered with the hands of war,
> All pity chok'd with custom of fell deeds.
>
> (3.1.265–9)

A concern with republicanism rather than monarchy can give voice to dissenting positions, however, and *Coriolanus*, written in the context of the uprising in 1607–8 of poor labourers in protest at the high prices of food, is sympathetic to more democratic answers to political problems. However, since the Roman plays were written during a period in Shakespeare's career when he was testing out new dramatic structures to express the changing national mood, it might be appropriate to consider them, as his editors did, as tragedies.

Shakespeare did write, probably in collaboration with John Fletcher, one more play about English history, *Henry VIII*, first performed in 1613. This is unlike the earlier plays in many ways. It has none of the popular elements of battle-scenes and heightened rhetoric or comic sub-plots, and shows in its interest in pageant and ceremony the influence of sophisticated Jacobean court masques, as if intended primarily for a court audience even though its first performance was at the Globe. It has a moralizing function in following the rise and fall of ambitious men, notably Buckingham and Wolsey, but its primary function is celebratory, since it ends with the prediction of Elizabeth's glorious reign and the equally illustrious rule of James who, phoenix-like, is to arise from Elizabeth's ashes to reign in 'peace, plenty, love, truth, terror' (5.5.47). It is as if Shakespeare's intention was to project history into the present, to show James's reign as the significant culmination of history. This may seem a rather un-sceptical position for Shakespeare to take, but it does provide a fitting conclusion to an analysis that has shown the relationship of drama to history: drama arises from a conflict of perspectives, and so in a real sense does history; drama allows us to understand the present moment by staging for us the conflict and contradictions (or inner conflict) of history. We do not see history as a set of facts to be resolved into truth, but as a process that shows us that there are many truths or, as the alternative title of *Henry VIII* implies, that *All Is True*.


## TRAGEDIES

Most accounts of Shakespeare's career agree that its climax occurred during the period from 1600 to 1606 because it saw the composition of his 'major' tragedies, *Hamlet, Othello, King Lear* and *Macbeth*. The writing of tragedy occupied much of Shakespeare's energy during these years and the two years following, which saw the appearance of *Antony and Cleopatra, Coriolanus* and *Timon of Athens*; for various reasons, these latter three tragedies have generally been treated by critical history as inferior to the earlier four. Before this period Shakespeare had already written five tragedies: apart from *Titus Andronicus* and *Romeo and Juliet*, *Richard II* and *Richard III* are certainly tragic in form, as is *Julius Caesar*. We should note too that the six years which saw the appearance of the four major tragedies were also a period of intense experimentation with form: Shakespeare wrote the last of the plays usually designated romantic comedies, *Twelfth Night*, leaving behind a genre that had served him well for most of the preceding decade, and produced the trio of so-called problem plays (one of which, *Troilus and Cressida*, is sometimes treated as tragedy) which, as we have seen, were clearly attempts to push at the limits of comic form by exploring the darker areas that had merely been hinted at in earlier comedies.

Why should Shakespeare's tragedies be considered his major achievement when he expended so much more of his creative energy on comedies? To answer this we need to go to Aristotle's *Poetics* and his idea that, in the hierarchy of dramatic kinds, tragedy is superior to comedy. Aristotle's justification for this was that tragedy represents people as better than the norm, while comedy represents them as worse.[32] Furthermore, tragedy is concerned with members of noble families, so the hierarchization is at least in part a reflection of social hierarchy. One might think that history plays, about which, of course, Aristotle knew nothing, shared these tragic elements. However, modern Shakespearean criticism has allocated them too to an inferior position: A.C. Bradley calls *Richard II, Richard III* and the Roman plays 'tragic histories or historical tragedies', containing 'undramatic material' and to be distinguished from the four plays that he calls 'pure tragedies'.[33]

In fact, the kind of value judgement implied in this ranking of dramatic genres is a little misleading. Dramatic form grows out of the conditions under which it is produced. There have been few periods in which great tragedy has been written, and consequently it is difficult to make general statements about it, but it tends to appear at times of unusual social stress. Shakespeare obviously found that histories and comedies provided him with a satisfactory way of representing his society until the last years of Elizabeth's reign. His movement into tragedy does not simply reflect an artistic maturing that allowed him to develop a higher dramatic form, but rather a need for a different form to represent a changing culture. The tragedies have to be seen in the context of a phase of Shakespeare's career during which he was responding to the intensified uncertainties of the last years of Elizabeth's reign and the first years of James's.

We should also note that Shakespeare was not alone in turning to experimental and tragic forms after 1600. John Marston produced his satirical tragedy *Antonio's Revenge*, which bears an interesting relationship to *Hamlet*, around 1600. George Chapman, previously known for his humours comedies, concentrated on tragedy after 1604, and Ben Jonson's only two tragedies date from this period: *Sejanus* (1603) and *Catiline* (1607). These were the forerunners of the Jacobean flourishing of revenge tragedies and tragedies of state in the work of Middleton, Tourneur and Webster. Furthermore, there is a marked darkening into satire in much of the comedy of these years. The theatres were obviously responding to a change in audience demands that was itself a response to a less stable time.

Tragedy is about personal and social anxiety. The simplest way to describe a tragic dramatic structure would be to say that it concerns a central figure who falls from a position of power or status into adversity that leads to death, and this would certainly apply to Shakespeare's tragedies. We have been taught, however, that because tragedy stirs deep emotions in us it must have greater significance than this rudimentary outline suggests, and there have been many attempts throughout the history of criticism to generate a theory of tragedy that would account for both its structure and its affective power. Most of these theories have their origins in Aristotle's *Poetics*. According to Aristotle, the plot of a tragedy must be an imitation of 'fearful and pitiable incidents' (18). The protagonist must be good, but not completely good, and he must fall from good to bad fortune. His fall comes about from what Aristotle calls *hamartia*, which has often been misleadingly translated as 'tragic flaw', but which seems more properly to refer to some error of the protagonist's. His experience must be such that it will, through pity and fear, purge these emotions, an event identified as *catharsis*. The protagonist's experience should also lead him from ignorance to knowledge, a process of recognition called *anagnorisis*; he will understand the progression of cause and effect that has given an inevitability to his experience.

Aristotle's definition of tragedy formed the basis of many subsequent theories and has frequently been applied to readings of Shakespeare's plays. The problem with this is that Aristotle derived his understanding of tragedy from observation of plays on the stage in his own time, and his work has too often been taken as somehow 'true' of all tragedy. But there are many ways in which it is an inappropriate model for a definition of Shakespearean tragedy, not least because Shakespeare was probably unfamiliar with it (he would have been far more familiar with the *de casibus* concept of tragedy). Furthermore, there is no universal agreement on what Aristotle meant by some of the terms he used, and yet they have become prescriptive, defining and limiting what constitutes tragedy. To take one large example: what did Aristotle mean by the enigmatic word *'catharsis'*? The Greek word can mean 'purgation', 'purification' or 'clarification', and in its context in the *Poetics* we are given insufficient information to be able to say which of these meanings is appropriate, although most readings of Aristotle understand him to mean the first of them. All of them seem to indicate that Aristotle believed in the affective nature of tragedy – that it generates responses in the audience that mimic in some way the experience of the tragic protagonist. But what does it mean to say that pity and fear are *purged* through the tragic action? Since no one has come up with a satisfactory answer to this, perhaps the most we can say is that tragedy generates an emotional, possibly empathetic, response in the spectator.

More disabling have been the problems created by the idea that the tragic hero must have a tragic flaw, that he is the victim of a fatal psychology. If this is true, what is Hamlet's tragic flaw? Neo-Aristotelian critics usually answer this question by indicating his indecisiveness, but what they term 'indecisiveness' is really an intellectual tendency to explore all the moral and spiritual ramifications of any proposed action, and it is difficult to see in what way this is a flaw. It certainly is not the initiating element in the chain of events that bring about his death. Through no fault of his own he is put into a dilemma – to kill his uncle or to fail in what is presented to him as a duty to avenge the murder of his father. He is understandably reluctant to commit an act himself that would be not just murder, but regicide. In the other major tragedies, the concept of a tragic flaw might seem more persuasive: Othello's jealousy, Lear's pride, Macbeth's ambition. But the idea that these 'flaws' are the fundamental source of the tragic events, a kind of psychological determinism, is severely limiting to the plays in question, for it places blame for the catastrophic events upon the hero's weaknesses, consequently diminishing the force of his tragedy.

The word *hamartia* appears to be derived from a term in archery which meant 'to miss or fall short of the target', and is thus more likely to imply an error or misjudgement, and therefore to refer to an action rather than a moral quality. Character is *not* fate; the tragic hero is not simply doomed by his own character, but by the situation in which he has to function. Furthermore, if we consider the question of the inevitability of what happens to the Shakespearean tragic hero, he is not the victim of a hostile universe, however much he might believe himself to be, as does Gloucester, for example, in *King Lear* when he says 'As flies to wanton boys, are we to th' gods, / They kill us for their sport' (4.1.36–7). There are, certainly, circumstances that are beyond his control, perhaps beyond any human control, but this is not the same thing as a malignant or unavoidable fate, and we are more likely to find discontinuity in a Shakespearean play than a tight line of cause and effect. Even the idea of *anagnorisis*, a final tragic awareness, creates problems: any response to the terrible ironies of Lear's final lines must ask what kind of understanding it is that Lear can be said to have achieved.

The fact is that Aristotle's prescriptions, at least as they have been popularly understood, are not very helpful as a guide to what Shakespeare was doing and only tempt us to apply limiting formulae to the plays. There is little evidence that Shakespeare knew Aristotle's work, but if he did he did not feel obliged to take any notice of it. And yet the effect of Aristotelian theories, both his own, so far as they can be known for certain, and those of generations of his followers, has been to encourage a view of tragedy as being concerned with 'the conflict between man and his destiny', when the artist, through his tragic protagonist, gazes into the abyss and learns that his fellow artists 'have stared into the same depths'.[34] This idea of a universal 'tragic vision' with 'man' engaged in a futile struggle against a hostile 'fate' serves to draw attention away from the particular, local elements of tragedy.

What we need is a way of describing what happens in the tragedies rather than a set of possibly inappropriate prescriptive terms. If tragedy is produced at moments of great social stress we would expect to find in Shakespeare's tragedies reflections of the cultural and ideological stress that came with the breakdown of the certainties of the great chain of being, with the erosion of belief in hierarchy and obedience and a universal force and frame that authorized human action, and with the implications that this had for monarchic rule. Established authority in Elizabethan and Jacobean England, with its myths and doctrines, clutched at the remnants of the old system, but the validity of the old truths was everywhere under pressure from radical and sceptical ideas like those associated with Machiavelli, which shifted the locus of authority from an enclosing universal order to the individual human will or even individual desire

The tragic protagonist or hero-victim is usually a head of state or someone close to the centre of power (an obvious exception is in *Romeo and Juliet*). He is caught in a conflict that is in some way related to the issue of moral authority or to a collision in codes of belief. He may, like Titus or Lear, be associated with traditional laws and the authority of the past, or he may be like Hamlet, a figure who explores the meaning of moral codes and is set the impossible task of restoring past truths. Because of his status his fate has larger ramifications in the state, and so tragedy is ideological or political in its broadest sense, and is anchored in a clear social context in which an alternative is sought for obsolescent ideas of moral order. The source of tragic experience can be located in human desire rather than universal malice. Characters may, like Gloucester, see themselves as victims of uncaring or hostile cosmic forces, but we see them as victims of fallible or perverse human will.

The fatal events of a Shakespearean tragedy have their cause in a specific social situation. The opening chorus of *Romeo and Juliet* calls the young lovers 'star-crossed', but it is the hostility between their families rather than the hostility of the stars that destroys them. Othello is indeed jealous, but it is Iago's manipulations that destroy the Moor, clearly motivated by his own sexual and social envy of Othello and set within a context of racial contempt: within the first two scenes Roderigo calls Othello 'the thicklips' (1.1.66); Iago conjures for Brabantio images of 'an old black ram . . . tupping your white ewe' (1.1.88–9) and 'your daughter covered with a Barbary horse' (111); and Brabantio responds by claiming that only magic could have drawn Desdemona into 'the sooty bosom / Of such a thing as' Othello (1.2.70–1). Othello's tragic end is not brought upon him by his jealousy (although that is undeniably a factor in the sequence of events) but by his anomalous position as a successful general and an alien in the fundamentally racist Venetian society.

Perhaps what is truly tragic is the opposite of what is implied by deterministic notions of a tragic flaw or a hostile destiny, since a fatal inevitability that brings undeserved ruin upon its victims generates melodrama rather than tragedy. What makes melodrama into tragedy is the hero's struggle to resist, whether against his enemies, his 'fate' or himself; however hostile the world may be to his needs, he responds with magnanimity, and his struggle to resist illuminates the incompatible meanings of his situation. His resistance is unsuccessful but not futile. Othello's end is not brought about by a hostile destiny or by a fatal flaw: he is the victim of human action, led to believe in the lies of Iago rather than in the virtue of his wife. Iago works hard for that belief, however, and it is not simply jealousy that allows Othello to be deceived: he also has doubts about his own value that are clearly rooted in his social conditions. Once we locate the tragic predicament in a specific context we can see that tragedy arises out of a politically-generated situation.

I do not want to make too many generalizations about what tragedy is, however. *Othello* has its own structure and way of working, and the same is true of each of the other tragedies. The differences rather than the similarities between particular tragedies are what make them interesting, and we must try to avoid simplifying them through preconceptions brought to them by an inappropriate application of a limiting theory of tragedy. It is more

helpful to consider them within the context of the theatre for which
Shakespeare was writing, in relation to the models that were more
immediately available to him. This is certainly the most illuminating way to approach *Titus Andronicus* which, on the one hand,
like his earliest comedy, *The Comedy of Errors*, parades its classical learning and, on the other, responds sharply to current theatrical fashion.

*Titus Andronicus* was published in 1594, but might have been
written as early as 1589. This play has often been characterized
as crude and immature, and there have been frequent attempts
to deny Shakespeare a part in its writing or to claim that he merely
revised an earlier play by another writer – Thomas Kyd, perhaps, or George Peele. This idea seems to arise, however, out of
a reluctance to believe that 'gentle' Shakespeare could have had
the bad taste to think up the graphic mutilations and blood-letting
that happen in the play. There seems otherwise to be no compelling reason to think that the play was not entirely Shakespeare's
work – quite, in fact, the contrary.

Some time during the late 1580s two immensely successful plays
had appeared on the London stage, Kyd's *The Spanish Tragedy*
and Marlowe's *The Jew of Malta*. Kyd's play set up a formula for
a sub-genre that has been called 'revenge tragedy' or 'the tragedy
of blood', but its central conflict has implications beyond the sub-
genre. Its protagonist, Hieronimo, suffers the murder of his son,
but when he seeks justice he finds it unattainable, first because
of the manipulative machiavellian cunning of the murderers and
then because they are connected to the ruling family. Driven mad
by his suffering, Hieronimo uses the methods of his enemies against
them: he tricks them into taking part in a play-within-the-play
and kills them as part of the performance. Hieronimo is thus a
hero who is corrupted, turned into a villain, when he embraces
machiavellian tactics. What seems to be important here, however,
is that Hieronimo is, from the outset, associated with a traditional moral code: as Knight Marshal of Spain he holds a legal
office in the royal household. When his son is murdered,
Hieronimo's struggle to attain justice leads him to confront the
fact that his code does not work and there is no justice for him.
This discovery drives him into madness because to defeat his
enemies he has to become like them. Thus the play's tragedy arises
out of the loss of established ideals in the face of the workings of
the real world.

*The Jew of Malta* reverses this situation by unapologetically bringing the machiavellian villain to the centre of the play and allowing him to mount an attack on established values. In Barabas, Marlowe created a figure of comic evil whose wit and energy, manifested in his language and in the grotesque traps he sets for his enemies, make him ambiguously attractive in spite of his villainy. We do not experience Barabas as a tragic figure in the same way that we do Hieronimo, however, because in *The Jew of Malta* the pressure on the moral code remains outside the protagonist, whereas in the case of Hieronimo the pressure is internalized, leading to his madness and death.

It is apparent, and hardly surprising, that in the early years of his career Shakespeare was anxious to make a name for himself. We have seen the great ambitions that lay behind his first history plays and it is clear that in writing *Titus Andronicus* Shakespeare was trying to outdo Kyd (*Richard III*, written about the same time, appears to have something of the same purpose in relation to Marlowe, having as its protagonist an outrageous machiavellian villain). In its violence and grotesque invention (which may have a satirical element), as well as in the disturbing and ambiguous responses it generates in the audience, Shakespeare's play certainly does outdo its model. We cannot know if the dramatist was pleased with it, but Ben Jonson's mocking reference more than 20 years later to the popular taste for 'Jeronimo or Andronicus' indicates that the audience was pleased with it.[35]

What quality of pleasure could an audience find in a play whose very plot can be outlined in terms of its atrocities? Titus himself commits the first of them in the opening scene by insisting on the sacrifice and dismemberment of the eldest son of Tamora, Queen of the Goths, whom he has just defeated. Implacable in his application of the law, he justifies an act that leads to horrifying revenge against him and his family: the murder of his son-in-law, the rape and mutilation of his daughter, the beheading of two of his sons, and a trick that has him cutting off his own hand in an attempt to gain mercy for the latter. Like Hieronimo, Titus goes mad and uses against his enemies their own extreme methods, killing Tamora's sons, his daughter's rapists, and baking them in a pie served to their mother.

Titus's refusal of mercy to Tamora's son reflects an unbending belief in the laws of republican Rome. This inflexibility also leads him to refuse the imperial crown and, in an affirmation of the right of primogeniture, to champion Saturninus, elder son of the late Emperor, who immediately shows his moral inferiority to his younger brother. In doing so Titus imposes upon the state a selfish and irresponsible leader who places his own desires above duty to the state and sets in motion the attack on traditional law that leads to Titus's tragedy. The play's visual horrors are an extreme representation of the chaotic conflict precipitated when the ethos of the past, with its rites and certainties, slips away, leaving nothing in its place, no sense, any longer, of what is right. It is this vacuum that drives Titus mad and internalizes the conflict so that he is set against himself, acting in ways that oppose his own deepest beliefs, a legitimate tragic figure.

*Romeo and Juliet*, written a couple of years later, presents the conflict between duty and desire in a different way. The two young lovers find that the fulfilment of their passion sets them against parental authority. This is the material of romantic comedy with which Shakespeare was concurrently occupied, and indeed there are comic elements of verbal excess in Romeo when he first appears that relate him to such Petrarchan lovers as Lucentio and the young men of *Love's Labour's Lost*:

> O heavy lightness, serious vanity,
> Misshapen chaos of well-seeming forms!
> Feather of lead, bright smoke, cold fire, sick health,
> Still-waking sleep that is not what it is!
>
> (1.1.176–9)

This is his response to Rosaline, a young woman with whom he is in love but who remains absent from the play. When he sees Juliet, he immediately transfers his affections to her, and although his language in speaking of her is a little less conventional, it is still marked by rhetorical excess:

> O, she doth teach the torches to burn bright.
> It seems she hangs upon the cheek of night
> As a rich jewel in an Ethiop's ear –
> Beauty too rich for use, for earth too dear.
>
> (1.3.43–6)

In comparison with Romeo's self-indulgent passion, Juliet's is tempered by her awareness of practicalities: 'If that thy bent of love be honourable, / Thy purpose marriage, send me word to-morrow' (2.2.143–4). There is much in this comparable to the relationship between Rosalind and Orlando in *As You Like It*.

What turns the play from its comic beginning into tragedy is the fact that conflict is not just generational but involves a feud between the Montague and Capulet families. We do not know what lies at the source of the feud but it is a matter of pride and status, and extreme and irrational hatred is elevated into a duty, as in Tybalt's response to Benvolio's call for peace: 'I hate the word / As I hate hell, all Montagues, and thee' (1.1.67–8). Even characters less hostile than Tybalt intensify the negative pressure on the lovers, imparting a certain ambiguity of tone to the play's comic and satirical elements. The romantic language of Juliet and Romeo is frequently counterpointed by the bawdy talk of the Nurse or the obscene cynicism of Mercutio, threatening to re-define their love as lust. But however immature their desire may be, it has its beauty in this bleak world of competition and violence. Despite the coincidences in the play, it is not fate that dooms their love but the fact that they must try to fulfil it outside the perimeters of this loveless society, a clear impossibility. They become victims, in effect, of family politics, the desire of youth thwarted by the material realities of their circumstances. It is perhaps ironic that the healing of the division between the families in response to the deaths of their children should be expressed in terms of material competition, as they re-embody the passionate lovers as golden statues.

*Julius Caesar* was described as a tragedy by the Folio editors, and this raises a number of questions about generic definition. As we have seen, the play has clear connections with the English history plays, but it also marks the beginning of a transitional period in Shakespeare's career. He moved away from romantic comedy at about the same time that he moved away from English history, towards the darker and more ambiguous comic forms of his so-called problem plays, and towards tragedy. *Julius Caesar* is a kind of triple tragedy: if we think of it as Caesar's tragedy, this is located mid-way through the play; the second half repeats Caesar's tragedy, with variations, in that of Brutus. Beyond these personal tragedies, however, is the larger public disaster of civil war, and it might be as well to think of *Julius Caesar* as what has been called a tragedy of state.[36] Caesar and Brutus are both flawed men caught between private ideals and political practicality. Caesar is a great leader and politician, and is seen by his enemies (as he sees himself) as a Colossus bestriding the world. The play also insists on all his human frailties: he is deaf and epileptic, over-confident and yet superstitious. Brutus, the republican idealist, allows himself to be convinced that Caesar's ambition is a threat to Roman freedom and that his assassination can be justified, but Brutus does not have the political wit or the military skill to cre-ate order out of what he has done. It is Mark Antony who shows, in his brilliant, cunning oration at Caesar's funeral, that the state is an arena for the machiavellian rather than the idealist.

What seems to be developing through these plays is a sense that the tragic protagonist is caught up in a dislocation of values that may also be understood as a dislocation between past and present. *Hamlet* is directly about this dislocation. On one level it is a play about succession, which in 1600 was the greatest source of anxiety for Elizabethan England; certainly, the loss of his chance to succeed his father is one practical aspect of Hamlet's motivation. In *Hamlet* the past is remembered (or imagined) as a golden age in contrast to the fallen world of the present, and the tragic hero has the duty of restoring the golden age. Hamlet's father, as ghost and memory, represents for Hamlet true authority and human perfection, a Hyperion in contrast to the drunken satyr and usurper Claudius. Hamlet's protest that 'The time is out of joint. O cursed spite, / That ever I was born to set it right' (1.5.196–7) states pre-cisely the protagonist's predicament. Part of his problem is that the values represented by his vision of the past inhibit him from restoring it. One of the questions frequently asked about Hamlet is why he delays in killing Claudius, but he gives us the answer in his first soliloquy. In a state of depression induced by his father's death and his mother's hasty re-marriage he wishes for death, or 'that the Everlasting had not fixed / His canon 'gainst self-slaughter' (1.2.131–2). Clearly, a man whose religious beliefs keep him from suicide will not easily be able to commit murder. Hamlet is a man of conscience and this puts him at a disadvantage in deal-ing with Claudius, who has a conscience but is not much moved by its workings.

Hamlet's dilemma is that it is his filial responsibility to avenge his father's death, but his moral duty not to commit murder. He delays because he tries to find a way of resolving this conflict of obligations. This leads him to try to understand Claudius, the master of duplicity. On his first appearance Hamlet insists that there is no deception in him, that he is distant from 'actions that a man might play' (1.2.84). But 'seeming', paradoxically, is the state of the 'real' world of Elsinore, and Hamlet can only confront this reality by absorbing it. Spied upon, apparently, by all, he responds by 'playing' for them, by feigning madness. The conflict between ideal and reality is thus internalized. This allows Hamlet to act as satirist, and there is a great deal of mordant humour in his character that rather belies the popular view of him as the 'melancholy Dane' and enables him to creatively mock his enemies. However, to the degree that he absorbs the condition of Elsinore, Hamlet is corrupted by it. His madness, whether real or feigned, leads him on a course of action that destroys Polonius and Ophelia.

Hamlet's probing of 'reality' expands into broader moral exploration of the meaning of life or, rather, of death. For all his belief in the canon of the Everlasting, he has a deep horror of 'The undiscover'd country, from whose bourn / No traveller returns' (3.1.79–80). He also goes through extensive self-examination, and this is partly the cause of his reputation as the great literary enigma. His actions within the concrete context of the play are not enigmatic, however. He emulates the machiavellian's use of illusion in order to pierce the political illusion represented by Claudius. But when he returns from England he has discarded these methods and no longer intends to seek revenge. His 'Mousetrap' was a play used to disclose the sinister 'playing' of Claudius, and in the final scene's fencing match Claudius responds with a play of his own, a sport that is intended to make Hamlet's death a reality. Hamlet is now confronting his enemies openly and honestly, having come to terms with death, and we see his true value. His opponent is Laertes, whose father Hamlet has killed. When asked by Claudius what he would be willing to do to get revenge upon Hamlet, Laertes replies 'cut his throat i' th' church' (4.7.125). Laertes has none of Hamlet's moral fineness: 'Conscience and grace, to the profoundest pit! / I dare damnation' (4.5.132–3). We are reminded that it is precisely conscience and grace that have hindered Hamlet's action and that make him the better man, and it is his deeper awareness of the implications of damnation that make him valuable to us. This does not save him from his tragic fate, however; caught in his conflict with reality he is destroyed by it. But he bears no blame for the final bloodbath in which he dies. He has reaffirmed his ideals in the face of the rotten state of Denmark and the cynical opportunism of its exemplars.

Part of what makes Hamlet an appropriate figure to embody the conflicting tensions of a changing culture is that his self-division comes from an existence that is simultaneously inside and outside his society. As Prince of Denmark he is obviously a central figure in the state. However, he has recently arrived from Wittenberg, where the university clearly nourished his capacity for radical thought, and he insists on his difference, wearing black at a wedding celebration, mocking Danish debauchery, satirizing fashions. In a different way, Othello is also both inside and outside his society, a Moor, an alien who through his military conquests has brought himself to the centre of Venetian society, and who also suffers the tragic consequences of self-division.

Of all Shakespeare's tragic heroes Othello starts out with the greatest dignity and magnetism, projected through the poetic assuredness of his speech. He can load with authority a line as deceptively simple as 'Keep up your bright swords, for the dew will rust 'em' (1.2.59), and when we hear of his military heroism we can understand how such a man would have found acceptance in the Venetian court. With these same qualities he has also conquered Desdemona, the highly-valued daughter of the Venetian senator Brabantio, whom he has married in secret, though there is no indication that Desdemona was mistaken in her choice or that it was lightly made. Defending her choice against the angry accusations of her father she says: 'I saw Othello's visage in his mind, / And to his honours and his valiant parts / Did I my soul and fortunes consecrate' (1.3.252–4). There is something significant about her wording here: she says she saw Othello's visage in his mind, not that she saw his mind in his visage. The noble mind revealed the noble face. Thus she shows that she well understands what the cause of her father's objection to Othello might be: his appearance.

I have already noted the hostility to Othello's blackness articulated by Iago, Roderigo and Brabantio, and I do not think it is possible, though many critics have done so, to separate his tragedy from his race. So outraged is Brabantio that his daughter could be in love with 'what she feared to look on' (1.3.98) that he believes Othello must have bewitched her, since she is not 'deficient, blind, or lame of sense' (1.3.63). The emphasis is entirely on what is *seen*, that is, on Othello's skin. To be sure, the Duke of Venice, before whom Brabantio makes his accusations, is sympathetic to Othello, but he needs the Moor to fight against the Turks. What might Othello perceive in all this? – perhaps that he is wanted for his military utility, but spurned for his race.

Unless we take some such view of the situation I do not see how we can explain the ease with which Iago is able to persuade Othello of Desdemona's infidelity. This is a matter of choice: Othello chooses, against all normal probability, to believe Iago rather than Desdemona. What Iago achieves is to make Othello perceive himself as he thinks Venice perceives him (and as Brabantio certainly perceives him). His problem is not jealousy but an insecure sense of his identity that re-situates him as an outsider in a society of which he had thought himself to be at the centre. In his vulnerable state the idea of Desdemona's infidelity is all too possible. It turns Othello in his own mind into a comic figure, a cuckold (it is notable that Shakespeare had recently written two comedies about jealousy, *The Merry Wives of Windsor* and *Much Ado about Nothing*), and his dignity, which had rested much upon his sense of his social worth, cannot bear this. Othello is thus divided from himself, his identity undermined; as Desdemona says, 'My lord is not my lord' (3.4.121). Desdemona's shift in his mind from 'fair lady' to whore makes her the visible sign of his division.

Although Iago's antecedents include the medieval Vice and the machiavellian stereotype, he cannot be explained simply as an embodiment of motiveless malignity. He himself gives a number of reasons for his hatred of Othello. Professional, social and sexual envy clearly underlie them, but his hatred goes beyond this, for he embodies all the resentment and suspicion of the Moorish outsider that are latent in the society and that demonize the Moor as alien. He is also deeply misogynistic, as we see in his treatment of Emilia, both desiring and hating what he desires. This is why it is so important for him to destroy Desdemona: to him she is Othello's undeserved 'reward'. He makes her the object of Othello's fear and rage, just as Othello is the object of his fear and rage.

Perhaps the play should be considered as much Desdemona's tragedy as Othello's. Her value is understood by both Othello and Iago in material terms, and even though Othello's love for her is genuine it has clear limitations: his remorse when he discovers that he has killed an innocent woman includes no sense that he would have had no right to kill her even if she had been guilty. He kills her because he thinks she has given away her body, and so Desdemona's body becomes the tragic sign and victim of a masculine struggle for authority. Both Othello and Desdemona are destroyed by those who fail or refuse to see what they truly *are*.

*King Lear*, like *Measure for Measure* and *Macbeth*, was written for performance during the first years of James I's reign. Like them it offers a profoundly ambivalent analysis of the rights and duties of rulers. Lear begins with a belief in the universal laws of traditional hierarchy, the macrocosmic web of connections of purposeful order, the bonds of what he calls 'nature'. In society the 'offices of nature' appear in 'bond of childhood, / Effects of courtesy, dues of gratitude' (2.4.180–1) and they demand obedience to him as king. What he fails to see is that his division of the kingdom is an act against the order that validates his power, an act of abdication. He wants authority without responsibility and, in imposing his own will against his duty, he dis-orders nature. The immediate effect of this is a draining of meaning from the language of love. The hypocrite daughters Goneril and Regan can speak the words of love, leaving the loving Cordelia nothing to say except the ambiguous-sounding truth that she loves him according to her bond. Lear knows which daughter truly loves him but, because Cordelia will not speak the words that he wills her to speak, he banishes her, so letting in the forces that crack the bond and invert the universe.

The forces that destroy Lear are defined by 'bastard Edmund', who has a quite different understanding of 'nature'. For him nature does not shape the human will but is shaped by it: 'I should have been that I am had the maidenliest star in the firmament twinkled on my bastardizing' (1.2.138–40). In Edmund, as in Goneril and Regan, is embodied a ruthless sense of self that persecutes the 'self-less' Cordelia and Edgar. The disorder that Lear has promoted divides generations and families as it divides the kingdom. It appears to Lear that it also divides the universe, the storm on the heath proving to him that the macrocosm shares his own madness.

What is happening is in reality a little different from Lear's perception of it, however. His act of 'divesting' himself of 'rule' (1.1.49) initiates a process of literal and metaphorical stripping. In stripping him of his retinue his daughters merely re-enact what has already happened, for his power goes with the word 'divest'. Stripped of his sanity he is also stripped of the beliefs that shaped his idea of power and is left with nothing, which he acknowledges when he strips off his clothing to expose the 'poor, bare, forked animal' (3.4.110) that constitutes a man. However, in the company of the dispossessed, a Fool and an apparent madman, he experiences the real meaning of hierarchy, for he sees it from the bottom, from the perspective of those who are oppressed by it, and he sees that its orderings are relative: 'see how yond justice rails upon yond simple thief. Hark, in thine ear: change places, and, handy-dandy, which is the justice, which is the thief?' (4.6.154–6).

This is a deeply pessimistic play, and not because it bears out Gloucester's belief that 'As flies to wanton boys, are we to th' Gods; / They kill us for their sport' (4.1.36–7). Edmund has already discredited the superstitious view that 'when we are sick in fortune, often the surfeits of our own behaviour, we make guilty of our disasters the sun, the moon, the stars; as if we were villains on necessity, fools by heavenly compulsion' (1.2.124–8); the fact that these sentiments are uttered by a villain does not invalidate them. If the only alternative order is that imposed by individualist will, however, what is to stop the Cornwalls of the world from blinding the Gloucesters, or the Edmunds from hanging the Cordelias? Lear's tragic understanding of the oppressed does not protect him from the inexpressible pain of his daughter's needless and irreversible death: 'Thou'lt come no more, / Never, never, never, never, never' (5.3.307–8); that terrible 'never' echoes the 'nothing' that has resounded through the play. And if Lear dies believing that his daughter still breathes, this only adds irony to the tragedy, which seems to offer nothing to hope for. Nowhere does Shakespeare come closer than this to giving us an image of 'the promis'd end'.

The extreme to which individualist will or desire can drive a man is illustrated in Macbeth's 'vaulting ambition'. Of all Shakespeare's tragedies, *Macbeth* gives the most compelling impression that evil has a universal existence, but this impression derives from the poetic passion with which Macbeth perceives the conflict or paradox within his own actions and experience. At the beginning of the play he is presented as the courageous and loyal servant of a king who, within a system of feudal ties, is 'the Lord's anointed Temple' (2.3.69). In spite of this mystification of the system, however, its existence depends on bloodshed and ruthless suppression of opposition, and Macbeth, 'Bellona's bridegroom' (1.2.55), is the best exponent of this. Paradoxically, his ambition sets him against the system of which he is the representative product.

Macbeth's course of action is freely chosen by him. The three witches are not a sign of an external evil that controls Macbeth; they should be seen as metaphorical rather than metaphysical in that they predict but do not cause what he will do. The conflict between conscience and ambition that brings him such terrible suffering is, as he is well aware, of his own making. Even before he kills Duncan, an act that he knows goes against all humane bonds of kinship and community, he imagines his action as a kind of suicide:

> But in these cases
> We still have judgement here; that we but teach
> Bloody instructions, which, being taught, return
> To plague th'inventor: this even-handed Justice
> Commends th'ingredience of our poison'd chalice
> To our own lips.
>
> (1.7.7–12)

So it proves; the murder sets him on a path to spiritual isolation that is a more dreadful torment than the fear of death could ever be, and what torments him the most is his knowledge of himself as the author of his fortune. Macbeth is, in all conventional senses of the word, evil, and his uncommon courage is not sufficient to redeem him as a hero. But if we compare him with Richard III, who in the crimes he commits is most like Macbeth, we can see what it is that makes Macbeth a tragic figure. Richard stands outside himself and mocks his own actions; only in his final moments does he show a tiny trace of conscience. What is different about Macbeth is the peculiar poetic intensity with which he is able to imagine the consequences of his actions. We are brought into his suffering and can pity him at the same time that we condemn him.

His imagination also distinguishes him from his wife. Lady Macbeth goads him to his action by mocking his manhood, undoing the differences between man and woman by 'unsexing' herself, denying her own femininity and offering her 'undaunted mettle' as a notion of masculinity that contains only the brutal courage to act on ambition. She does not see that his reluctance to kill Duncan arises from an imaginative grasp of the spiritual implications of what he will do and not out of cowardice. In murdering Duncan he murders sleep, and he knows he is doing so. He murders his wife's sleep too, but she does not know this until after the act, after she has seen how much blood the old man had in him.

To function in the world of masculine power Lady Macbeth tries to take on the role of a man, but she gets it wrong. Cleopatra also tries to function in a world of masculine power but the roles that she plays are all versions of the feminine, some of them parodic. *Antony and Cleopatra* was written shortly after *Macbeth* but there has been a critical reluctance to include it amongst the major tragedies. The play is flawed, we are told, and the source of the flaw is often identified as Cleopatra, a great comic figure who stands at the centre of the play and deflates Antony's tragedy. But the play is also Cleopatra's tragedy and her presence complicates our responses in intriguing ways.

Antony's tragedy does arise from a conflict between duty and desire, between the military code of Rome embodied in Caesar and the pull of erotic love embodied in Cleopatra, between public and private worlds. Unfortunately, at this political level the public and the private cannot easily be separated, and Antony wants both worlds. Indeed, his failure to make a clear distinction between the two leads to a collision that destroys him when he allows Cleopatra to make military decisions for him. For all her boggling, however, we can see why he throws his lot in with Cleopatra; the Roman world, at least as represented by the coldly efficient Caesar, has ceased to hold a place for Antony.

Caesar's rigidity stands in stark contrast to Cleopatra's infinite variety. She is a queen who can play at being a strumpet or a maid, and the idea of playing is the key to what she is, for almost all of what she does is an act. She is also the most intelligent character in the play, aware that if she is to survive in a man's world she has to fill all the roles that men expect of her. She does not entirely commit herself to any of them, however. Her attempt close to the end of the play to hide half of her fortune from Caesar is clearly an act because she has already made plans for her suicide; she leads him away from her true intentions by pretending feminine vanity. She plays for Antony because she knows that is the way to keep him. Enobarbus's famous description of her (2.2.191–240) might seem overdone, but it defines her extraordinary powers of illusion, and is all the more convincing coming from this satirical, even cynical soldier.

It is the alloying of the tragedy with comedy that gives the play its extraordinary quality. Antony's death-scene contains much moving poetry but even here Cleopatra upstages him, interrupting him when he tries to say a few last words:

> *Ant.* I am dying, Egypt, dying.
>    Give me some wine, and let me speak a little.
> *Cleo.* No, let me speak, and let me rail so high,
>    That the false huswife Fortune break her wheel,
>    Provok'd by my offence.

(4.15.41–5)

Her own death is presented almost as if it were a parody of Antony's, the Clown's refusal to leave and let her get on with it echoing her treatment of Antony. It is a consciously theatrical death but for Cleopatra playing has been a serious business, her way of surviving in a harsh masculine world. And why should not a comic character have a tragic fate? In this play the tragic and the comic are not different modes but inextricable components of each other.

*Coriolanus* is a tragedy in form but its interests are close to those of the history plays, and it appears to be closely related to contemporary social and political concerns: the uprisings of the poor in 1607–8 and the struggles between James and his increasingly intransigent parliaments, which raised troubling questions about the distribution of power and resources. *Coriolanus* differs from the English histories, however, in that it dramatizes competing ideological positions rather than competing ambitions. No contender for the English crown questioned the authority of the hierarchical system itself, and even Jack Cade wanted to be king. Different ideologies might be implied but were not stated. In *Coriolanus* the people have an understanding of social order that is different from the aristocratic view of Coriolanus.

The play is remarkable for an unusual degree of detachment. Because it is interested in the ideological argument it does not engage our sympathies with any character, although it is possible to maintain that to dramatize a popular position at all indicates a degree of sympathy with it. This detachment affects our response to the play as tragedy, however. Coriolanus's aristocratic virtues disable him, his pride translating into arrogance; indeed, setting aside machiavellian monsters like Richard III, he is Shakespeare's most extreme embodiment of individualism, living 'As if a man were author of himself / And knew no other kin' (5.3.36–7). He refuses to see that his 'self' – his reputation – has no existence outside the system that confers it. His stance proves meaningless and his existence becomes pointless, so his death at the end of the play does not generate any tragic pity or fear, or even sympathy, in an audience that is alienated from him.

Although *Timon of Athens* is classified as a tragedy it is like *Troilus and Cressida* in that its satirical component distorts its generic form. Its date of composition is uncertain and it appears to be incomplete, but it has affinities with *King Lear* in the ferocity of its attack on social corruption and greed. Timon treats men with an undiscriminating generosity that brings about his own fall from prosperity, and when he discovers human ingratitude he flays men with undiscriminating vituperation. As with Lear, his experience pushes him into misanthropy, but unlike Lear he never moves beyond this, never finding compassion for others who suffer from social inequity. His death imparts tragic form to the play, but there is no redeeming relaxation of its misanthropy, and his epitaph lays a curse on all who pass by.

If *Timon of Athens* was Shakespeare's last attempt at tragedy it provides a rather inconclusive ending to his tragic period, but it is clear from the experimentation of *Antony and Cleopatra* and *Coriolanus* that he was not anxious to keep to any formula, no matter how successful it had been. Certainly, in these later tragedies he began to push harder against generic limitations, as he had done in his problem comedies. After 1608 he turned his attention to the problematic sub-genre of romance or tragicomedy. No matter what we call them, they remind us again that satisfactory generic demarcation is sometimes, perhaps even usually, impossible, and that if we are to deal justly with Shakespeare our concern should always be with the play rather than the slot that it might fit.

# Notes

## Introduction

1. The elegy, entitled 'To the Memory of My Beloved, the Author Mr William Shakespeare: And What He Hath Left Us', can be found at the beginning of many editions of the *Complete Works*. Quotations here are from George Parfitt (ed.), *Ben Jonson: The Complete Poems* (Harmondsworth: Penguin Books, 1975) pp. 263–5.
2. A.D. Culler (ed.), *Poetry and Criticism of Matthew Arnold* (Boston: Houghton Mifflin, 1961) p. 26.
3. Newbolt Report, *The Teaching of English in England* (London: Report of the Board of Education, 1921) p. 312.
4. Jonson, *Complete Poems*, pp. 462, 394.

## Chapter 1

1. *Greene's Groats-worth of Wit* (1592), reprinted in E.K. Chambers, *William Shakespeare: A Study of Facts and Problems* (Oxford: Oxford University Press, 1930) Vol. 2, p. 188.
2. See W. Frazer, 'Two Studies of *Greene's Groatsworth*', *The Shakespeare Newsletter*, 44, 3 (1994) pp. 48, 56.
3. S. Schoenbaum, *William Shakespeare: A Documentary Life* (Oxford: The Clarendon Press, 1975) p. 155.
4. Jonson, *Complete Poems*, p. 476.
5. For an entertaining account of the amazing range of pseudo-Shakespeares, read S. Schoenbaum, *Shakespeare's Lives* (Oxford: Clarendon Press, 1991) pp. 385–451.
6. E.M.W. Tillyard, *The Elizabethan World Picture*, 1943 (rpt. Harmondsworth: Penguin Books, 1970) p. 18.
7. D.M. Palliser, *The Age of Elizabeth: England under the Later Tudors, 1547–1603*, 2nd edition (London and New York: Longman, 1992) p. 98.
8. For an excellent study of this issue see A.L. Beier, *Masterless Men: The Vagrancy Problem in England, 1560–1640* (London and New York: Methuen, 1985).
9. Palliser, *The Age of Elizabeth*, p. 74.
10. Palliser, *The Age of Elizabeth*, p. 83.
11. L. Stone, *The Family, Sex and Marriage in England, 1500–1800* (Harmondsworth: Penguin Books, 1982) p. 70.
12. P. Laslett, *The World We Have Lost* (London: Methuen, 1971) pp. 56, 58.
13. R.B. Bond (ed.), *Certain Sermons or Homilies (1547) and a Homily against Disobedience and Wilful Rebellion (1570)* (Toronto: University of Toronto Press, 1987) p. 161.
14. King James I, 'A Speech to ... the Parliament', in C.H. McIlwain

(ed.), *The Political Works of James I* (Cambridge, Mass.: Harvard University Press, 1918) pp. 307–8.

15. John Donne, *The Epithalamions, Anniversaries and Epicedes*, ed. W. Milgate (Oxford: Clarendon Press, 1978).

16. Sir Philip Sidney, *The Defence of Poetry*, in K. Duncan-Jones and Jan Van Dorsten (eds), *Miscellaneous Prose of Sir Philip Sidney* (Oxford: Clarendon Press, 1973) p. 79.

17. Niccolò Machiavelli, *The Prince*, ed. G. Bull (Harmondsworth: Penguin, 1962) p. 91.

18. Christopher Marlowe, *The Complete Works*, ed. Irving Ribner (New York: The Odyssey Press, 1963).

19. Quoted in P. Thomson, *Shakespeare's Professional Career* (Cambridge: Cambridge University Press, 1992) p. 146.

20. McIlwain, *Political Works of James I*, p. 43.

21. Attributed to George Ferrars. Reprinted in A.F. Kinney, *Elizabethan Backgrounds: Historical Documents of the Age of Elizabeth I* (Hamden, Conn.: Archon Books, 1975) p. 16.

22. 'A Letter of the Authors' prefaced to *The Faerie Queene* in H. Maclean (ed.), *Edmund Spenser's Poetry* (New York: W.W. Norton, 1982) p. 2.

23. R. Strong, *Gloriana: the Portraits of Queen Elizabeth I* (London: Thames and Hudson, 1987) p. 147. This book provides an invaluable survey and analysis of the portraits.

24. Jonson, *Complete Poems*, pp. 70–1.

## Chapter 2

1. For a discussion of the problems surrounding pageant-wagon presentation, see W. Tydeman, *The Theatre in the Middle Ages* (Cambridge: Cambridge University Press, 1978) pp. 102–13.

2. A useful account of the Rose excavations is in C. Eccles, *The Rose Theatre* (London: Hern Books, 1990).

3. Quoted in A.M. Nagler, *A Source Book in Theatrical History* (New York: Dover Publications, 1952) p. 117.

4. Nagler, *Source Book*, pp. 117–18.

5. R.A. Foakes, and R.T. Rickert (eds), *Henslowe's Diary* (Cambridge: Cambridge University Press, 1961) pp. 291–4.

6. For the beginning of this debate, and a statement of the formalist position, see M.C. Bradbrook, *Elizabethan Stage Conventions* (Cambridge: Cambridge University Press, 1933) p. 109. The strongest statement of the realist position is to be found in M. Rosenberg, 'Elizabethan Actors: Men or Marionettes?', *PMLA*, 69 (1964) pp. 915–27.

7. Sir Thomas Overbury, *Characters* (1614–16). Reprinted in J.D. Wilson, *Life in Shakespeare's England* (Harmondsworth: Penguin Books, 1968) p. 219.

8. For an account of company sizes and the demands of doubling, see T.J. King, *Casting Shakespeare's Plays: London Actors and Their Roles, 1590–1642* (Cambridge: Cambridge University Press, 1992).

9. See David Wiles, *Shakespeare's Clown: Actor and Text in the Elizabethan*

*Playhouse* (Cambridge: Cambridge University Press, 1987) p. 146.

10. G.E. Bentley, *The Profession of Dramatist in Shakespeare's Time* (Princeton, N.J.: Princeton University Press, 1971) p. 199.

11. A. Harbage, *Shakespeare and the Rival Traditions* (Bloomington and London: Indiana University Press, 1952); A.J. Cook, *The Privileged Playgoers of Shakespeare's London, 1576–1642* (Princeton, N.J.: Princeton University Press, 1981). A useful counter to the arguments of both of these books can be found in Appendix II of M. Butler, *Theatre and Crisis 1632–1642* (Cambridge: Cambridge University Press, 1984).

12. See C. Leech and T.W. Craik (eds), *The Revels History of Drama in English, Volume Three, 1576–1613* (London: Methuen, 1975) p. 48.

13. For a list of years in which the plague affected playhouse performances, see Leech and Craik, *Revels History*, pp. 34–5.

14. J. Clare, *'Art Made Tongue-tied by Authority': Elizabethan and Jocobean Censorship* (Manchester and New York: Manchester University Press, 1990).

15. Ben Jonson, *Bartholomew Fair*, ed. Maurice Hussey (London: Benn, 1964).

16. Clare, *Elizabethan and Jacobean Censorship*, p. 215.

## Chapter 3

1. *Edmund Ironside* has been championed and edited by E. Sams (Aldershot: Wildwood House, 1986). The other plays listed here can be found, with five more, in W. Kozlenko (ed.), *Disputed Plays of William Shakespeare* (New York: Hawthorn Books, 1974).

2. This is usually included with other prefatory documents in collected editions of Shakespeare's works. My source is P. Alexander (ed.), *William Shakespeare: The Complete Works* (London and Glasgow: Collins, 1951) p. xxvii.

3. E.A. Honigman, in the New Penguin edition of *Richard III* (Harmondsworth: Penguin Books, 1968) p. 242.

4. The texts of the known sources and analogues of Shakespeare's plays are collected in the eight volumes of G. Bullough's *Narrative and Dramatic Sources of Shakespeare* (London: Routledge & Kegan Paul, 1957–75). Also useful is K. Muir, *The Sources of Shakespeare's Plays* (London: Methuen, 1977).

5. M.E. Novak and G.R. Guffey (eds), *The Works of John Dryden, Vol. XIII: Plays* (Berkeley and London: University of California Press, 1985) p. 228.

6. Thomas Nashe, prefatory note to Robert Greene's *Menaphon* (*ES* 234).

7. S. Greenblatt, *Renaissance Self-Fashioning* (Chicago: University of Chicago Press, 1980) p. 3.

8. A.C. Bradley, *Shakespearean Tragedy*, 1904 (rpt. Greenwich, Conn.: Fawcett Books, 1968) p. xi.

9. L. Scragg, *Discovering Shakespeare's Meaning: An Introduction to the Study of Shakespeare's Dramatic Structures* (London and New York: Longman, 1994) p. xi.

10. Scragg, p. xii.
11. T. Hawkes, *Meaning by Shakespeare* (London, Routledge: 1992).
12. For an interesting account of the fortunes of Shylock, as well as of actors who have played him, see J. Gross, *Shylock: Four Hundred Years in the Life of a Legend* (London: Chatto and Windus, 1992).
13. Sidney, *The Defence of Poetry*, p. 81.
14. Dryden, *Works, Vol. XIII*, p. 226.
15. Sidney, *The Defence of Poetry*, p. 115.
16. Ben Jonson, 'Discoveries', in *Complete Poems*, p. 455.
17. C.H. Holman and W. Harmon (eds), *A Handbook to Literature*, 5th edition (New York: Macmillan Publishing Company, 1986) pp. 436–7.
18. N. Frye, *A Natural Perspective* (New York and London: Columbia University Press, 1965) pp. 119, 104.
19. C.L. Barber, *Shakespeare's Festive Comedy* (Princeton, N.J.: Princeton University Press, 1959).
20. Quoted by R.B. Heilman in the introduction to his edition of *The Taming of the Shrew* (New York: Signet, 1966) p. xxx.
21. Muir, *Sources*, p. 14.
22. Philip Stubbes, *The Anatomie of Abuses* (1583), in J.D. Wilson (ed.), *Life in Shakespeare's England* (Harmondsworth: Penguin, 1968) pp. 225–6.
23. P. Hyland, *Shakespeare: Troilus and Cressida* (Harmondsworth: Penguin, 1989) pp. 91–3.
24. Thomas Heywood, *An Apology for Actors*, 1612 (London: Reprinted for the Shakespeare Society, 1841) p. 52.
25. L.B. Campbell (ed.), *The Mirror for Magistrates*, 1938 (rpt. New York: Barnes and Noble, 1960), pp. 65–6.
26. For a very useful examination of Shakespeare's history plays, their sources and context, see I. Ribner, *The English History Play in the Age of Shakespeare* (London: Methuen, 1965).
27. E.M.W. Tillyard, *Shakespeare's History Plays* (London: Chatto and Windus, 1944).
28. A Harbage and S. Schoenbaum, *Annals of English Drama*, 2nd edition, rev. (Philadelphia: University of Pennsylvania Press, 1964) pp. 50–92.
29. S. Greenblatt, *Shakespearean Negotiations: The Circulation of Social Energy in Renaissance England* (Berkeley: University of California Press, 1988) p. 65.
30. Thomas Nashe, *The Unfortunate Traveller and Other Works*, ed. J.B. Steane (Harmondsworth: Penguin Books, 1972) p. 113.
31. A. Patterson, *Shakespeare and the Popular Voice* (Cambridge: Basil Blackwell, 1989) p. 120.
32. Aristotle, *Poetics*, tr. L. Golden (Englewood Cliffs, N.J.: Prentice-Hall, Inc., 1968) p. 5. All references to the *Poetics* are to this translation.
33. Bradley, *Shakespearean Tragedy*, pp. xii–xiii.
34. R.B. Sewall, *The Vision of Tragedy* (New Haven and London: Yale University Press, 1959) pp. 7, 8.
35. Jonson, *Bartholomew Fair*, Induction, 104.
36. J.W. Lever, *The Tragedy of State* (London: Methuen, 1971).

# Chronology

All dates of composition are approximate. The date of first publication appears in brackets after each title. In some cases the earliest quarto is a corrupt version, usually because it is a memorial reconstruction. These are the so-called 'bad' quartos, though there is not universal agreement on their status and cause.

| | |
|---|---|
| 1589–92 | *1 Henry VI* (1623) |
| | *2 Henry VI* (1594) 'Bad' Quarto |
| | *3 Henry VI* (1595) 'Bad' Quarto |
| | *Titus Andronicus* (1594) |
| 1590–4 | *Richard III* (1597) |
| | *The Comedy of Errors* (1623) |
| 1593–5 | *The Taming of the Shrew* (1623) |
| | *The Two Gentlemen of Verona* (1623) |
| | *Love's Labour's Lost* (1598) |
| | *Romeo and Juliet* (1597) 'Bad' Quarto |
| 1594–6 | *King John* (1623) |
| 1595–6 | *Richard II* (1597) |
| | *A Midsummer Night's Dream* (1600) |
| 1596–7 | *The Merchant of Venice* (1600) |
| | *1 Henry IV* (1598) |
| | *The Merry Wives of Windsor* (1602) 'Bad' Quarto |
| 1598–9 | *2 Henry IV* (1600) |
| | *Much Ado about Nothing* (1600) |
| | *Henry V* (1600) 'Bad' Quarto |
| 1599 | *Julius Caesar* (1623) |
| | *As You Like It* (1623) |
| 1600–1 | *Hamlet* (1603) 'Bad' Quarto |
| | *Twelfth Night* (1623) |
| 1601–2 | *Troilus and Cressida* (1609) |
| 1602–3 | *All's Well That Ends Well* (1623) |
| 1604–5 | *Measure for Measure* (1623) |
| | *Othello* (1622) |
| 1605–6 | *King Lear* (1608) |
| | *Macbeth* (1623) |
| 1606–7 | *Antony and Cleopatra* (1623) |
| 1607–8 | *Coriolanus* (1623) |
| | *Timon of Athens* (1623) |
| | *Pericles* (1609) |
| 1608–10 | *Cymbeline* (1623) |
| 1610–11 | *The Winter's Tale* (1623) |
| 1611–12 | *The Tempest* (1623) |
| 1612–13 | *Henry VIII* (1623) |
| | (*The Two Noble Kinsmen*) (1634) |

# Suggested Reading

There are far too many publications on Shakespeare to make possible a representative reading list. The following list contains some useful books on the background to Shakespeare's theatre, a few 'classic' books on Shakespeare and some recent studies, including a few that have been controversial. All of them, I hope, will be found stimulating.

Adelman, J. *Suffocating Mothers: Fantasies of Maternal Origin in Shakespeare's Plays.* London and New York: Routledge, 1992.

Bamber, L. *Comic Women, Tragic Men: A Study of Gender and Genre in Shakespeare.* Stanford: Stanford University Press, 1982.

Barber, C.L. *Shakespeare's Festive Comedy.* Princeton: Princeton University Press, 1959.

Bate, J. *Shakespeare and Ovid.* Oxford: Clarendon Press, 1993.

Bentley, G.E. *The Profession of Dramatist in Shakespeare's Time.* Princeton: Princeton University Press, 1971.

Berry, E. *Shakespeare's Comic Rites.* Cambridge: Cambridge University Press, 1984.

Bevington, D. *Tudor Drama and Politics: A Critical Approach to Topical Meaning.* Cambridge, Mass.: Harvard University Press, 1968.

———. *Action is Eloquence: Shakespeare's Language of Gesture.* Cambridge, Mass.: Harvard University Press, 1984.

Bradbrook, M.C. *Elizabethan Stage Conventions.* Cambridge: Cambridge University Press, 1933.

Bradley, A.C. *Shakespearean Tragedy.* 1904; rpt. Greenwich, Conn.: Fawcett Books, 1968.

Bradshaw, G. *Shakespeare's Scepticism.* Brighton: Harvester, 1987.

Brennan, A. *Shakespeare's Dramatic Structures.* London: Routledge, 1986.

Bristol, M.D. *Carnival and Theatre: Plebeian Culture and the Structure of Authority in Renaissance England.* London and New York: Methuen, 1985.

Brockbank, J.P. *On Shakespeare.* Oxford: Blackwell, 1989.

Bullough, G. *Narrative and Dramatic Sources of Shakespeare.* London: Routledge and Kegan Paul, 1957–75 (8 vols).

Calderwood, J.L. *Shakespearean Metadrama.* Minneapolis: University of Minnesota Press, 1971.

Clare, J. *'Art Made Tongue-tied by Authority': Elizabethan and Jacobean Dramatic Censorship.* Manchester and New York: Manchester University Press, 1990.

Cook, A.J. *The Privileged Playgoers of Shakespeare's London, 1576–1642.* Princeton: Princeton University Press, 1981.

Dawson, A.B. *Indirections: Shakespeare and the Art of Illusion.* Toronto: University of Toronto Press, 1978.

Dollimore, J. *Radical Tragedy: Religion, Ideology and Power in the Drama of Shakespeare and His Contemporaries.* Brighton: Harvester, 1984.

——— and A. Sinfield (eds). *Political Shakespeare*. Manchester and Ithaca: Cornell University Press, 1985.

Drakakis, J. (ed.). *Alternative Shakespeares*. London and New York: Methuen, 1985.

Eagleton, T. *William Shakespeare*. Oxford: Blackwell, 1986.

Frye, N. *A Natural Perspective*. New York and London: Columbia University Press, 1965.

Girard, R. *A Theater of Envy*. Oxford: Oxford University Press, 1992.

Goldberg, J. *James I and the Politics of Literature: Jonson, Shakespeare, Donne, and their Contemporaries*. Baltimore: Johns Hopkins University Press, 1983.

Greenblatt, S. *Renaissance Self-Fashioning: From More to Shakespeare*. Chicago: University of Chicago Press, 1980.

———. *Shakespearean Negotiations: The Circulation of Social Energy in Renaissance England*. Berkeley: University of California Press, 1988.

Gurr, A. *The Shakespearean Stage 1574–1642*. Cambridge: Cambridge University Press, 1970.

———. *Playgoing in Shakespeare's London*. Cambridge: Cambridge University Press, 1987.

Harbage, A. *Shakespeare and the Rival Traditions*. Bloomington and London: Indiana University Press, 1952.

Hawkes, T. *Shakespeare's Talking Animals: Language and Drama in Society*. London: Edward Arnold, 1973.

———. *Meaning by Shakespeare*. London: Routledge, 1992.

Hibbard, G. *The Making of Shakespeare's Dramatic Poetry*. London and Toronto: University of Toronto Press, 1981.

Hillman, R. *Shakespearean Subversions: The Trickster and the Play-text*. London: Routledge, 1992.

Holderness, G. (ed.). *The Shakespeare Myth*. Manchester: Manchester University Press, 1988.

Howard, J.E. *Shakespeare's Art of Orchestration*. Urbana and Chicago: University of Illinois Press, 1984.

Jardine, L. *Still Harping on Daughters: Women and Drama in the Age of Shakespeare*. Brighton: Harvester, 1983.

Kastan, D. *Shakespeare and the Shapes of Time*. Hanover: New England University Press, 1982.

——— and P. Stallybrass (eds). *Staging the Renaissance: Reinterpretations of Elizabethan and Jacobean Drama*. Durham: Duke University Press, 1991.

King, T.J. *Casting Shakespeare's Plays: London Actors and Their Roles, 1590–1642*. Cambridge: Cambridge University Press, 1992.

Leggatt, A. *Shakespeare's Comedy of Love*. London: Methuen, 1974.

———. *Shakespeare's Political Drama: The History Plays and the Roman Plays*. London: Routledge, 1988.

Lenz, C.R.S., G. Greene and C.T. Neely (eds). *The Woman's Part: Feminist Criticism of Shakespeare*. Urbana: University of Illinois Press, 1980.

Marcus, L.S. *Puzzling Shakespeare: Local Reading and Its Discontents*. Berkeley: University of California Press, 1988.

Muir, K. *The Sources of Shakespeare's Plays*, London: Methuen, 1977.

—— and S. Schoenbaum (eds). *A New Companion to Shakespeare Studies.* Cambridge: Cambridge University Press, 1971.

Mullaney, S. *The Place of the Stage: License, Play and Power in Renaissance England.* London and Chicago: University of Chicago Press, 1987.

Patterson, A. *Shakespeare and the Popular Voice.* Oxford: Basil Blackwell, 1989.

Rabkin, N. *Shakespeare and the Common Understanding.* New York: The Free Press, 1967.

Rackin, P. *Stages of History: Shakespeare's English Chronicles.* London: Routledge, 1990.

Ribner, I. *The English History Play in the Age of Shakespeare.* London: Methuen, 1965.

Righter, A. *Shakespeare and the Idea of the Play.* London: Chatto and Windus, 1964.

Ryan, K. *Shakespeare.* Brighton: Harvester, 1989.

Salingar, L. *Shakespeare and the Traditions of Comedy.* Cambridge: Cambridge University Press, 1974.

Schoenbaum, S. *William Shakespeare: A Documentary Life.* New York: Oxford University Press, 1975.

——. *Shakespeare's Lives.* Oxford: Clarendon Press, 1991.

Strong, R. *The Cult of Elizabeth: Elizabethan Portraiture and Pageantry.* London: Thames and Hudson, 1977.

Thomson, P. *Shakespeare's Professional Career.* Cambridge: Cambridge University Press, 1992.

Tillyard, E.M.W. *The Elizabethan World Picture.* London: Chatto and Windus, 1943.

Traub, V. *Desire and Anxiety: Circulations of Sexuality in Shakespearean Drama,* London: Routledge, 1992.

Vickers, B. *Appropriating Shakespeare: Contemporary Critical Quarrels.* New Haven and London: Yale University Press, 1993.

Weimann, R. *Shakespeare and the Popular Tradition in the Theatre.* Baltimore and London: Johns Hopkins University Press, 1978.

Wells, R.H. *Shakespeare, Politics and the State.* London: Macmillan, 1986.

Wells, S. (ed.). *The Cambridge Companion to Shakespeare Studies.* Cambridge: Cambridge University Press, 1986.

Wiles, D. *Shakespeare's Clown: Actor and Text in the Elizabethan Playhouse.* Cambridge: Cambridge University Press, 1984.

# Index